# Protest in Democratic India

# Westview Special Studies

The concept of Westview Special Studies is a response to the continuing crisis in academic and informational publishing. Library budgets are being diverted from the purchase of books and used for data banks, computers, micromedia, and other methods of information retrieval. Interlibrary loan structures further reduce the edition sizes required to satisfy the needs of the scholarly community. Economic pressures on university presses and the few private scholarly publishing companies have greatly limited the capacity of the industry to properly serve the academic and research communities. As a result, many manuscripts dealing with important subjects, often representing the highest level of scholarship, are no longer economically viable publishing projects—or, if accepted for publication, are typically subject to lead times ranging from one to three years.

Westview Special Studies are our practical solution to the problem. As always, the selection criteria include the importance of the subject, the work's contribution to scholarship, and its insight, originality of thought, and excellence of exposition. We accept manuscripts in camera-ready form, typed, set, or word processed according to specifications laid out in our comprehensive manual, which contains straightforward instructions and sample pages. The responsibility for editing and proofreading lies with the author or sponsoring institution, but our editorial staff is always available to answer questions and provide guidance.

The result is a book printed on acid-free paper and bound in sturdy library-quality soft covers. We manufacture these books ourselves using equipment that does not require a lengthy make-ready process and that allows us to publish first editions of 300 to 1000 copies and to reprint even smaller quantities as needed. Thus, we can produce Special Studies quickly and can keep even very specialized books in print as long as there is a demand for them.

# About the Book and Author

This book explores radical challenges to Indian governments' legitimacy and power and the responses of the Indian state and central governments to those challenges. Dr. Calman describes the unintended role Indian governments have played in fostering the emergence of radical movements and analyzes the effectiveness of governments in combating their growth. Light is shed on the power of newly developing decentralized movements to politicize impoverished groups and ultimately to challenge the legitimacy of the Indian mode of governing. These new movements, represented in this book by Shramik Sanghatana and Bhoomi Sena of Maharashtra, have more power to effect change than movements that attack the military force of government, like the Naxalites of Srikakulam District, Andhra Pradesh. The book draws upon government documents, a variety of unpublished sources, and extensive interviews with government officials and key participants in radical groups.

Leslie J. Calman is assistant professor of political science and women's studies at Barnard College, Columbia University.

*To Isobel and Joshua Calman*

# Protest in Democratic India
Authority's Response to Challenge

Leslie J. Calman

Westview Press / Boulder and London

*Westview Special Studies on South and Southeast Asia*

All rights reserved. No part of this publication may be reproduced or transmitted in any form or by any means, electronic or mechanical, including photocopy, recording, or any information storage and retrieval system, without permission in writing from the publisher.

Copyright © 1985 by Westview Press, Inc.

Published in 1985 in the United States of America by Westview Press, Inc.; Frederick A. Praeger, Publisher; 5500 Central Avenue, Boulder, Colorado 80301

Library of Congress Cataloging in Publication Data
Calman, Leslie J.
   Protest in democratic India
Westview special studies on South and Southeast Asia
   Bibliography: p.
     1. India—Politics and government—1947–
2. Radicalism—India—History. I. Title.
DS480.84.C28   1985     954.04     85-3216
ISBN 0-8133-7060-4

Printed and bound in the United States of America

10   9   8   7   6   5   4   3   2   1

# CONTENTS

Acknowledgments .................................................. ix

1 Introduction: The Struggle for Legitimacy ................... 3

## PART 1
## THE SRIKAKULAM NAXALITE MOVEMENT

Introduction to Part 1 ........................................ 17

2 The Development of Tribal Poverty ....................... 21

3 The Early Girijan Movement ............................. 45

4 The Naxalite Movement in Srikakulam ................... 63

5 After the Armed Struggle: Continuing Suppression of the Naxalites .................................................. 87

6 Government Recognizes the Legitimacy Crisis .............. 99

Conclusion to Part 1 ........................................ 133

## PART 2
## THE MAHARASHTRA MOVEMENTS: SHRAMIK SANGHATANA AND BHOOMI SENA

Introduction to Part 2 ................................. 137

7 The Development of Tribal Poverty in Maharashtra ....... 145

8 The Development and Organization of Shramik Sanghatana and Bhoomi Sena ........................... 163

9 State and Movement Interactions: Issues of Tribal
  Landlessness............................................. 185

10 State and Movement Interactions: Work and Wages.........211

   Conclusion to Part 2..................................... 231

11 Conclusion: Protest's Challenge........................... 235

   Appendix A .............................................. 241
   Glossary ................................................ 243
   Bibliography............................................. 247

# ACKNOWLEDGMENTS

This book is the product of many years of thinking, researching, writing, and, inevitably, re-thinking and re-writing. The task would likely not have been accomplished without the personal, intellectual and financial support that I was lucky enough to receive and for which I am very grateful.

My research in India was financed by a Columbia University Travel Grant. The American Institute of Indian Studies provided important institutional support. In India, many libraries and research institutes allowed me the privilege of using their resources. I would particularly like to thank the staffs of the Nehru Museum Library, the National Labour Institute, and Sapru House, all in New Delhi; the Maharashtra State Archives and the invaluable B.U.I.L.D. Documentation Centre in Bombay; the Gokhale Institute of Politics and Economics, and the Tribal Research and Training Institute in Pune; and the Tribal Cultural Research and Training Institute in Hyderabad.

The intellectual odyssey leading to this book began at Barnard College in New York under the influence of two extraordinary teachers: Dennis Dalton and Peter H. Juviler. Both are exceptional in their ability to impart to students not only knowledge, but values. I have been enriched by their appreciation of human life and dignity and have taken to heart their belief that political action can make a positive difference. As my teachers and now colleagues, they have been unfailing sources of personal and professional generosity; every young scholar should have such mentors.

This study had an earlier life as a doctoral dissertation for the Columbia University Department of Political Science. During my incarnation as a doctoral candidate, my work was aided by W. Howard Wriggins, who offered incisive advice and steady encouragement over a number of years. Philip K. Oldenburg shared with me his considerable expertise in matters scholarly and bureaucratic. He and his wife Veena Talwar Oldenburg shared, too, their infectious enthusiasm for Indian life, culture and politics. Ainslie Embree gave me a friendly push towards publication. Stephen Rittenberg and Demetrios Caraley read the manuscript and offered valuable criticism and encouragement.

Once in India, I found the concept of "networking" taking on new dimensions. Casual acquaintances would take the time to introduce me to acquaintances of theirs, who in turn led me to an ever-widening circle of scholars, journalists and government officials. I would particularly like to thank Kuldeep Mathur, Amrita Basu, Shanta Sinha, V. Chandramowli, Kannan Srinivasan, Niranjan Mehta and K.G. Kannabiran for their help. Many who graciously consented to be interviewed requested anonymity; I thank them for their trust and their insight.

Happily, networking was not limited to professional interests; it also extended to friendships. Many people provided me with a home away from home: in New Delhi, the Nath family and Manju and Suman Dubey; in Bombay, Sonal and Haresh Shah and Padma and Vasant Shah; and in Hyderabad, Amy and Edi Chinoy. The generosity, warmth and friendship I received from them surpassed any expectations. Joan Lintault and Merrilyn and Rob Wasson gave me emotional support during some rough times and contributed to many happy ones. Thanks, too, to Dan O'Dell, Kalpana Sharma, Mridula and Aditya Mukherjee, Rama and Ben Behel, and the Alladi family of Madras.

In New York, many friends endured the writing of the dissertation and the book. Isabelle Wilkins, Marsha Hurst, and Flora and Aryeh Davidson for the most part overlooked the author's crabbiness. Kathryn Yatrakis nurtured sparingly, but well. Jane Gruenebaum provided friendship and moral and practical support, while Ann Eisenstein patiently and skillfully explored the contradictions. Carole Christie has given much loving support and the best of times.

After the writing comes the production: without the able assistance of Deborah Bell, Andrea Trisciuzzi and Lee Sloan it would have been much more trying; without a grant from Barnard College, much more expensive.

My parents, Isobel and Joshua Calman, have given me a love of intellectual life, the means to begin its pursuit, loving support, and a fair share of *nudzhing*. Because of (and despite) this, the paper is finished and dedicated to them with love and thanks.

*Leslie J. Calman*

# Protest in Democratic India

# 1
# INTRODUCTION: THE STRUGGLE FOR LEGITIMACY

A major challenge facing Indian elites since independence has been to bring India's rural poor into loyal participation while at the same time holding their expectations within manageable boundaries. From the beginning, it has been understood that if the desires of India's masses became too quickly politicized the political system would be unable to comply with the demands, and the result would be chaos.[1]

As independence dawned in India only a small number of committed communists pushed for a class-based revolution. Within Congress ranks, Gandhians and socialists, including Nehru, believed instead that only a slow, nonviolent and indirect attack on landed privilege in the countryside would both prevent horrible carnage and lead to economic development.[2] As a first step in this process the Indian government created new institutions of self-government in the villages. Nehru and other Congress elites hoped that gradual politicization would generate a responsible local leadership which would work within the framework of established government institutions for the gradual transformation of rural life.[3]

This scheme counted heavily on the patience of the rural poor and their emerging leaders. For the most part, rural India has been patient. But on occasion leaders who are the products not of a slowly changing countryside but instead of more sophisticated urban life have attempted to speed along the process of change. Some leaders have tried to create immediate revolution; the Naxalites working in Srikakulam District, Andhra Pradesh attempted to initiate the violent overthrow of the state. Other movements, including Shramik Sanghatana in Dhule District, Maharashtra and Bhoomi Sena in Thane District, Maharashtra, hope for radical change but proceed more slowly to politicize the agrarian poor, to press legal demands on the government that cannot be wholly met and, in so doing, to cast doubt on the capacity and the legitimacy of the democratic system in India. In the long run, they hope, this strategy may lead to revolutionary change.

## The Struggle For Legitimacy

This book, through the study of the Srikakulam Naxalites, Shramik Sanghatana and Bhoomi Sena, explores the interaction between the emergence and development of movements based among the rural poor and the governments, local, state and central, upon which they hope to have an impact. If the analysis that follows achieves its author's goals it should serve as a guide of equal value for those in government who work to maintain its strength and legitimacy, those who seek to generate movements, and those of less energetic commitment who wish only to understand the interaction between the two.

Recent social science literature has suggested a number of ways to explore the phenomenon of revolutionary challenge to state authority. Three approaches in particular are often cited: the social psychological (most often represented by Ted Gurr, *Why Men Rebel*), the social structural (whose most cited work is Chalmers Johnson's *Revolutionary Change*), and the group conflict theorists (notably Charles Tilly, *From Mobilization to Revolution*).[4] Of these, structural analysis is most helpful for exploring the system changes that make the growth of a revolutionary movement possible, while a conflict approach best addresses the continuing interactions between movements and government.

Ted Gurr's psychological theory rests on the importance of a sense of relative deprivation among the population. He is not as concerned with objective conditions as he is with the subjective perceptions of people who may become participants in political violence. People feel deprived when they perceive that their capabilities, or opportunities, are not adequate to achieve the goods and positions to which they feel entitled; in Gurr's language, their value expectations exceed their value capabilities. Should a group of people who experience deprivation blame their problems on the political system, a revolutionary political movement may result. Gurr's theory, however, offers little guidance to explain how the sense of deprivation, once felt by individuals, is transformed into mass political activity. There is little light shed on the mobilization or organization of movements.

Not much of this gap is filled by social structural theory, either, but the structuralist emphasis on the strains that may cause a society's "disequilibrium" is useful for explicating the preconditions that may give rise to the emergence of movements and particularly for highlighting the activity of political elites as they seek to maintain the system. For the key to structuralist thinking is the notion that elites, if clever and alert, may avert revolution by prompt action to correct a disequilibrated society. The present study questions whether this is always possible, and suggests that some contemporary movements in India may present a model for gradual but ultimately radical change that the elite cannot prevent.

Chalmers Johnson's *Revolutionary Change* argues that a society is normally in a state of equilibrium, with its values and its environment comfortably synchronized. In this circumstance, one might also say that the state has legitimacy. Should the values and environment become dissynchronized, an event which may occur if new values are introduced or if the environment changes either from within or from outside the country, then the authorities can act to re-establish the equilibrium by adjusting either values or environment.

A prerequisite for the on-going adjustments that are required for system maintenance, then, is a perceptive elite that recognizes the first signs of system disequilibrium. As will be discussed below, if the disequilibrium has become more severe, and movements have emerged to exacerbate the problem, the government may still have recourse to the use of force.

One of the findings of the present study is that Indian elites, particularly at the state and local levels, not only have failed to recognize disequilibrium but must bear considerable responsibility for *creating* disequilibrium by allowing a deterioration in the environment of their poorest citizens. This deterioration has occurred, in many instances, because government has failed to implement the laws intended to forestall it. By flouting the rule of law, by not acceding to accepted standards of governmental behavior, the government has forfeited its own legitimacy in the eyes of citizens who have then become available for mobilization by a political movement.

While the structuralist approach is thus helpful in understanding the causes of the disequilibrium which is a prerequisite for the emergence of successful revolutionary movements, and government's role in creating or correcting it, conflict theory proves to be more useful in understanding first, how a political movement emerges to challenge the system and second, the struggle that ensues between movement and government.[5] For revolution occurs not only because of structural dislocations, but also because of organized political activity. Structural disequilibriums provide opportunity, but for that opportunity to be realized, political mobilization and organization must occur. Charles Tilly has persuasively criticized Johnson's inadequate attention to the question of collective action; in the final analysis, a revolution is a battle among groups contending for power. The relative strengths of these groups determine the outcome.

In our examination of the Naxalites, Shramik Sanghatana and Bhoomi Sena, we will identify the resources the movements brought to bear against the government, and how they mobilized those resources. Of particular interest will be the modes of leadership and organization utilized by the different groups, as well as the ideologies that have provided the focus for movement organization and strategy.[6] For each movement, too, we must examine the strength of the movement's opponent. What branch of government did the movement try to influence, and what were the resources the government could bring to bear

## The Struggle For Legitimacy

to fight the movement?[7]

A variety of factors may create increased opportunity for a revolutionary group. Theda Skocpol presents the argument that developments within the international state system, such as defeat in war or threat of invasions, may weaken the coercive power of the state, and thus provide critical opportunities for revolutionary groups.[8] The present study's discussion of the Naxalite failure lends weight to the importance of this factor. It will be argued below that the Naxalites' use of force against the state failed in substantial part because the Indian state, unlike the Chinese state at the time of the Maoist revolution, had not been weakened by external enemies.

While it is agreed that government can lose power through events in its external environment, it is also argued here that government can lose power through the internal loss of legitimacy. The coercive power of the state on which in a crisis the government will have to rely is not a constant measure, but exists relative to the powers of other contending groups. Thus, it can be affected negatively either by an actual diminution of government's power through, for example, loss in war to outside enemies; or by an actual increase in a revolutionary group's power through, for example, the organization of a wider constituency.

In its examination of resources that affect the powers of contending groups, this study places particular emphasis on legitimacy. The government begins with the clear advantage here. It is almost axiomatic that for government to function it must be perceived by most of its citizens to be legitimate; citizens must share "the belief that in spite of shortcomings and failures the existing political institutions are better than any others that might be established and that they therefore can command obedience."[9] In addition, citizens must feel that only government may use force, if necessary, to influence the behavior of citizens.

Max Weber's concept of the state rests on these dual characteristics of legitimacy (or authority) and force.

> ...a state is a human community that (successfully) claims the *monopoly of the legitimate use of physical force* within a given territory.[10]

While the state must have the means to exercise physical power, "the use of physical force is neither the sole, nor even the most usual, method of administration of political corporate groups."[11]

> Organized domination, which calls for continuous administration, requires that human conduct be *conditioned to obedience* towards those masters who claim to be the bearers of *legitimate power*.[12]

## The Struggle For Legitimacy

A state seeks legitimacy because legitimacy makes the use of force unnecessary or minimal. A regime that is seen as legitimate has time on its side; even when it is inefficient or ineffective in its attack on problems, citizens will continue to acknowledge and obey the authority of the state.[13] But should a group of citizens cease to accept the legitimacy of the regime they may organize to overthrow it, and government may have to use violence to defend the system. If force does become necessary, the more widespread and deep the commitment of the citizenry to the state's legitimacy, the more "conditioned" they are to obedience, the more able the state will be to mobilize force against that minority which has revolutionary goals. While the use of violence is thus indicative of a weakened regime, and while in a democracy in particular the use of governmental violence against citizens must be carefully explained and defended, if important segments of the population accept the government's explanation (and if the violence is successful) the system will remain intact.

> While policies for adjusting the system are being created and implemented, phenomena such as rising rates of deviancy, increased status protests, the circulation of ideologies, and so forth, will appear. In order to control these and maintain some systematic integration under stress, the elite must use its legitimate means of force more frequently. But *so long as confidence in future improvements is maintained among non-deviant actors, this increased use of force will be regarded as legitimate* and tolerated as a necessary concomitant of social change.[14]

The "monopoly of the legitimate use of physical force" is the state's ultimate defense. An attempted revolution is not likely to occur if in the judgment of potential revolutionaries the incumbent regime's resources for the use of force far outweigh the resources of the revolutionaries. Attempted revolutions are rare, in part, because only if the revolutionaries believe that they have the physical force necessary to overthrow the state are they likely to take violent action.

It is for good reason that attempted revolutionary change in India has been limited. The Indian state is strong in that it enjoys both widespread legitimacy and considerable resources of force. The Indian government's legitimacy stems from several sources. With the brief exception of 1977-1979, the few years of Janata rule, Congress, the party of the independence movement, has ruled India. The Congress governments have inherited the mantle of the nationalist movement, and have further cultivated the legitimizing tie between the Congress governments and the nationalist movement through the Nehru family's dominance of politics in the post-independence era. This source of legitimacy may, in Weberian terms,[15] be seen as a routinization of the charisma of the nationalist movement and its key leaders, Gandhi and Nehru. Adding to this charismatic heritage is the appeal that Indira Gandhi, Nehru's daughter, obviously held for many Indians and Rajiv Gandhi seems to have inherited.

These charismatic sources of legitimacy are combined with several legal sources. The Indian government is a parliamentary democracy, with a democratic-socialist constitution that has provided ongoing mechanisms for the selection of governments; those mechanisms are widely acknowledged as legitimate. Even when the procedures have been breached, as they were during the 1975-1977 Emergency, homage was still paid to the constitution by the offenders, who argued strenuously, if unconvincingly to many, that their actions in fact *were* within the legal limits set by the constitution; the concern with stressing their adherence to the constitution demonstrates the constitution's power to legitimize political acts.

Another cause of the continuing legitimacy of the Indian state is its successful defense of the nation's security and territorial borders against international threats. This is a primary responsibility of any government. One need only look to a few historical examples to see how failure to protect a country against foreign encroachments has led to a severe weakening of the regime's legitimacy. The inability of the Manchu dynasty to protect its borders against European invasion, and the blame shouldered by the German Weimar Republic for the loss of World War One and the resultant loss of territories are two instances in which military defeat by foreign enemies and the loss of territory fatally crippled a government's legitimacy and aided the rise of revolutionary movements.

India's government, in wars against Pakistan, and in diplomatic relations, has proved itself a strong defender of the nation's integrity. In the 1962 border war with China, India's military capability was not adequate to check the Chinese; but fortunately for India and its government, the Chinese unilaterally ended the fighting. India emerged from the war "united as never before": "By and large the official explanations for the debacle were accepted, the blame put on the Chinese rather than on the Indian Government or on the military leadership."[16] The fact that some of India's revolutionary movements, including the Naxalite movement discussed below, have claimed allegiance to Chinese leadership has reinforced the legitimacy of the Indian government in its struggle against these internal allies of a foreign enemy.

It may be argued further that the government retains its legitimacy not only because of the democratic manner in which governments have been selected, but also because of its stated commitment to socialist goals. The Indian political culture demands of government that it work for the uplift of the poor. Government is expected to take an active leadership role in the socio-economic development of its people. Not only has this vision been put forward by the nationalist movement and a succession of politicians since independence, it is also set down specifically in the non-justiciable Directive Principles section of the Constitution. Article 38 directs the state to

> strive to promote the welfare of the people by securing and protecting as effectively as it may a social order in which justice, social, economic, and political, shall inform all the institutions of the national life.

The government is exhorted specifically to ensure that citizens have an adequate means of livelihood; that the operation of the economic system does not result in the concentration of wealth; and that the ownership and control of the material resources of the country subserve the common good.[17] The right to work, a living wage, and free and compulsory education are also goals to which the government is pledged.[18]

A political party or an individual politician, to maintain public trust and popularity, must appear to be working toward these goals. Ultimately, the legitimacy of the governmental system as a whole rests not only on the heritage of the nationalist movement, the process of democratic elections, and the maintenance of national security, but also on its commitment to this redistributive, democratic-socialist vision. As will be seen below, it is this last component of legitimacy to which the Maharashtra political movements have directed their attention.

Because a government has two sources of strength, force and legitimacy, it may be attacked on either of these fronts. The Naxalite movement in Srikakulam, Andhra Pradesh, while challenging the legitimacy of government, concentrated most of its efforts on armed attack on government; the Naxalites attacked the government with force. The movement fatally underestimated the spontaneous armed support that would arise to join with it, and was equally deficient in its understanding of the force available to the Indian government. The Naxalites' attempt to overthrow the government through force was utterly futile.

At the same time that the government committed its resources of armed force to the Naxalite problem, it also recognized that the Naxalites posed an implicit threat to the legitimacy of government as well. It was widely noted in the press, as well as in government circles, that the Naxalites could enjoy the amount of support they did only because of a failure of government to uphold its own laws and, more broadly, to move towards the socio-economic uplift of the poor. It was widely charged that government's activities in the

## The Struggle For Legitimacy

Naxalite-afflicted areas had served to benefit the rich at the expense of the poor tribals whom government was especially pledged to protect.

While the Naxalite's physical threat was minimal relative to the resources of force available to the government, its threat to governmental legitimacy was potentially more serious, and government plainly recognized this threat. As will be seen below, government's response to the crisis was thus two-pronged: it fought force with force, and it fought the threat to its legitimacy with a rapid increase in social welfare measures. Just as important, if not more important, than the social welfare measures for the poor tribals who were the victims of government neglect and of Naxalite opportunism was the public relations effort which accompanied them. The audience for government's response was not only the poor tribals, but interested onlookers throughout the country. In the short run, at least, the reality of change is less important than the appearance of change for government's retention of its legitimate right to rule. The immediate success of the effort is less important to the wider audience than the appearance that the effort is sincere.

Others intent on creating political change have learned from the Naxalite experience that the use of force against the present Indian government is fruitless; the vacuum of power described by Johnson as a pre-requisite to revolution does not exist, and the Indian government has proved fully capable of protecting itself against the force of localized armed struggles. Consequently, rather than attack government's force, other movements have begun to focus on government's legitimacy. The strategy of the movements in Maharashtra that will be examined below is multi-faceted. On the one hand, through gradual politicization of the poor, the movements' leaders hope to mobilize and educate what will become a self-led, self-sufficient and widespread movement, eventually capable of creating revolutionary change. At some future time, the hope is, India will experience a total, class-based revolution through, if necessary, the use of force. These movements recognize, however, that present efforts to overthrow the government through armed struggle would be futile. Thus, the politicization of the population serves a second, and more immediate purpose: to begin a process of casting doubt on the government's legitimacy.

The movements hope to spread an awareness of the contradiction between the socio-economic progress to which the government is pledged, and the government's inability to achieve that progress. Shramik Sanghatana, in particular, believes that because the system of government is closely tied to the interests of the landed and wealthy, government does not have the capacity to implement substantive change. Through political mobilization, they hope to increase both the demand for change, and the realization among the poor that the present structure of government is incapable of creating such change. The movements hope, too, to instill a sense of political efficacy in the poor;

this will be accomplished through the achievement of medium-range goals, such as the passage and implementation of legislation. The result over time, the movements hope, will be the collapse of the system, as masses of people come, first, to see the government as illegitimate because of its fundamental incapacity and, second, to aggressively demand change.

The Maharashtra movements, through strikes, demonstrations, and other forms of agitational activities, first attempt to influence the passage of laws that are beneficial to the socio-economic well-being of the tribals who predominantly make up their constituency. Once those laws are in place, the movements agitate to obtain the implementation of those laws. None of this activity, viewed narrowly, is revolutionary or illegitimate. Indeed, a number of observers of the Indian scene have noted that extra-constitutional methods of protest are quite acceptable in the Indian context. Rajni Kothari has written,

> As a system and as a people we have shown a high tolerance of dissent, including a whole lot of "extra-constitutional" forms of opposition, thoughtless invectives against the elite and the establishment, and not a little violence. Perhaps more than anywhere in the world, the legitimacy of opposition and dissent seems to be an integral part of our national political idiom. It represents our inherently anarchic and anti-collectivist trait as a political culture.[19]

Thus, because the movements' goals for the creation of better economic conditions through the passage and implementation of improved laws are within the legitimate boundaries of political demands, and because their methods, although extra-constitutional, are also within a legitimate tradition, the movements cannot be suppressed by government without considerable political cost. Furthermore, because they are demanding the rule of law, the movements have the potential to cast widespread doubt on government's capabilities and, ultimately, legitimacy. A government that does not uphold the law of the land, and that does not appear to be making sincere, intelligent efforts to create socio-economic change, may cease to be legitimate in the eyes of a politically mobilized population.

A government beset with shortages and insufficient capacities will respond more quickly where the demand is loudest and best organized. But when government responds positively to a movement's demands, there is a danger that its positive response will add to the popularity of the movement. Paradoxically, through actions designed to maintain its own legitimacy, such as the passage of more progressive laws, or the implementation of existing laws, government aids the legitimacy of the movements, and provides them with the tools to further challenge the government. It is through such small vic-

## The Struggle For Legitimacy

tories that the movements hope to teach the efficacy of organized political action, and to build their strength.

In the short run, the movements play a reformist role; indeed, in the short run, they may even aid the cause of governmental legitimacy by forcing government to live up to the standards expressed in the constitution. Speaking of the United States' democratic system, Theodore Lowi has noted,

> ...government's capacity to change things is really limited to its use of positive law—that is, to its willingness to directly and coercively use the powers of the state on society in a way that is unmistakably clear to all. Ironically, the above describes the rule of law...Yet, this rule of law is the very thing that most social movements seek. Governments in the United States...have never moved with greater certainty or with greater effectiveness than when pushed by movements....A nation that is in need of stability is also in need of change. It follows that such a nation needs law and *dis*order.[20]

But, in India, if the movements demanding redistribution of wealth and social justice were to become too widespread, the government would cease to be able to meet their demands even to the limited extent it now does for the Maharashtra movements. It simply does not have the capacity to insure than minimum wages are paid, to provide public works jobs, to provide land. If the challenge became too widespread, if too many demands were made simultaneously, the present state would be incapable of responding in a way that would support its legitimate right to rule. The ability to politicize the poor to make demands that the government cannot fulfill is the basis for the movements' potentially radical impact. Because their demands are legal, and are made legally, government cannot legitimately suppress them as they struggle towards this goal.

In structuralist terms, the present Indian government can respond adequately with force if it is challenged with force; there is no vacuum of power. It can also act to re-legitimize itself, to re-establish the equilibrium between values (i.e., the right to employment) and environment (i.e., lack of employment) if the dissynchronization becomes politically significant for small pockets of the population. But no matter how clever, the elites would be incapable of creating synchronization if the movements that work to politicize the poor and thus create forceful demands become too widespread.

The present state could be trapped in an insolvable dilemma. India is a political democracy and to retain its legitimacy the government must allow free political association and organization. If it does not respond positively to legitimate demands, it risks forfeiting its legitimacy with a wide audience of onlookers. But when it does respond positively to movement demands, it strengthens and broadens the movements, which then have the capability to politicize more people and activate more demands. The demands, eventually, could outstrip government's capacity to respond. The government might then cease to be legitimate in the eyes of many of its citizens and would rest more heavily on force. While a government relying primarily on force to maintain itself in power is possible, it is a much shakier pedestal on which to rest.

The chapters that follow attempt to demonstrate the validity of the proposition that while violent action against the Indian government is, at present, doomed to failure, a more gradual mobilization of the poor to question government's capacity might eventually result in government's delegitimation, and structural change.

## The Struggle For Legitimacy

### NOTES

1. Robert L. Hardgrave, Jr., *India: Government and Politics in a Developing Nation* (New York: Harcourt Brace Jovanovich, Inc., 1980). p. 4 relates to India the theory Samuel Huntington developed in *Political Order in Changing Societies* (New Haven Cn: Yale University Press, 1968).

2. Francine Frankel, *India's Political Economy 1947-1977* (Princeton, N.J.: Princeton University Press, 1978), ch. 2 *passim*.

3. Ibid., p. 110.

4. Ted Gurr, *Why Men Rebel* (Princeton, N.J.: Princeton University Press, 1970); Chalmers Johnson, *Revolutionary Change* (Boston: Little Brown, 1966); Charles Tilly, *From Mobilization to Revolution* (Reading, Mass.: Addison-Wesley, 1978). Ted Gurr names these groups of theories in his "The Revolution-Social Change Nexus," *Comparative Politics*, April 1973, pp. 359-392. Theda Skocpol renames them the "aggregate-psychological," "systems/value consensus," and "political conflict" theories in *States and Social Revolutions* (New York: Cambridge University Press, 1979), p. 9.

5. In *States and Social Revolutions* Skocpol supplements her structural analysis (in her case, a Marxist analysis) with conflict theory in order to understand "how and when class members find themselves *able* to struggle effectively for their interests." p. 13.

6. The focus on leadership, ideology and organization is based on a course, Modern Political Movements, developed by Peter Juviler and Dennis Dalton at Barnard College. To some degree these categories overlap with Tilly's emphasis on "mobilization" (leadership), "interest" (ideology) and "organization." *From Mobilization to Revolution*, p. 7.

7. Tilly, p. 7, speaks of "opportunity" — "the relationship between and group and the world around it."

8. Skocpol, p. 23.

9. Juan Linz, *The Breakdown of Democratic Regimes: Crisis, Breakdown and Reequilibration* (Baltimore: The Johns Hopkins Press, 1978), p. 16.

10. Max Weber, "Politics as a Vocation," in H.H. Gerth and C. Wright Mills, eds., *From Max Weber* (New York: Oxford University Press, 1946), p. 78. Emphasis in the original.

11. Max Weber, *The Theory of Social and Economic Organization* (New York: Free Press, 1947), p. 154.

12. Max Weber, "Politics as a Vocation," p. 80. Emphasis added.

13. Linz, p. 45.

14. Johnson, p. 92. Emphasis added.

15. Weber described three sources of elite legitimacy: traditional, legal-rational and charismatic. "Politics as a Vocation," p. 78.

16. Neville Maxwell, *India's China War* (New York: Anchor Books, 1972), p. 469.

17. Article 39.

18. Articles 41, 43, and 45.

19. Rajni Kothari, "More Opposition," *Seminar*, January 1971, p. 22. The legitimacy of agitational politics is also noted by David Bayley and Satish Arora. Bayley writes: "Agitational politics has become a customary coercive force supplementing, sometimes supplanting, the orderly processes of parliamentary government." David Bayley, *The Police and Political Development in India* (Princeton: Princeton University Press, 1969), p. 278. Satish K. Arora, "Political Participation: Deprivation and Protest," *Economic and Political Weekly*, Annual Number, January 1971, p. 341, writes: "Political participation, generally considered to be symbolic of the extensiveness to which democratic ideals are applied, also includes a dimension which, in fact, lies outside the scope of constitutional activity. In this respect mass protests have become a conventional—if not legal—form of participation..."

20. Theodore Lowi, *The Politics of Disorder* (New York: Basic Books, 1971), p. 57.

# PART 1
# THE SRIKAKULAM NAXALITE MOVEMENT

# INTRODUCTION TO PART 1

The Naxalite rebellion in Srikakulam District of Andhra Pradesh was a self-described Maoist movement aimed at the immediate overthrow of state power. In reality, the movement never posed a significant revolutionary threat; it was easily crushed by state and central police forces. But the state did acknowledge its own responsibility for allowing the development of economic and political conditions that had led to the movement, and it understood that the movement posed a threat to its legitimacy. Consequently, the government not only took measures to forcefully suppress the movement, it also acted to correct the conditions that had led to revolt and, in so doing, to re-establish its own legitimacy. The government on both the state and union level plainly articulated its understanding that violent suppression of the movement, while necessary, was not sufficient. Efforts to capture the loyalties of the tribal population affected by the Naxalite revolt through a rapid infusion of economic aid were begun even before the military defeat of the movement. These efforts, while considered essential to retain the allegiance of the tribals, also represented an attempt to legitimize governmental authority in the eyes of Indian public opinion more generally.

The Srikakulam Naxalite movement was not a totally isolated event. It followed soon after an uprising in the Naxalbari area of Darjeeling District in West Bengal.[1] The "Naxalite" revolutionaries, under the ideological leadership of Charu Mazumdar, the District Communist Party of India (Marxist) Secretary, began their struggle in March 1967 by organizing village committees to seize lands and begin armed revolution.

> Some twenty thousand peasants and agricultural and tea garden workers were working vigorously to organize these committees and some ninety percent of villagers were armed to function as village defence squads against "reactionary subversion." The weapons used by the insurgents were traditional, like bows and arrows and spears and guns snatched from landlords. Feudal and government lands were redistributed. Legal documents including mortgage deeds were burnt.

Work cattle, farm implements and hoarded grains of landlords and usurers were confiscated and distributed among poor peasants and workers. Oppressive and notorious landlords, usurers, and the "enemies of the revolution" were publicly tried and executed.[2]

Aside from the obvious challenge to government power and authority, the Naxalbari revolt was especially unacceptable to the Indian government for three reasons. First, Naxalbari occupies a location of strategic importance; it is only ninety-six kilometers from China's Tibetan border, and Darjeeling borders Nepal in the west, Sikkim and Bhutan in the north, and Bangladesh in the south.[3] Darjeeling is a vital link between the main peninsula of India and its eastern region. For strategic reasons, then, the Union government was gravely concerned that governmental authority in the district not be lost.

Second, the Naxalites enjoyed the support of the Chinese communist government, against whom India had fought a war in 1962, and with whom relations were still severely strained. Chinese support for the Naxalites, argues Biplab Dasgupta, confirmed the worst fears of India's elites that through them China was trying to subvert the Indian government.[4] On June 28, 1967 Peking Radio hailed the uprising in Naxalbari, calling it "the front paw of the revolutionary armed struggle launched by the Indian people under the guidance of Mao Tse-tung's thought"; this endorsement was noted with considerable alarm in India's press.[5] Thus, Naxalbari's close physical proximity to China, in combination with the Chinese support the revolutionaries enjoyed, made the task of ending the rebellion urgent for the union government.

Third, the Naxalbari revolt began just as a coalition government with prominent CPI(M) participation came to power in West Bengal. The rebellion was led by disaffected CPI(M) members who were incensed at the CPI(M)'s alliance with non-Marxist parties and the pro-Moscow CPI.[6] However, to the general public, Naxalbari appeared to be led by the CPI(M):

> Many thought at the time that they were part of a well-laid nationwide conspiracy to seize power in the country under the CPI(M) leadership, which was also using its position in the state government to subvert the administration to facilitate the objective of revolution.[7]

This fear of revolutionary intent by an established political party that had just achieved significant power in two state governments was a third cause for extreme anxiety on the part of the Congress government at the center.

Although the CPI(M) had chosen the parliamentary path of political action, Jyoti Basu, CPI(M) leader and Home Minister of West Bengal, was reluctant to use police force against the revolutionaries and made efforts to negotiate with Mazumdar and the local Naxalbari leader, Kanu Sanyal. As the negotiations were being initiated, the national press was increasingly playing up the CPI(M)'s cooperation with the revolt.[8] The negotiations were unsuccessful,

## The Srikakulam Naxalite Movement

and the Central government put tremendous pressure on the government of West Bengal to order massive police action.[9] The order was made on July 5, and full scale police action began on July 12, 1967. Within a fortnight, the movement was fully suppressed.[10]

The Srikakulam movement, which erupted in violence in 1968, was of longer duration and involved greater violence than Naxalbari. It too was suppressed by the police, and did not pose a significant threat to government force. But coming soon after Naxalbari, it posed a threat to government greater than its armed strength would indicate. These eruptions of violence indicated that government's legitimacy was not unquestioned. To regain its legitimacy, government had both to suppress the movements with violence and regain its monopoly on the legitimate use of force, and it had to take steps to correct the economic and political conditions that had led to the disequilibrium. After the initial rebellion in Srikakulam, members of the judiciary and elected officials plainly acknowledged the culpability of government in creating the conditions of poverty and exploitation that had driven many impoverished people to accept armed revolution. Consequently, to regain legitimacy and support, government had to initiate steps to correct the deplorable conditions under which the tribals of Srikakulam lived.

The discussion of the Srikakulam rebellion that follows is divided into five segments. In Chapter 2, the economic, social and political conditions in Srikakulam prior to the Naxalite rebellion in 1968 are detailed with special attention to the nature of government's responsibility for the development of these conditions. Chapter 3 describes the pre-Naxalite political movement that was formed in the Agency area of the district from the mid-1950s onward; again, government's role, this time in thwarting the movement, is highlighted. Chapter 4 analyzes the shift of the local movement to Naxalism, the leadership, organization and ideology of the Naxalites, and their armed struggle. Chapters 5 and 6 move beyond the initial confrontation with police and the issue of power to the question of governmental legitimacy by examining ways in which government sought to re-establish its authority in the area. Since the conditions that allowed for the Naxalite's emergence are not unique, since that disequilibrium exists elsewhere in India, the issue of governmental legitimacy remains the most compelling.

## The Srikakulam Naxalite Movement
### NOTES

1. In addition to the works cited in this study, there are numerous valuable sources on the Naxalbari uprising. Among them are Asish Kumar Roy, *The Spring Thunder and After* (Calcutta: Minerva Associates, 1975); Sankar Ghosh, *The Naxalite Movement* (Calcutta: Firma K.L. Mukhopadhyay, 1975); Sohail Jawaid, *The Naxalite Movement in India* (New Delhi: Associated Publishing House, 1979); Mohan Ram, *Maoism in India* (Delhi: Vikas Publications, 1971).

2. Haridwar Rai and K.M. Prasad, "Naxalism: A Challenge to the Proposition of Peaceful Transition to Socialism," *Indian Journal of Political Science*, October-December 1972, p. 464.

3. Manoranjan Mohanty, *Revolutionary Violence: A Study of the Maoist Movement in India* (New Delhi: Sterling Publishers Pvt. Ltd., 1977), p. 32.

4. Biplab Dasgupta, *The Naxalite Movement* (Bombay: Allied Publishers, 1974), pp. 11-12.

5. Mohanty, p. 45; and *Statement Filed by the Inspector General of Police on Behalf of the Police Department of Andhra Pradesh*, 1977, p. 4. This document was presented to the Bhargava Commission. See Chapter 5 below.

6. Dasgupta, p. 7.

7. Ibid., pp. 8-9.

8. Mohanty, p. 45.

9. Under the Seventh Schedule of the Constitution of India, public order is the responsibility of state governments.

10. Mohanty, p. 45.

# 2
# THE DEVELOPMENT OF TRIBAL POVERTY

When, in the late 1960s, the tribals of Srikakulam District—called *girijans*, or "hill people"—became part of a violent Naxalite movement, government officials at state and national levels accused the Naxalites of exploiting the poverty and despair of these Scheduled Tribes. Government did not at any time deny that the tribals had excellent reasons for being desperately unhappy; only the method for the redress of what were acknowledged to be legitimate grievances was questioned.

The poverty they experienced was extreme, with chronic hunger a severe problem. One 1971 government-sponsored study noted, in reference to tribals throughout Andhra Pradesh, that "although agriculture is the main source of livelihood, it is not giving sufficient returns to save the tribals from starvation....Chronic poverty and destitution have become the patterns of tribal life."[1] *The Statesman* observed in 1969 that in Srikakulam "the Girijans are so poor that for part of the year many of them live on mango kernels and tamarind seeds."[2] A 1969 government survey of one tribal development block in the area most involved with the Naxalite uprising found that the per capita income of tribals there was only Rs. 123.21, while the State per capita income was Rs. 354.31.[3]

The girijans' impoverished condition is attributable to a number of factors, of which several are humanly created. The loss of girijan lands to non-tribal outsiders and widespread indebtedness are of particular importance. Although both British and post-independence governments created numerous laws designed to protect the tribals from exploitation at the hands of more sophisticated outsiders, these laws were virtually ignored by the local officials whose responsibility it was to implement them. In light of its failure to prevent slippage in the tribals' economic condition as non-tribals prospered, and, more concretely, its failure to uphold the law, government's claim to legitimacy was extremely fragile.

# The Development Of Tribal Poverty

This chapter will analyze the development of the tribals' intense poverty, and will especially consider government's role in the creation of their increasing impoverishment.

## The Loss of the Land

Through a combination of government actions beginning in the nineteenth century that favored a class of large landholders, and the unchecked usury and corruption of non-tribal moneylenders from the plains areas adjoining the Agency tracts,[4] tribals progressively lost the use of agricultural lands.

> The tribal belt in Srikakulam district is an area of 400 square miles of mountains, vallies [sic] and jungles declared as "Agency" more than fifty years ago by the British Government who appointed the District Collector as the Agent to the Governor General to administer the area. The entire land in this tribal belt belongs either to the Government or to the tribals and its alienation to plainsmen was prohibited under the Land Regulation Act, 1917, except under certain circumstances. But plainsmen started to settle at the fringe of the Agency more than half a century ago as petty tradesmen and moneylenders and used to go into the interior as opportunity gave them passage....The plainsmen started to exploit [the tribals] by selling them articles on credit and lending them money at a very exhorbitant [sic] rate of interest. The stage was reached when tribals could not repay the loans and hence they had to give away their lands to the plainsmen. The plainsmen thus came into possession of their land and settled down in the interior Agency.[5]

By the time of the Naxalite rebellion, the per capita share of cultivated land in one block of Parvathipuram Taluk, Srikakulam that was closely examined by government was only 0.39 acres; the size of this holding was deemed "uneconomic." "The man-land ratio is very low," stated a government report, "it is not even just sufficient for the subsistence of a single person throughout the year."[6] The following is a summary of how the tribals lost their lands, and of the ineffective government measures that addressed the problem prior to the Naxalites.

In 1802-1803, the British introduced a land system of Permanent Settlement in the area. The harsh judgment of the Srikakulam *Gazetteer* is that "this system which created a class of territorial landlords...became riddled through and through with every species of corruption and malpractice during the subsequent years." One source of abuse was the Muttadari system, in which the right to collect rents from the tenants in the Agency areas was auctioned off to a middleman, a Muttadar, who agreed to pay a certain sum to the Zamindar.[7] In addition, the Muttadars were also made responsible for maintaining "law and order" among the hill tribes; as representatives of the law, there was nothing to prevent their harassment of the tribals.[8] While, legally, the Zamindari system was abolished under the Estates Abolition Act of 1948, by the late 1960s, the government had failed to survey and re-settle the tribal areas; the tribals still had no *patta* rights, no legal rights, to the land they cultivated.[9] A government report claimed that "the traditional feudal type of 'Muttadari' system has almost reduced [the tribals] to serfdom."[10] Another author condemned the government's failure to survey and settle the tribal areas, noting

> the Muttadari system has met with such a universal condemnation that it is a matter of surprise that no action has been taken to end it. . . . The poor tribals who are engaged in the cultivation of lands for generations together have no protection against the high-handedness of the Muttadars either in the matter of exacting levies or outright evictions.[11]

The Muttadar issue is relevant to those tribals who retained access to agricultural lands; but by the time of the Naxalite rebellion, only about one-third did. While in 1961, 48 percent of the working tribals in Srikakulam were cultivators, by 1971, that percentage had shrunk to 34 percent. The percentage of workers who were agricultural laborers had correspondingly risen over the same period from 40 percent in 1961 to 53 percent in 1971. The *Integrated Tribal Development Plan for Tribal Areas of Srikakulam District* stated that "This decrease in the number of cultivators is largely because of alienation of tribal land by non-tribals which was one of the major factors contributing in large scale unrest in the latter half of 1960s." [sic][12]

The British and post-independence Andhra government did take some steps designed to stem the alienation of land from tribals to non-tribals; by all accounts, these efforts were completely ineffective. The British as early as 1917 realized that "by taking advantage of the illiteracy and backwardness of hill tribes, the plainsmen have been exploiting them by charging exorbitant interest on debts and that ultimately they are obtaining the transfer of the immovable property from the hill tribes."[13] Consequently, the British passed the Agency tracts Interest and Land Transfer Act of 1917, prohibiting the transfer of land from tribals to non-tribals unless the transfer was agreed to in writing by a prescribed officer of the government. This law, in the words of a 1961 government evaluation, "was not effective and gave ample scope for many underhand transactions."[14] *The Times of India* reported that the 1917 law "was

## The Development Of Tribal Poverty

more honored in the breach than in the observance. As a result, vast stretches of land passed into the hands of plainsmen who went and settled in the Agency areas."[15] The plainsmen continued to obtain the transfer of land by extending loans to the tribals at "exorbitant rates of interest." When the tribals could not repay the loans, they were compelled to give away their lands.[16]

In 1959, the Andhra Pradesh government passed a law designed to strengthen government's ability to protect tribals against this exploitation by moneylenders. The Andhra Pradesh (Scheduled Areas) Land Transfer Regulation, 1959, enabled local officials to commence legal action to restore alienated lands on their own initiative; the 1917 law had required a complaint from the aggrieved party.[17] In addition, the 1959 law stated that no immovable property owned by a member of a Scheduled Tribe could be attached and sold in execution of a money decree.[18]

In his 1961 government-sponsored report, V. Raghavaiah noted with complacency that "there has been a genuine effort on the part of the Andhra Pradesh Government to employ the special powers vested in the Governor under the fifth Schedule of the Constitution. Though lapses have occurred here and there."[sic][19] By the end of the decade, the same author, then a member of the Government of India's Study Team on Tribal Development Programmes, had become dismayed by government's inaction:

> the rules for carrying out the purpose of the Regulations under the Andhra Pradesh Scheduled Areas Land Transfer Regulation of 1959...[have] not been framed so far and...this lacuna [has] come in the way of effective implementation of the protective provisions of the Regulations.[20]

The 1959 Regulation proved as ineffective as the 1917 legislation; again, government failed to stem the activities of the non-tribals from the plains bent on obtaining land. In the shadow of the rebellion in Srikakulam, some government officials put the blame for the failure of the 1959 Regulation jointly on the ruthlessness of the moneylenders and the innocence of the unworldly tribals. Other government officials, however, have been willing to acknowledge government's failure to govern.

An example of the first mode of analysis is found in a study undertaken in 1971-72 by the Tribal Cultural Research and Training Institute of the Tribal Welfare Department, *Indebtedness Among Scheduled Tribes of Andhra Pradesh*. This document acknowledges that

> the non-tribals found ways and means to circumvent the legislation and they have been grabbing much of the fertile lands from tribals...Most of the land alienation cases are the result of indebted-

ness. The non-tribals settle down in tribal areas with the motive of grabbing lands. Though the lands are in the name of tribals as per records, the actual possession is in the hands of non-tribals and the usufruct is enjoyed by them till the tribal completely repays the loan. Most of the tribals cannot repay the debt due to abysmal poverty. After a lapse of several years, the sowcars declare themselves as de facto owners of the lands.[21]

As the analysis continues, the government's efforts to relieve the situation are seen as thwarted by the simplicity of the tribals; even here, though, there is some acknowledgment that the tribals' unwillingness to testify against the moneylenders may be based not on naivete, but on necessity:

> Whenever any enquiry is made, the tribals *due to moral binding to creditors* gave false evidence that they own those lands but not the sowcars or moneylenders. Thus the operation of the Regulation becomes difficult *in spite of the best wishes of Government*.
>
> Further, most of the tribals in Agency Areas are not aware of this regulation. Even if they are aware of this regulation they cannot but [remain] silent with a fear that they may not get loans in future from sowcars and moneylenders in the hour of need.[22]

Other government officials familiar with the local scene offer a picture of government non-involvement. Mr. Lakshminarayana, who was appointed Special Deputy Collector for Tribal Welfare in Srikakulam in 1968, in direct response to the threat posed by the Naxalites, suggests that "a tribal area was a *distant* area that was *ignored* unless and until there was tension in the area. The essence of tribal protective legislation is that it is expected to be implemented by officers, not by the tribals themselves, who are assumed to be unable to assert their own rights. But officials didn't go much into the area."[23] A document prepared for the police in the wake of the Naxalite uprising also commented on the failure of the government to be present in the region:

> . . . revenue officials rarely went into the interior either for collection of revenues or for any other purpose because of the bad terrain and lack of communications....police officers of all ranks found it difficult to go deep into the Agency. Thus *the writ of the Government failed to run through the tribal belt.*[24]

Mr. V. Chandramowli, I.A.S., was a Sub-Collector in Srikakulam in 1964-66, and in 1969 became the Director of the Girijan Cooperative Cor-

## The Development Of Tribal Poverty

poration, the body at the forefront of government's efforts to wean the tribals away from the Naxalites by introducing a number of welfare and development schemes. Chandramowli is less inclined to place the blame for government's failure to implement the land alienation law on local officials, but instead points to the state government and, particularly, the courts. Local officials, he says, would decide in favor of the return of land to the tribals, but the landlords would then get stays from the courts. De facto possession always remained with the non-tribal. The state officials did not pay any attention to this problem. Srikakulam, says Chandramowli, was "too distant, too obscure."[25]

Thus the tribals in Srikakulam in the years prior to the Naxalite rebellion experienced a continuing loss of their land to non-tribals. Government, despite the passage of legislation designed to prevent this land alienation and to restore already alienated land, offered no effective assistance.

### *Tribal Indebtedness*

The loss of land was usually attributable directly to the endemic indebtedness in the tribal areas. The indebtedness was so severe that in addition to losing their land, tribals sometimes lost their individual freedom, becoming bonded to the service of a moneylender. Although legislation designed to alleviate tribal indebtedness came into force in 1960, it was virtually ignored by government officials responsible for its implementation. Neither the Andhra Pradesh (Scheduled Areas) Moneylenders Regulation, 1960 nor the Andhra Pradesh (Scheduled Tribes) Debt Relief Regulation, 1960 had any measurable effect.

Both the degree of indebtedness and the legislations' ineffectualness are clearly documented in a number of Andhra Pradesh government-sponsored studies. One such study published by the state's Tribal Cultural Research and Training Institute, *Survey of Tribal Development Block: Bhadragiri, Srikakulam District*, analyzed data collected in 1965-65 and 1967. Bhadragiri is a block in the Parvathipuram Taluk, the taluk in which the Naxalites were most active. The TCRTI study found that 34 percent of the tribal households in the block were indebted, with Rs. 159 the average indebtedness per household.[26] The per capita income of a tribal was Rs. 123.21, and the average annual income of a tribal household was Rs. 553.[27] Therefore, the amount owed by the average indebted household amounted to 29 percent of the annual household income. Most of the debts were owed to private moneylenders; 75 percent of the tribal households had borrowed from private moneylenders, while only 18 percent had borrowed from government agencies.[28] The *Survey* acknowledged that the Andhra Pradesh Scheduled Tribes Cooperative Finance and Development Corporation, founded in 1956 for the purpose of extending credit to the tribals and purchasing agricultural and minor forest products from them, was "not in a position to meet the credit needs of the tribals to a greater extent...[Due] to various handicaps and limited financial resources the Corporation has yet to become a dependable major source to tribals for meeting the credit needs."[29] Because the credit facilities provided by government were "insufficient and inadequate,"[30] and because tribal income was not adequate to meet basic needs, "the majority of the tribal people...living at marginal subsistence...have no other easy and ready way out except to borrow loans [sic] from money lenders."[31]

As a result of this indebtedness, some tribals became virtually enslaved to moneylenders:

> Some of the tribal families are so much indebted to the moneylenders that they cannot repay the amount in full even if they render their services to the creditor throughout their life. Due to exorbitant rates of interest the tribals are unable to repay the debt either in cash or in kind and...they become the "Gothis" or "serfs" for the Sowcars for whom they have to work. These tribals get only food and nothing else in return. The Money Lenders always take utmost care to manipulate their accounts in such a manner that it becomes impossible for the Tribal to repay the debt. Many of the tribals have alienated their lands to non-tribals for redemption of debt.[32]

Nor was there any escape for the tribal from this enslavement. A 1971 government study reported that the moneylenders "take recourse to means including intimidation and assault for recovery of loans. [They] have a network of agents, both tribal and non-tribal, in tribal areas....[When] the tribal fails to repay the amount, the Agent...collects the loan amount from the debtor by beating him up."[33] In addition to losing his land and performing agricultural labor, "the tribal has to do whatever his master tells, whether it is good or bad. It is reported in some cases that the non-tribal money-lender uses him as a weapon whenever any social disturbance arises."[34]

These slave-like conditions of indebtedness were documented not by radical extremists, but by the Government of Andhra Pradesh in the years just before and after the revolt. In government sources, too, one finds evidence of the utter failure of government, prior to the Naxalite revolt, to take effective remedial steps.

Laws were passed but were not implemented. Important provisions of the Andhra Pradesh (Scheduled Area) Money-Lenders Regulation, 1960 provided for the annual licensing of moneylenders, the prohibition of moneylending without a license, the prohibition of interest rates exceeding 12 percent, and the maintenance of accurate accounts by the moneylenders.[35] "In actual practice," wrote V. Raghavaiah, "these provisions are honoured more in the breach than in observance."[36] In a book published in 1971 he noted that the rules for carrying out the regulation had not yet been framed, and that "the rate of interest charged by the money-lender usually varied from 25 to 50 percent and was sometimes as high as 100 percent."[37] The Tribal Cultural Research and Training Institute's study *Indebtedness Among Scheduled Tribes of Andhra Pradesh* also found, with reference to the 1960 Moneylenders Regulation, that "in spite of the provisions of the regulation, moneylending has been taking place on an unprecedented scale at exorbitant rates of interest in Scheduled areas."[38]

The government's legislation for relieving indebtedness—the Andhra Pradesh (Scheduled Tribes) Debt Relief Regulation, 1960—was equally ineffective. The law provided for the scaling down of debts owed by Scheduled Tribe members to non-governmental lenders. Section 4(5) provided for the scaling down of debts incurred before January 1, 1951; the level of usury that was common is reflected in subsection (b):

> Where any member of a Scheduled Tribe has paid to any creditor twice the amount of the principal whether by way of principal or interest or both, such debt...shall be deemed to be wholly discharged.

Debts incurred on or after January 1, 1951 were to be scaled down so that the interest due would be no more than five percent per annum; the amount the tribal had already paid was to be credited toward the payment of this rate.

To implement this Regulation, Special Deputy Tehsildars were to be appointed in the Agency areas; they would obtain applications from the tribals and apply on their behalf to the Civil Courts for the scaling down of debts.[39] But "the Regulation," writes V. Raghavaiah, "proved to be a nullity."[40] A government of Andhra Pradesh document, *Note on Protective Legislation-Srikakulam District* came to the same conclusion that because of fear that "the non-tribal may not advance loans at times of need," the suits filed by the Tehsildars had to be dismissed by the courts "owing to the fact that there was a collusion between the creditor and the debtor who deposed before the Court that the debt was discharged." Thus, during 1964-65, 341 of the 380 cases the government brought before the courts were withdrawn.[41]

While it may be true that the reluctance of the tribals to bring suit limited the government's ability to successfully prosecute cases, one must also question the commitment of government to the law's implementation. According to the 1961 census, there were 192,276 tribals in Srikakulam district.[42] The average size of a tribal household in Andhra Pradesh is 4.9 people.[43] This

## The Development Of Tribal Poverty

means that there were, in 1961, approximately 39,240 tribal families in the district of Srikakulam. If one uses as a rough estimate of indebted families the figure of 34.63 percent cited in the *Survey of Tribal Development Block: Bhadragiri, Srikakulam District*,[44] one finds approximately 13,482 tribal families in debt. If one instead calculates the frequency of indebtedness according to the 1971 study, *Indebtedness Among Scheduled Tribes of Andhra Pradesh*,[45] which found that 70.54 percent of tribal households in Srikakulam were indebted, one can calculate approximately 27,679 indebted tribal families. The government, in 1964-65, brought 380 cases. This means that the government brought between 1.3 and 2.8 percent of the possible cases. This certainly seems to indicate only the most minimal government effort to actively implement this legislation.

### Diminished Access to Forest Lands

In addition to their chronic indebtedness and the loss of their agricultural lands, the tribals suffered from limits imposed by government rules and sometimes by corrupt local officials on tribal access to forest land for the collection of forest products and for cultivation.

Prior to 1894, tribals enjoyed unlimited rights to the forest. In 1894, for the first time, the Government of India became concerned with the problem of erosion and the desire to preserve and cultivate timber for commercial purposes; some restrictions were consequently put on the unlimited use of the forests by their inhabitants. In 1952 the Government of India, which had attained ownership of all forest lands from their zamindari owners in 1948 as a result of the Andhra Pradesh (Andhra Area) Estates (Abolition and Conversion in Ryotwari) Act,[46] further limited tribal rights to forest access in an effort to restore 33.3 percent of India's total land area to forest.[47] Some areas were therefore declared reserved; shifting cultivation was banned as was the collection of minor forest produce for commercial purposes; collection of minor forest produce for personal use was made subject to government regulation.[48]

In the process of reserving forest lands, government sometimes declared reserved areas in which tribal villages already existed. The tribals were then forced to leave their homes; they were not given homestead rights.[49] Tribals wishing to remain on what historically had been their land were subject to continual harassment by forest officers. In short, while the goal of resuming forest land in order to preserve the ecological balance may have been sound, the implementation of this process had a harsh impact on those citizens—the tribals—least able to defend their interests and already experiencing the most severe deprivation.

Historically, the forests were important to the tribals for the collection of minor forest produce for both commercial and personal use. In 1961 an

## The Development Of Tribal Poverty

Andhra Pradesh government document reported on the wide range of economic activities provided by forest access:

> [Tribals in Srikakulam's Agency areas] keep themselves busy collecting and selling minor forest produce like nuxvomica myrabolams [a fruit], Adda and Beedi leaves, tamarind, pipallu, pea-cock feather, gum, bee wax, deer skins and horns, porcupine bristles, stag hoofs, soap leaves, and nuts and several kinds of medicinal herbs. They also collect and sell forest grasses, snare and sell birds, peacocks and deer.[50]

In 1969, the *Survey of Tribal Development Block: Bhadragiri, Sirkakulam District* found that even with the legal restrictions, 44.1 percent of the tribals engaged in the collection of minor forest produce, and 10.4 percent of all tribals had the collection of minor forest produce as their main occupation.[51]

The economic necessity of continuing to collect minor forest produce led to a situation in which local officials had considerable power to coerce and bribe the tribals:

> Innumerable taxes, some having legal sanction and some collected without proper sanctions from Government were levied on the tribals. Money was collected and bribes...taken for cutting...grass to build roofs for the house, for felling wood for fuel, for having used forest pastures for feeding sheep and cattle, for using tamarind trees for fuel wood, for cutting any small tree to make a plough or any other instrument. If bribes were not given, cases were booked. The tribals had to give fuel and wood to the forest officials and share with them their produce, supply them with chickens, and in many cases work as unpaid labour for laying roads, etc. To pay their obligations to the forest officials most of the tribals became indebted and fell into the clutches of moneylenders.[52]

Since the commercial cutting of timber became the sole province of the government, and the private contractors to whom it leases coupes, tribals have also been continually exploited by these agents. The 1961 *Report of the Andhra Pradesh Tribes Enquiry Committee* states unequivocally that in the Agency areas of Srikakulam and neighboring districts tribals were

> employed by the forest department in felling and transporting timber from inaccessible jungle heights to the plains below in difficult, rocky and even precipitous terrain, though they are *invariably cheated*

## The Development Of Tribal Poverty

in these operations *by unscrupulous officials and blood sucking contractors.*[53]

Another of the tribals' traditional occupations which was subject to harassment was *podu*, or slash and burn cultivation. In the effort to limit damage to the forests, government in 1952 prohibited shifting cultivation.[54] However, having lost their settled agricultural land to moneylenders, the tribals had little other choice. Two government reports—the 1948 *Report on the Socioeconomic Conditions of the Aboriginal Tribes of the Province of Madras* (known as the Aiyappan Report) and the 1952 *Report of the Special Agency Development Officer* (the Malayappan Report)—acknowledged the conditions which made podu cultivation necessary for the tribals.

> Podu cultivation did not arise out of "any perversity of the tribesmen." It was because the best lands suitable for permanent cultivation had "all passed into the hands of the sowcars and other plainsmen who managed to get a stranglehold over them; from a commonsense point of view, there is little prospective gain, if the tribals spend their capital and labour in improving land."...On the other hand, the forests had to be preserved and developed, and podu cultivation could not therefore be allowed to continue. Aiyappan, therefore, makes the thoughtful suggestion that podu "should not be suddenly stopped, but it may be slowly restricted while the tribesmen are provided with suitable land for permanent cultivation and helped with credit facilities."[55]

The government did not carry out Aiyappan's suggestion. Therefore, given the loss of their best land, the failure of government to provide alternative land, and the tribals' limited access to forest produce, podu became an economic necessity. Vempatapu Satyanarayana, who in the late 1950s became the major political organizer of Srikakulam's girijans, wrote that no matter how many bribes to government officials had to be paid and how many court cases had to be faced, the girijans *could* not stop shifting cultivation.[56]

Thus, the steady loss of tribal access to forest land, and the accompanying opportunities for harassment and exploitation by private contractors, moneylenders, and government officials, was another crucial influence in the early radicalization of Srikakulam girijans.

### The Role of Government in the Development of Tribal Poverty

This chapter has thus far described the loss of land, the increasing indebtedness, and the loss of access to forest that the girijans experienced in

*The Development Of Tribal Poverty*

the years prior to the first efforts to politicize them. The deterioration of the girijans' ability to maintain the minimum necessities of life is apparent. As these events proceeded, what was the role of government in allowing them to unfold?

The most striking fact about governmental activity with regard to the girijans in Srikakulam was government's total ineffectualness; indeed, in many respects, government was virtually absent. The rugged terrain of the forest areas made access difficult, and not until the Naxalites made the Agency areas of Srikakulam a matter of concern to government was much attention paid to the area by responsible officials. Until then, a number of accounts attest, local moneylenders and traders had virtually free reign to exploit the tribals however they liked. A paper written for a Law and Order Seminar of the National Police Academy during the time of the Naxalite rebellion in Srikakulam pointed to the lack of governmental authority in the region:

> . . . the normal type of revenue administration found in most of the villages in this district *was not there* in the Agency and many villagers were without village Headmen or Talyaris. The "village munsif" or "village karnam" having his jurisdiction over a tribal village used to stay miles away in some plains village. The other *revenue officials rarely went into the interior* either for collection of revenues or for any other purpose because of the bad terrain and lack of communications. Elwynpet, Kurupam, Palankonda and Kothur Police Stations in the plains used to exercise jurisdiction over the unwieldy terrain and *police officers of all ranks found it difficult to go deep into the Agency. Thus, the writ of government failed to run through the tribal belt.*[57]

This governmental vacuum helps explain why, although legislation was passed in 1959 and 1960 to protect tribals' land, regulate moneylending and limit indebtedness, these laws remained largely inoperative. Mr. Lakshminarayana, who during the Naxalite uprising was assigned to Srikakulam to expedite the implementation of land legislation, had this to say about the failure of government prior to the revolt:

> Tribals are poor, uneducated, lethargic compared to plainsmen. The tribal area was inaccessible. Administration generally remained out of the tribal area. The tribals themselves were not aware of the laws; and officers remained away from the area. It was almost an anarchistic situation. The powerful locals were free to do whatever they wanted.[58]

To the extent that government officials did operate in the area, they often acted on behalf of the local influentials, not on behalf of the tribals.[59] Although, as will be discussed below, there were government-sponsored programs aimed at tribal development, the consensus of those familiar with the area seems to be that government programs to aid the tribals would be initiated only if such programs did not detract from the wealth and power of the moneylenders and landowners. Measures such as the prohibition of land transfers from tribal to non-tribal that would hurt those interests were not implemented.

> Money and power were on the side of the landowners. Police and administration respond to better placed persons, rather than to the tribals. The tribals are also very timid and unassertive.

> It's not like government had been ignoring the area completely. Block development *was* there. But they performed tasks that didn't interfere with the interests of the others—i.e., the moneylenders, the landowners. But the land problem—alienation of tribals' land—*did* benefit one section at the expense of the tribals. And not until after the Naxalite movement was there enough pressure to go against the interests of this section. Where money only is required to be given, it is done; but where other interests are involved, it's not so easy.[60]

Mr. Chandramowli corroborated this viewpoint in his acknowledgment that while during the 1960s the government did build ashram schools, initiate some health and nutrition programs, and build high school boarding houses—worthwhile projects to be sure—government took no action on three issues critical to girijan welfare which *also* affected the interests of local powers: minimum wages, land alienation, and land development.[61] Thus the local influentials—the moneylenders, landowners and traders—faced no opposition from the state government to their illegal activities that drove the tribals into progressively deepening poverty.

On the local level, non-tribals came to completely dominate the governmental apparatus. "In the elections since 1951 and also in the panchayat elections since 1963, most of the persons acquiring leadership positions have been non-tribals."[62] Anthropologist N. Patnaik of the National Institute of Community Development commented after a visit to Sirkakulam that the panchayat system was alien to the tribals and had little effect on their welfare.[63] Thus, on all levels of government tribals had little if any voice.

To the extent that government operated at all in the Agency areas, it did so in ways that favored the more powerful "ruling elite" of traders and rich

## The Development Of Tribal Poverty

farmers "who monopolised the politics as well as the economy of Srikakulam."[64] Government did not itself actively oppress and impoverish the tribals, but through its neglect, its failure to implement the law, government gave free reign to those who would exploit them.

### The Failure of Development Efforts

While government activity in the Agency areas was notable primarily for its absence, there were some economic development efforts sponsored by government. Up until the time of the Naxalite revolt, however, these efforts were extremely inadequate. The limitations and failures of these programs have been starkly outlined in several studies sponsored by the government of Andhra Pradesh.

Tribal development had been a very low priority since the very first Five Year Plan, consistently receiving a lower percentage of the budget allocation than the population of tribals would seem to warrant. According to the Government of Andhra Pradesh's *Special Program for the Development of Scheduled Areas and Scheduled Tribes of Andhra Pradesh in Fourth Five Year Plan, Volume I*

> With the adoption of community development as the instrumentality of national development, a systematic attempt was made for the first time to develop the tribal areas....But the plans [i.e., the first three Five Year Plans] could not make a perceptible impact on the tribal areas as the investment made was very meager.[65]

Although 5.11 percent of the population of Andhra Pradesh belong to scheduled tribes,[66] the percentage of the budget allocated to their needs was considerably smaller than 5.11 percent. In the First Five Year Plan, "the total expenditure incurred for the development of all the sectors of Scheduled Tribes in Andhra Pradesh was...0.65 percent of the total State outlay."[67] In the Second Five Year Plan, with the introduction of four Multipurpose Projects under the community development program, the percentage of budget expenditure for tribal development rose to 1.35 percent.[68] In the Third Five Year Plan, the allocation was reduced to 0.56 percent of the State Plan outlay.[69]

Not only were the funds allocated small, but even these funds were not fully utilized. For example, under the Second Five Year Plan, Rs. 27 lakhs were allocated for each of the four Multi-purpose Projects, for a total of Rs. 108 lakhs. But total *actual expenditure* amounted to only Rs. 83.70 lakhs.[70] During the Third Five Year Plan, 20 additional Tribal Development Blocks were started in Andhra Pradesh, of which three were in Srikakulam: Bhadragiri, Seethampet, and Pachipenta.[71] A government study published in 1968,

*Assessment of the Tribal Development Blocks in Andhra Pradesh*, found that the funds allocated for these Blocks were underutilized. Table 1 indicates the percentage of allocated funds that were actually spent, from the time of the inception of the Tribal Development Blocks through 1966.

**Table 1**
Percentage of Expenditure in
Tribal Development Blocks

| Scheme | Amount Budgeted (Rs. in lakhs*) | Percentage of Expenditure |
|---|---|---|
| 1. Agriculture and Animal Husbandry | 36.90 | 64.33 |
| 2. Irrigation, reclamation and soil conservation | 40.73 | 71.70 |
| 3. Co-operation | 36.40 | – |
| 4. Communication | 36.27 | 68.83 |
| 5. Education | 12.17 | 88.54 |
| 6. Social Education | 8.21 | 89.71 |
| 7. Rural Arts, Crafts and Industries | 20.73 | 64.96 |
| 8. Health and Sanitation | 13.60 | 73.35 |
| 9. Rural Housing | 13.62 | 25.09 |

*One lakh is the equivalent of one hundred thousand. Thus, 36.90 lakhs equals 3,690,000.

Source: Manohar Rao, *Assessment of the Tribal Development Blocks in Andhra Pradesh*, p. 15.

Not only was the implementation of programs limited, but the effects of those programs that were introduced often were not as intended. The *Assessment of the Tribal Development Blocks in Andhra Pradesh* argued that "in general it can be safely concluded that it is the *non-tribal who is benefitting more* from the programmes" introduced into the Tribal Development Blocks.[72] The study suggests that the structure of local political power constitutes the "choking bottlenecks and glaring pitfalls which have a crippling effect on the pace of progress." Power too often resides in the hands of non-tribals:

> In the three tier system only the Samithi President's Office is reserved for the tribals whereas there is no such reservation regarding the office of the sarpanch at Gram Panchayat level. This has resulted in

### The Development Of Tribal Poverty

> a peculiar set up in some of the samithis in which the President is a tribal while the majority of the members are non-tribals thus making the President a pawn in their hands.

The author of the Assessment therefore recommended that the Panchayat President's office also be reserved for tribals.[73]

But the implementation of programs was hampered, too, not only by the self-interest of some local officials, but by their incompetence. On the local level:

> because of the inability of the Samithi members to properly assess their felt needs and lack of a deliberate effort on the part of the officials to elicit the required information from the tribals, the programmes are implemented haphazardly.[74]

On the district level, in part because of the "frequency in change in personnel...in tribal areas," the effectiveness of the officials was no better:

> programmes are not fruitfully implemented due to lack of sufficient interest and supervision of the district officials who are expected to guide the Block extension team in technical matters.[75]

The overall assessment seems to point not to corrupt or rapacious local officials, but, instead, to chronic underfunding, official ignorance of local conditions, and frequent incompetence and disinterest:

> Suitable strains of seeds have not been evolved for the hilly regions...The stereotyped implements supplied throughout the tribal areas do not take into consideration the local requirements....The loan provision...cannot be spent as the lands have not been surveyed and settled in many areas. Most of the minor irrigation works suffer on account of the monetary ceilings fixed for new constructions, maintenance and special repairs....Supply of improved varieties of bulls and poultry are intended to vitalize local breeds, but they are not maintained on sound lines by providing them suitable feed and protection due to the poverty of the tribals....Loans [given by the government] are neither issued in time nor collected at the appropriate moment. The proverbial official red tape, the cumbersome procedures and the vagaries of the non-tribal members and moneylenders make it ineffective in implementation....Even though large sums are spent on education, the expected results are not achieved. Stereotyped cur-

riculum and syllabi are introduced...without taking into consideration peculiar conditions prevailing . In spite of the recommendations of many an expert committee to give a tribal bias to the system of education, nothing tangible has been done....The Industries Programme suffers mainly on account of paucity of funds for the follow-up works. Moreover the stipends paid at the rate of Rs. 25 a month to each trainee is insufficient.[76]

The end result of this litany of failed effort was that "in spite of a decade of planned development the 'gap' between the stages of development of the tribal and the non-tribal still remains as wide as ever."[77] This assessment, published as it was on the eve of the Naxalite rebellion, is an especially compelling critique of government ineptness.

Not all official reports written in the late 1960s, however, shared the sense of outrage and urgency communicated in the *Assessment of the Tribal Development Blocks in Andhra Pradesh*. A case in point is the *Survey of Tribal Development Block: Bhadragiri, Srikakulam District*, published by the Tribal Cultural Research and Training Institute in 1969.[78] Part of this report evaluates the "landmark"[79] Andhra Pradesh Tribes Cooperative Finance and Development Corporation, and one of its subsidiary organizations, the Gummalakshmipuram Agency Produce Cooperative Marketing Society, which operated in Bhadragiri. Although the report is at times critical, there is also considerable failure to analyze problems and obfuscation of trouble areas.

The task of the Corporation was to develop the tribal economy by purchasing at fair prices the minor forest produce collected by the tribals and agricultural produce grown by them; and to sell, at fair price, the goods meeting the agricultural and domestic needs of the tribals.[80] The final conclusion of the *Survey* with regard to the workings of the Gummalakshmipuram Agency Produce Cooperative Marketing Society in Bhadragiri is quite sanguine:

> While playing the role of benevolent monopsonist in the purchase of minor forest produce from tribals of the block and being an effective competitor in the purchase of the agricultural produce and sale of domestic requirements, this Society is offering fair and better prices to the saleable commodities of the tribals and is holding the price line of minor forest produce, agricultural produce, and domestic requirements.[81]

While this is the overall conclusion presented in the *Survey*, the data contained therein does not warrant such equanimity. For example, the *Survey* reports the following data, which records the continual decline in the volume of pur-

## The Development Of Tribal Poverty

chases of the tribals' agricultural produce made from the years 1963-64 to 1966-67: the amount, in rupees, purchased was 23,649 in 1963-64; 22,994 in 1964-65; 6,715 in 1965-66; and 4,103 in 1966-67.[82] Despite the obvious problem represented by these figures, the report offers no explanation of, nor even comment on, the decline.

Elsewhere in the report it *is* noted that "The Andhra Pradesh Scheduled Tribes Cooperative Finance and Development Corporation is not in a position to meet the credit needs of the tribals to a greater extent...due to various handicaps and limited financial resources."[83] While 75 percent of the tribal households in the Bhadragiri Block had borrowed from private moneylenders, the *Survey* notes, only 18 percent had borrowed from government sources.[84] The report does recognize that despite the deception used by the sowcars in weighing the minor forest produce they purchase from the tribals, the tribals are still likely to sell their produce to the sowcars rather than the Cooperative, because the "Tribal feels more attached to the sowcar as he extends loans at any time, and the Tribal is bound to repay the amount to the sowcar in kind."[85]

So, while this *Survey* does cite specific problem areas, its overall tone is lacking any sense of urgency, or any hint that the problems of the area might necessitate particular attention. And, as will be seen in the next chapter, attempts by the girijans to peacefully draw the attention of government to these problems met with no positive response; not until Naxalite violence erupted did government's attention turn more urgently to the region. Until that time, government, through its neglect, contributed to the rise of non-tribal exploiters and the corresponding development of the girijans' poverty.

## The Development Of Tribal Poverty

### NOTES

1. Government of Andhra Pradesh Tribal Welfare Department, Tribal Cultural Research and Training Institute, *Indebtedness Among Scheduled Tribes of Andhra Pradesh* (Hyderabad, undated), p. 28. The research for the study was done in 1971-72.

According to Government of Andhra Pradesh Information and Public Relations Department, *Tribals Join the Mainstream* (Hyderabad, September 1979), p. 31, "The Tribal Cultural Research and Training Institute was estalbished at Hyderabad in 1963 under Centrally Sponsored Schemes. It has two wings for Research and Training. The Research wing undertakes studies on various tribes in order to probe into the cultural patterns and assess their basic problems and needs besides evaluating the performance of the various development programmes. The Research programmes of the Institute have been mainly oriented towards plan formulations, building up of Techno-economic and Socio-cultural data, Evaluation studies, Studies on Castes and Communities, etc." A number of the studies that will be cited in this and subsequent chapters were issued by the Tribal Cultural Research and Training Institute.

2. V.M. Nair, "Time Yet to Wean Girijans from the Naxalites," *The Statesman*, December 11, 1970.

3. Tribal Cultural Research and Training Institute, *Survey of Tribal Development Block: Bhadragiri, Srikakulam District* (Hyderabad, 1969), p. 30. The data for this survey was collected in 1964-65 and 1967. Although the number fluctuates, there are approximately eight rupees to one U.S. dollar.

4. Srikakulam District is divided into two geographic regions, the plains and the hills. The hilly areas of the northwestern taluks of Palakonda, Parvathipuram and Salur are known as Agency tracts. *Andhra Pradesh District Gazetteers: Srikakulam* (Hyderabad, 1979), p. 2. It was primarily among the tribals living in these hills, particularly in Parvathipuram, that the Naxalite movement took place.

5. "Naxalite Activities and the Police." An unpublished paper written for the Law and Order Seminar of the 19th Senior National Police Academy Officers' course, October 1969-March 1970, pp. 14-15.

6. *Survey of Tribal Development Block: Bhadragiri, Srikakulam District*, p. 45.

7. *Andhra Pradesh District Gazetteers: Srikakulam*, pp. 125, 127.

8. N.Y. Naidu, "Tribal Revolt in Parvatipuram Agency," *Economic and Political Weekly*, November 25, 1972, p. 2343.

9. Ibid.

10. P. Kamala Manohar Rao, *Assessment of the Tribal Development Blocks in Andhra Pradesh* (Hyderabad: Government of Andhra Pradesh, 1968), pp. 12-13. The author is Director of Tribal Development.

11. V. Raghavaiah, *Tribal Revolts* (Nellore, Andhra Pradesh: Andhra Rashtra Adimajati Sevak Sangh, 1971), pp. 55-56. Raghavaiah quotes the *Report of the Study Team on Tribal Development Programmes (1967-68)* created by the Committee on Plan Projects of the Government of India Planning Commission, with which Raghavaiah was associated, as stating, "No satisfactory explanation has been advanced for delaying the survey and settlement of the tribal areas." p. 55.

12. Government of Andhra Pradesh Tribal Welfare Department, Tribal Cultural Research and Training Institute, *Integrated Tribal Development Plan for Tribal Areas of Srikakulam District* (Hyderabad, May 1977), p. 6. The language cited does not specify if it refers only to settled cultivators, or also to those engaged in shifting cultivation. If the latter are included in the figure of 34 percent, this means that the number of tribals with access to land that would be affected by legislation concerning muttadar ownership would be even less than 34 percent.

13. Koka Raghava Rao, *The Law Relating to Scheduled Areas in Andhra Pradesh* (Hyderabad: Andhra Pradesh Law Publishers, 1972), p. 6. See also C. Subba Rao,

## The Development Of Tribal Poverty

"Revolt in Srikakulam," *The Times of India Magazine*, January 4, 1970.

14. Government of Andhra Pradesh Education (S.N.) Department, *Report of the Andhra Pradesh Tribes Enquiry Committee, Volume I, 1961-62* (Hyderabad), p. 56. The chairman of the committee was V. Raghavaiah.

15. C. Subba Rao, "Revolt in Srikakulam."

16. *Naxalite Activities and the Police*, p. 15.

17. *Report of the A.P. Tribes Enquiry Committee, Volume I, 1961-62*, p. 56.

18. *Indebtedness Among Scheduled Tribes of Andhra Pradesh*, p. 105.

19. *Report of the A.P. Tribes Enquiry Committee, Volume I, 1961-62*, p. 56.

20. Raghavaiah, pp. 56-57, citing the *Report of the Study Team on Tribal Development Programmes (1967-68)*. Rules had also not been framed for the Andhra Pradesh (Scheduled Area) Money-Lenders Regulation, 1960, to be discussed below.

21. *Indebtedness Among Scheduled Tribes of Andhra Pradesh*, pp. 105-106.

22. Ibid., pp. 107-108. Emphasis added.

23. Interview with Lakshminarayana, March 27, 1980, March 31, 1980.

24. *Naxalite Activities and the Police*, p. 15. Emphasis added.

25. Interview with Chandramowli, April 3, 1980.

26. *Survey of Tribal Development Block: Bhadragiri, Srikakulam District*, pp. 89-90. The figure of 34 percent may be taken as an extremely conservative estimate. The figure derives from the investigations of the Deputy Tehsildar appointed under the Andhra Pradesh (Scheduled Areas) Debt Relief Regulation, 1960. But as will be shown below, the debts were often severely under-reported under this law, a law generally acknowledged to have been of no effect. Thus the figure of 34 percent is almost certainly a bare minimum. In contrast, the 1971 government study, *Indebtedness Among Scheduled Tribes of Andhra Pradesh*, revealed that 63 percent of the households throughout the state were indebted; in the sample households in the tribal regions of Srikakulam and the neighboring district of Visakhapatnam, 71 percent were found to be indebted. Pp. 29-30.

27. *Survey of Tribal Development Block: Bhadragiri, Srikakulam District*, p. 30.

28. Ibid., p. 95.

29. Ibid., pp. 95, 98.

30. Ibid., p. 67.

31. Ibid., p. 87.

32. Ibid., p. 88.

33. *Indebtedness Among Scheduled Tribes of Andhra Pradesh*, p. 85.

34. Ibid., p. 84.

35. Andhra Pradesh Legislature (Assembly Secretariat) Committee on Welfare of Scheduled Tribes 1976-77, *First Report on Educational Facilities, Representation in Services, Medical Facilities and Other Socio-Economic Schemes Implemented for the Welfare of Scheduled Tribes* (Hyderabad, June 28, 1977), p. 23.

36. Raghavaiah, p. 57.

37. Ibid., pp. 56-57. The *Survey of Tribal Development Block: Bhadragiri, Srikakulam District*, pp. 93-94, describes several systems of loan payments that bear this out: "There are two types of loans, viz. 'Kattubadi' and 'Faida' given by the Money Lenders to the tribals. Moneylender advances loans to the tribal at the time of sowing and in off seasons. The tribal is expected to repay the loan as soon as the harvesting is over. The Moneylender determines the price of paddy or any other food grains while advancing loans and the tribal is obliged to surrender his paddy or other food grains to the moneylender at the stipulated rates irrespective of the market fluctuations. With the result the tribal loses more than 50 percent of the profitable price. This type of loan is locally called as 'Kattubadi.' There is another type of loan, referred to as 'Faida' system. According to this system, the tribal borrows food grain from Sowcar on the

condition that he would repay the debt in kind, together with interest. For example, if a tribal borrows 60 kgs of paddy the tribal has to pay 15 kgs of paddy towards the interest. In case the tribal fails to repay the loan in kind the total quantity, i.e. 75 kgs of paddy, will be treated as principle amount. This rate of interest is only for a period of one year. During the subsequent years the tribal will be asked to pay a penalty of 3 kgs for every 20 kgs of Principle quantity and this mode of repayment is called as 'Namu' system [sic]."

38. *Indebtedness Among Scheduled Tribes of Andhra Pradesh*, p. 113.
39. Ibid., p. 114.
40. Raghavaiah, p. 57.
41. The cyclostyled document, undated, is cited in Shanta Sinha, "Maoists in Andhra Pradesh," Diss. Jawaharlal Nehru University, 1976, p. 202.
42. Cited in Government of Andhra Pradesh, Integrated Tribal Development Agency, Srikakulam, *Medium Term Tribal Sub-Plan, 1978-83: Srikakulam District*, p. 6.
43. *Indebtedness Among Scheduled Tribes of Andhra Pradesh*, p. 56.
44. *Survey of Tribal Development Block: Bhadragiri, Srikakulam District*, p. 89.
45. *Indebtedness Among Scheduled Tribes of Andhra Pradesh*, p. 30.
46. *Andhra Pradesh District Gazetteers: Srikakulam*, p. 75.
47. In 1952, it was estimated that only 20 percent of the total land area was forest, a proportion considered ecologically unsound. This data, and the preceding paragraph, drawn from *Report of the A.P. Tribes Enquiry Committee, Volume I, 1961-62*, pp. 196-197.
48. Naidu, p. 2339.
49. Interview with Chandramowli, April 3, 1980. *Report of the Andhra Pradesh Tribes Enquiry Committee, Volume I, 1961-62*, p. 199 also reports: "In several places the tribals represented to us that while demarcating the boundary of the taken-over forests, the interests of the tribals living very close to their forest areas have not been taken into consideration. In their attempt to grabble [sic] as much area as possible for the forest resumes the boundary line has been taken by their forest subordinates very close to the residential area without leaving any moving space worth the name for the villagers or their cattle." Chandramowli, in "Highlights of the Girijan Problem (Srikakulam Since '64)," Inaugural Address at the Cooperation and Applied Economic Association, Andhra University at Waltair, September 16, 1971 (unpublished) points out that the decision that a certain percentage of land be preserved *throughout India* has been applied across the board to individual *districts*, even when "this policy leaves no land whatsoever to the tribal tillers of the soil."
50. *Report of the Andhra Pradesh Tribes Enquiry Committee, Volume I, 1961-62*, pp. 91-92.
51. *Survey of Tribal Development Block: Bhadragiri, Srikakulam District*, p. 27.
52. Sinha, pp. 188-189. Chandramowli explained in an interview, April 3, 1980, that any movement of wood—considered "major" forest produce—is governed by the Forest Department under the Timber Transit rules. *Any* movement of timber has to be covered by a permit. "Therefore, the tribal can be harassed everywhere by the forest department."
53. *Report of the Andhra Pradesh Tribes Enquiry Committee, Volume I, 1961-62*, p. 91. Emphasis added.
54. Ibid., p. 197.
55. The reports are cited in Organization for the Protection of Democratic Rights, Andhra Pradesh, Fact Finding Committee, *Srikakulam Movement: A Report to the Nation* (OPDR, April 1978), p. 43. This thinking is echoed in Chandramowli, "Highlights of the Girijan Problem (Srikakulam Since '64)": "It is wrong to say that the tribal cultivators are fond of doing 'Podu' or rotation of cultivation over the de-forested hilltops. No Girijan ever cultivates the patches of podu if only good wet land is made

## The Development Of Tribal Poverty

available to him. There are a large number of case-studies which prove this point." Chandramowli believes the loss of tribal land was the primary grievance that allowed the extremists to gain the sympathy they did in Srikakulam.

56. *Srikakulam Girijanodhyama Sankshipta Charitra* (Socialist Publications). Cited in Sinha, p. 189.
57. *Naxalite Activities and the Police*, p. 15. Emphasis added.
58. Interview with Lakshimarayana, March 31, 1980.
59. Some observers have been harsher in their assessments of government officials, condemning their corruption at the local level. C. Subba Rao, "Revolt in Srikakulam," *The Times of India Magazine*, January 4, 1970, commented on the Srikakulam girijans: "They have had little contact with the district administration; until recently they have seen only forest guards, who behave with them like little Hitlers."
60. Interview with Lakshminarayana, March 31, 1980.
61. Interview with Chandramowli, April 3, 1980.
62. Naidu, p. 2343.
63. *Patriot*, April 21, 1971, cited in Manoranjan Mohanty, *Revolutionary Violence: A Study of the Maoist Movement in India* (New Delhi: Sterling Publishers Pvt. Ltd., 1977), p. 50.
64. Mohanty, p. 50.
65. Government of Andhra Pradesh, *Special Program for the Development of Scheduled Areas and Scheduled Tribes of Andhra Pradesh in Fourth Five Year Plan* (Hyderabad, 1970), p. 1.
66. The Director, Information and Public Relations Department, Government of Andhra Pradesh, *Tribals Join the Mainstream* (Hyderabad, September 1979), p. 4.
67. *Special Program for the Development of Scheduled Areas and Scheduled Tribes of Andhra Pradesh in Fourth Five Year Plan*, p. 9.
68. Ibid., p. 10. Two of these "Special multipurpose tribal development blocks" were in Visakhapatham District, one was in Warangal, and one in Adilabad; none was in Srikakulam.
69. Ibid., p. 68.
70. P. Kamala Manohar Rao, Director of Tribal Welfare, Government of Andhra Pradesh, *Assessment of the Tribal Development Blocks in Andhra Pradesh* (Hyderabad, 1968), pp. 5-6.
71. Ibid., pp. 10-11.
72. Ibid., p. 19. Emphasis added. The data for the study were gathered in 1966. The study reached this conclusion by counting how many of the following goods had reached tribals and non-tribals: improved seeds, iron ploughs, seed drills, weeders, sprayers, oil engines, electric motors, other implements, bulls, bucks, rams, and boars. It also counted the members of cooperative societies. The study summarized its findings: "...non-tribals are also deriving the benefit of the developmental programmes, in equal measure along with the tribals. In case of improved seeds, oil engines and electric motors, the non-tribals have benefitted more while for other items the share of the non-tribals is quite sizeable considering the percentage of non-tribal population living in the T.D. Blocks. For most of the items attended to by the Blocks there are no authentic records to indicate the position regarding the benefits accrued to the tribals and the non-tribals. In general it can be safely assumed that it is the non-tribal who is benefitting more from the programmes." pp. 18-19.
73. Ibid., p. 19.
74. Ibid.
75. Ibid., p. 20.
76. Ibid., pp. 20-22.
77. Ibid., p. 22.

78. The field work for the study was conducted in 1964-65 and 1967.
79. *Survey of Tribal Development Block: Bhadragiri, Srikakulam District*, p. 65.
80. Ibid., pp. 65-68.
81. Ibid., p. 84.
82. Ibid., p. 77.
83. Ibid., pp. 95, 98.
84. Ibid., p. 95.
85. Ibid., p. 76.

# 3
# THE EARLY GIRIJAN MOVEMENT

Beginning in the late 1950s, a school teacher named Vempatapu Satyanarayana organized the girijans of Parvathipuram taluk of Srikakulam district into a non-violent movement to seek redress of a variety of economic and political grievances. For the next decade, the movement enjoyed some limited success, but suffered from substantial landlord and police repression. The frustrations that Satyanarayana encountered in his peaceful struggle, his inability to move the government, led to his willingness to consider violent methods.

The story is told that in 1968 an anthropologist came to Parvathipuram to study the causes of the Naxalite revolt. In his interview with one of Satyanarayana's two tribal wives, he showed her a picture of Mahatma Gandhi, and asked her, "Why do you go the way of violence? Why don't you do like Gandhiji?" She explained to him that for many years they had tried, but without result; only then did they turn to violence. She felt they had been forced to turn to violent methods. The anthropologist emerged from the interview saying that if *he* had been a tribal, he too would have become a Naxalite.[1]

This chapter will examine the development of the moderate phase of the movement and the limits of government's positive response. Why did this generally legal, peaceful movement fail? How did this experience lead Sattyanarayana and his followers to Naxalism? How much responsibility must the government bear for the development of Naxalism in Srikakulam?

Vempatapu Satyanarayana, also known as Satyam, was born in the plains area in Bobbili, the taluk adjoining Parvathipuram. In the mid-1950s he settled in the Agency area and began work as an elementary school teacher. Although not himself a tribal, "his encounter with Girijans was a sort of love at first sight."[2] He soon married a woman from one of the two major tribes in the area, the Jatapu, and came to identify himself with the culture and the problems of the girijans. In fact, he subsequently married a woman from the other major tribe, the Savara, as a symbolic enactment of the political and social unity that, he felt, should exist between the two tribes.[3]

## The Early Girijan Movement

Resolved to organize the girijans to improve their economic position, he first began to gain their support by arranging a variety of cultural events; only after thus attaining a high level of popularity and trust did he begin to organize politically.[4] His initial actions were aimed at economic improvement. He organized several cooperative labor contract societies, through which he hoped to secure higher wages for the girijans from forest contractors, government contractors, and landowners.[5] These cooperatives were completely unsuccessful, however, because local contractors and government officials vigorously opposed them:

> local MLAs...bombarded the Chief Minister with telegrams making adverse comments on [Satyanarayana's] activities. The result was that the co-operative societies remained without work. The PWD [Public Works Department] and forest departments which would have given contracts to the societies, refused to have anything to do with them. It was quite clear that vested interests were able to influence the Government.[6]

The contractors also brought pressure to bear on the District Education Officer, who in turn wrote to Satyanarayana, warning him that he could not be a teacher and the president of the cooperatives at the same time. In response, Satyanarayana gave up his job as a teacher, and became a full-time organizer.[7]

When Satyanarayana entered the Agency area, he was not a Communist; the then undivided Communist Party came to him.[8] The Communist organization had been very strong in the Agency since the early 1950s;[9] prominent Andhra Communist leaders, including T. Nagi Reddy, journeyed to Parvathipuram and persuaded Satyanarayana to join with them. When Satyanarayana, along with another school teacher, Adibhatla Kailasam, organized the Girijan Sangham (the Hill People's Association), he did so as a Communist.[10] In 1960 Satyanarayana and Kailasam were among those elected to the Communist Party Srikakulam District Committee.[11] The increasing radicalism of Satyanarayana and the Srikakulam group is evidenced by their joining with Nagi Reddy and other Andhra left Communists in the formation of the Communist Party of India (Marxist) in 1964.[12]

The Girijan Sangham worked initially to raise the sociopolitical consciousness of the tribals and to give them increased confidence in their own capability to struggle effectively for improvement in their lives. To this end, cultural troops gave performances in tribal villages "depicting the woes of the tribals and exposing the people responsible for this and exhorting the tribals to rise and rebel."[13] Sangham workers urged tribal women to change their dress to garments that covered their whole bodies, and tribal men to cut their hair, for they felt these actions would "instill a sense of self-respect, dignity and self-identity."[14] The importance of daily bathing was stressed, as was the value of basic education. The Sangham set up night schools in many villages to teach basic educational skills as well as to impart political information and to debunk superstitious beliefs. Sangham workers also acted as "barefoot doctors," spreading modern ideas of hygiene and medicine.[15]

Particular efforts were made to unify the girijans and give them a heightened sense of identity. Satyam's marriage to women from each of the two major tribes worked to this end. The Sangham taught all the tribals to address each other as "comrade" as a sign of equality and mutual respect. The unity of the tribals was also underscored by the Sangham's creation of "people's courts." Members of the Sangham were told that they should not bring any arguments that arose among them to the government courts, but should instead bring their disagreements before village or Agency committees of Sangham members.[16] The "people's courts" served to create an authority within and of the tribal Agency area that set the tribals apart from the justice system administered by outsiders. This would not only give the tribals a sense of unity, and separateness from the non-tribal population, but also would give the Sangham its beginnings as an alternative government, a replacement for the existing government that did not serve the tribals' needs.

Once the Girijan Sangham was organized, with a beginning membership of 1,000,[17] Vempatapu Satyanarayana began a decade of agitations around specific economic issues. While he did meet with some successes—notably in the area of wages for coolie labor—the decade was marked by landlord violence that was, at best, overlooked by the local government authorities. At times, the government authorities, particularly local police and forest officials, themselves were engaged in harassing the girijans' leaders. Ultimately, more than the painfully slow progress in making economic changes, and the attending frustrations of that, it was the violence of gundas (goons or thugs) organized and paid for by the landlords, coupled with the obvious failure of the police to put an end to the violence or to bring the landlords to justice, that was the spark that drove Satyanarayana, and with him, his girijan followers, to violent action. Thus, much more than the failure to protect the girijans economically, it was government's failure to protect them from landlord violence that caused violent rebellion. The government's legitimacy was certainly in doubt because of the daily economic exploitation the girijans experienced; but it was government's seeming acquiescence in murderous violence that pushed Satyanarayana over the edge of legal action.

In the charge sheet that made up the accusations in the Parvathipuram Conspiracy Case, the major case pertaining to the Srikakulam Naxalties, the

## The Early Girijan Movement

government presented the history of the girijan movement incorrectly by claiming that "Till 1967 the agitation was peaceful. From 1967 onwards Communists infiltrated in the area and under their leadership agitations were launched and meetings were held."[18] This false history suggests that the infiltration of radical outsiders brought violence immediately in its wake. But, in reality, Satyanarayana had identified himself as a Communist, been active in Party committees, and had been in touch with Communist leaders in Hyderabad since the late 1950s. The government's charge sheet fails to note the gradual evolution of radicalism, a phenomenon that resulted from the continuing frustration with legal methods that was an outgrowth of police backing for the landlords. The government's history fails, most specifically, to note the 1967 incident which will be discussed below, in which two tribals were shot by landlords who were never brought to justice. This incident, not a swift Communist infiltration, was the spark that prompted violent response.

The cumulative disappointment of fighting without success to gain that which was rightfully theirs, in the absence of help from the government, was the cause of the girijan's smoldering anger:

> Until 1967 the communist cadres in Srikakulam were persuading the tribals *only to assert what had been granted them by law*, namely, relief from debts, recovering their own land from non-Girijans, facilities for cooperatives, higher wages, and greater shares in crops, etc.[19]

The first action of the Girijan Sanghams came in 1959 in the form of a propaganda effort against *vetti*, or forced labor. The Sanghams were successful in gaining the positive attention of the girijans, and the number of Sanghams increased.[20] Next, the Sanghams organized a campaign to physically resist forest officials who demanded bribes and private usurers who demanded excessively high interest rates. There were several thrashings of moneylenders and forest officials who demanded payments and bribes.[21]

In 1960, Satyanarayana began a militant campaign to reclaim girijan lands that had been lost to moneylenders; the Sanghams informed the girijans that the landlords were in violation of the law when they seized girijan land, even if the girijan had failed to pay off his debt. The seizure of land, they told the girijans, correctly, was in violation of the 1917 law. In November 1960 the girijans made plans to seize the harvests from the lands that had been taken from them in lieu of debt payments. The landlords first tried to bribe Satyanarayana to call off the plan; when this tactic failed, an unsuccessful attempt was made to murder him.[22] When the girijans moved to harvest the crop, the local police station was at first powerless to prevent the action, because as many as three hundred girijans were involved. The girijans, according to *Liberation*, the Naxalite monthly publication, were able to seize the crop on one hundred fifty acres.[23] Soon afterward, a larger police camp was established, and many girijans were arrested.[24]

The Sangham responded by calling for a strike of farm laborers[25] in order to prevent the harvest. The laborers responded, and the landlords, fearful that they would lose their crop, gave in to the laborers' demands so that the harvest could proceed. The demands included a raise from the three to ten putlu of grain per year then being paid, to 25 putlu per year; the cancellation of interest on old debts; the cancellation of charges arising from the seizure of the harvest; and the removal of the police camp.[26] Thus, organized action against the landlords did yield some temporary victories of increased wages and reduced indebtedness.

The next step the Sangham took, in 1962, was to organize girijans to occupy and freely use the forest lands. The target here was not the landlords, but government forest regulations and forest officials. The Sangham claimed that its actions resulted in the occupation of 4,000 acres of forest lands by the tribals.[27] Numerous warrants were issued, but the girijans, acting on instructions from the Sangham, refused to go voluntarily to court. The forest officials called in the police, but, again, the task of making so many arrests among a hostile population was too much for the local police forces, and the girijans prevailed.[28]

The years 1960 to 1967 witnessed a series of actions designed to increase the wage rates paid to agricultural laborers.[29] Although there is disagreement about the exact degree to which these actions were successful, all observers agree that, by 1967, the wage rates had risen dramatically.[30] There also seems to be widespread agreement that the landlords repeatedly used violence in the attempt to break the strikes, and that the government offered no assistance to the girijans in their attempts to gain the minimum wage due them by law.

V. Chandramowli, who in 1964-66 was the subcollector in Srikakulam, recalled Satyanarayana's failed attempts to move government to intervene in order to raise the wage rates of agricultural laborers:

> There is a minimum wages act under which landowners can be prosecuted for not paying. Satyanarayana would hold demonstrations against the government. Specifically, he would march to the subdivisional headquarters at Parvathipuram.
>
> The normal response of government was to send the labor officer to go and inquire into the complaint. He would go, conduct an oral inquiry, and send in a report. Generally, he would draw the conclusion that by and large everything was OK. The normal tendency of any

## The Early Girijan Movement

tribal administrator was to collaborate with non-tribal interests in the tribal areas. Even a very honest officer with a normal background of non-tribal schooling, knowing nothing about tribals, would think only in terms of cooperating with the existing power structure rather than confronting it.

Despite repeated marches, "the government did nothing" to encourage the landlords to pay the minimum wage required by law.[31]

While government sided with the status quo, the landlords, for their part, repeatedly used violence in the attempt to destroy the Girijan Sanghams and end the wage demands. V.M. Nair, writing in *The Statesman*, noted that while "the communists did much that was wrong and high-handed...they did succeed in bettering the lot of a lowly and exploited tribe. Today Girijan labourers in Elwinpet and Parvathipuram get the highest wages in the area..." While repeatedly deploring the "militant and disturbing activities of the communists," Nair contended that "it is possible to argue that the unthinking militancy of the landlords not only triggered off the tribal unrest but also provided a justification for the communist tactics."[32]

A girijan witness for the prosecution in the Parvathipuram Conspiracy trial recalled the violence with which wage demands were met:

> The landlords used to beat the workers of the Girijan Sanghams with a view to completely annihilate them. The landlords with the same end in view used to foist false cases against the workers of the Girijan Sanghams.[33]

Strikes would be broken up by the importation of scab labor and by threats; the government, at best, stood idly by and took no steps to intervene in the troubles:

> Under the leadership of VS [Satyanarayana] we observed strikes to enhance the wages....When we asked for higher wages the landlords used to get coolies from outside areas. When we were objecting to outside coolies working in our area, the landlords used to threaten us with dire consequences in case we prevent the outside coolies from working [sic]...Though we made representations in this regard to Government officials, nothing was done for us.[34]

Often, the predisposition of the government to "collaborate with non-tribal interests" led it to actively support the landlords against the girijans through

## The Early Girijan Movement

the use of police harassment and intimidation. According to the investigations of the Fact Finding Committee of the Organization for the Protection of Democratic Rights,

> When the Girijans launched a struggle for higher wages in 1964, and called a public meeting on December 2, hoodlums set up by landlords attacked a procession heading towards it. C.P.I. leaders V. Ramalingachari and others were injured but were charged with dacoity. Ramalingachari was let out on bail but was detained under D.I.R. [Defense of India Rules]...Police camps were set up throughout the Agency area. Large scale arrests on false charges supplemented police violence.[35]

Police harassment of the activists is also evident in Mr. Chandramowli's recollection that, when he was a subcollector, he twice had occasion to release two prominent activists who had been arrested by the police on evidence he deemed to be insufficient.[36]

By 1967, repeated girijan activities had forced the landlords to pay higher wage rates. In response, some landlords developed a tactic far more effective than violence; rather than pay the new rates, some landlords simply let their fields lie fallow.[37] This was a strategy against which the Sanghams had little recourse.

The government was equally unhelpful to the efforts of Kailasam, Satyanarayana and others to start a forest laborers' contract cooperative. Their idea was to begin the cooperative so that the girijans could receive contracts for forest labor directly from the government, instead of having to use the intermediary of a private contractor. But two prominent people in the area successfully worked to prevent the success of this enterprise. Medida Satyanarayana, a forest contractor, and Gudlea Satyanarayana, a moneylender, forest contractor, and sarpanch of Gummalaxmipuram village (no relation to Medida or to Vempatapu Satyanarayana) together saw to it that the cooperative could not get working capital. As Chandramowli explained, several government departments cooperated with this effort:

> They would wean off some tribal families to come work for them. Then the forest department would write that the cooperative wasn't working efficiently. The sarpanch of the village has a lot of power with the local administration. The Cooperatives Inspector (who works for the State Department of Cooperatives) would cooperate with the local powers....The Cooperatives Department accused Satyanarayana's labor cooperative of embezzlement; a notice was served, and this kept him out of business.[38]

## The Early Girijan Movement

The Girijan Sangham was more successful in organizing against corruption in the Andhra Pradesh Scheduled Tribes Cooperative Finance and Development Corporation, and in obtaining fair market price for their forest produce. The government had banned private trading in the region and given a monopoly to the Corporation to buy the girijans' goods. The Sangham, contending that the corporation was cheating the girijans in the weighing of their produce, stationed workers at the markets to watch over the transactions.[39] The Sangham also complained that the Corporation paid less than market rate. This complaint was later affirmed by V.M. Nair in *The Statesman*. He wrote that the Corporation

> was set up to provide Girijans with an assured market for minor forest produce, but in practice it has compelled the Girijans to sell at prices lower than they would have been paid by the landlords. Not all the employees of the Corporation have been scrupulous in their dealings with the tribals.[40]

Many tribals tried to circumvent the government agency by selling directly to private buyers who would pay higher prices. The government put a stop to this by bringing the traders to court, until the Sangham responded by threatening, and in some cases beating, Corporation officials. This tactic resulted in the Corporation's "not only accepting the prices demanded by the Sangham but also agreeing to accept Sangham's recommendation to employ Sangham people." In addition, the Sangham created five shandies (markets) of their own, and declared that from these shandies "goods can be sold to Corporation or to traders—whoever pays the higher price." The Corporation was unable to put a stop to these. "Thus by the mid-1960s the Sangham was practically running the Corporation in the area around Mondemkhal."[41]

The Sangham also took militant steps to obtain foodgrains for reasonable prices from the landlords. The tribals would customarily sell to the landlords at low prices at harvest, and then buy from them at high prices later. As Sinha notes, "The tribals due to ignorance and illiteracy were not very good tradesmen."[42] The landlords would sell two *addas* of grain for one rupee. (Five addas equals three and a half kilos.) The Sangham demanded that the landlords sell grain at the rate of six addas per rupee. The landlords retaliated by transporting their grains to markets outside of the area. The Sangham began stopping the trucks en route and, in one case, distributing the grain to the tribals. The police made arrests, but the landlords came to a compromise settlement in which they sold some grain to the Sangham at the rate of six addas per rupee, with the understanding that the Sangham would allow the safe transport of the remaining grain.

## The Early Girijan Movement

The Sangham opened twelve selling depots to distribute the grain it had so acquired. The members of the Sangham were given chits, and the grain was rationed among them. The Sangham, however, soon decided that it was not receiving enough grain and forcibly seized more. The landlords resisted, there were clashes, and the police arrested many Sangham workers. But despite the arrests, the landlords were still finding it difficult to transport their grain.

Again, as when the landlords decided to leave some fields fallow rather than pay higher wages to agricultural laborers, some landlords began to passively resist; they started hoarding grain and would not sell to the tribals at any price. At this point the government intervened. It began to purchase grain from the landlords and sell it through the corporation.[43]

Thus, by 1967, the movement had had some successes, especially in the area of wages and in the occupation of thousands of acres of forest and hundreds of acres of private land. There were also major failures, such as the labor cooperative. Most important for the future, the landlords had discovered a new and powerful weapon which, because of their superior economic power, boded poorly for the tribals: they would try to starve out the Sanghams by leaving land fallow and hoarding grain.

The landlords were consistently backed by government and police officials, even when the landlords were breaking the law. And, of course, there were plenty of opportunities for the police to take legitimate action against the movement which, while often engaging in legal protest, was also not above violence.[44] As Chandramowli's recollections have made clear, the government was equally unresponsive to girijan demands whether the tactics were non-violent or violent; no matter which tactic was tried, the government and police seemed firmly on the side of the landlords. The result was continuing frustration for the movement's leaders and followers.

Although they had only limited success in gaining their objectives, the Girijan Sanghams continued to have appeal to the girijans because the need was so great, and because no help was forthcoming from any other source. Interestingly, even the charge sheet in the Parvathipuram Conspiracy Case seems to acknowledge this need. Of the Savara and Jatapu tribals of Srikakulam it states:

> *They are neglected.* There is no impact of modern civilization on them. There was prohibition on their traditional Podu cultivation. They were subjected to exploitation at the hands of merchants and moneylenders who hailed from the plains. Their lands slowly passed into the hands of Sahukars. *Out of necessity* the Tribals from Girijan Sanghams agitated for restoration of their lands...distribution of Banjar [waste] lands...abolition of debts, fair market price for their forest produce,

## The Early Girijan Movement

> lifting of prohibition on the use of forest timber, and for declaring the Agency area as an autonomous region to be administered by the Girijans...[45]

But however great their needs, systematic girijan violence did not begin until girijans were murdered by the landlords, and the police and the legal system protected the guilty. It was at this stage that the girijans came to believe that their immediate physical safety could be guaranteed only by forming armed bands and attacking the landlords. The leaders of the movement, who organized the girijans into *dalams*, or guerrilla bands, of course had a different perspective, a vision of broader revolution. Before examining their ideology and strategic understandings, however, the point must be made that the girijans themselves did not share these understandings; their vision was more local, more immediate, and it is likely that had the violence of the landlords and police collaborators not been so brutal and swift, the leaders of the movement would not have been able to gain the girijans' cooperation. The judgment in the Parvathipuram Conspiracy trial, which convicted a number of the leaders of the Naxalites, acquitted most of the girijan members of the dalams. The judge ruled that "they were made to think that they were members of those dalams only to resist the attacks of the gundas employed by the landlords."[46] Their own resistance seemed to be essential because of the obvious failure of the law to protect them, not only from the slow violence of hunger and poverty, but from the swift violence of landlord murderers.

It was an incident in 1967 that clearly provided the spark that led to the girijan willingness to take up arms. Throughout 1967, tensions had been increasing. An account written by T. Nagi Reddy, who in 1967 was a leader of the opposition in the Andhra Legislative Assembly, but who later resigned his seat to become a revolutionary, describes increasing organization and militancy on the part of the girijans; this was met with escalating landlord and police violence:

> In the sowing and plantation season of 1967, the Girijans under the leadership of Girijan Sangh announced the wage rates which the Girijans demanded from the landlords. Meetings and processions proclaiming the new rates were the order of the day...The landlords were flabbergasted...Direct attacks on the Girijans were started. The landlords visited Hyderabad [the capital of Andhra Pradesh]. Additional police force was injected into the areas. Section 144 was imposed in 200 villages...of this mountainous area from July 24 to August 25, 1967.

## The Early Girijan Movement

In the Assembly, Nagi Reddy appealed to the government to withdraw Section 144 and to initiate impartial investigations into what he contended were "thousands of instances" of "police atrocities and landlord violence."[47] A spokesman for the Srikakulam District Police responded to Nagi Reddy's request by putting the blame for the troubles in Parvathipuram on the shoulders of the "left communists" who had been "inciting the farm labourers to revolt."[48]

On October 31, 1967, a procession of girijans on their way to the third Annual Conference of Srikakulam District Girijan Sangh at Mondemkhal were fired upon by a group of landlords intent on stopping them; two girijans were killed.[49] C. Subba Rao reported in *The Times of India* that

> Practically everyone in the area knew who had fired on the procession but because of the culprits' money and influence the police were tardy in arresting them.[50]

In fact, not only were the culprits not arrested immediately, but a number of tribals were arrested for unlawful assembly and rioting as a result of the incident.[51] The men who were eventually arrested for the crime were subsequently acquitted.[52]

In response to the murders at Levidi, Satyanarayana began to organize the girijans into guerrilla bands.[53] He was joined at this juncture by two communist activists from outside the Agency area, Chaudari Tejeswar Rao and Vasanthada Ramalingachari.[54] A girijan prosecution witness at the Parvathipuram Conspiracy trial recounted:

> VS exhorted the girijans that because Government was not doing justice even when some girijans were killed by landlords and because the landlords were out to grab their lands and because the courts were also not doing justice to the girijans when some of them were murdered by the landlords, the only alternative and honourable course left open to the girijans was to lead armed struggle against the Government. The girijans were convinced...VS formed the dalams in order to make the fight effective and through the dalams the girijans began their revolt.[55]

In January 1968 dalams began to raid and loot the government shandies. A paper written for the Police Academy, *Naxalite Activities and the Police*, describes a "lightening dacoity in broad daylight in the heart of the village Sithampeta on 22-1-1968 when hundreds of tribals armed with sticks and axes

## The Early Girijan Movement

raided the 'shandy,' looted the merchants and beat them up." On February 2, more than one thousand girijans marched to Kurupam, and again looted a shandy. This was followed by a raid on a landlord's house; articles worth Rs. 8000 were taken.[56] On March 4, 1968, the first encounter between the police and the primitively armed girijans took place.

> On 4-3-1968 a contingent of A.P.S.P. [Andhra Pradesh Special Police] led by the S.P. [Superintendent of Police] went to Pedakarja to apprehend the accused involved in the dacoities and to recover the property looted. A mob of about 1000 Girijans then descended in batches from the adjoining hills and showered battle axes, bows and arrows on the police. They opened fire on the police, forcing the police to return fire in self-defence. This exchange of fire resulted in the death of two tribals.[57]

The Organization for the Protection of Democratic Rights later claimed that the police firing was "altogether unprovoked," and was "part of a planned offensive on the movement at the instance of landlords."[58] According to their account, three hundred policemen surrounded Pedakarja village and simply opened fire on the girijans working in the fields, killing two.

> ...it was found on investigation that some years prior to the incident, the villagers had lost possession of a large amount of land which had been mortgaged to the landlord. As a result of the organized movement in the area, the Girijans had re-occupied 70 acres of this alienated land and distributed it among the 100 households occupying the village. The respondents alleged that the landlord concerned had been instrumental in directing the police to take repressive steps in order to terrorize the villagers and suppress their movement to re-occupy and distribute the land illegally held by the landlords.[59]

However, the Naxalites' own account, as published in the May 1969 *Liberation* in a story signed by the District Communist Committee, Srikakulam, is closer to the police's account:

> The people of Pedakarja village took up arms. They resisted the raiding police bands openly. The police resorted to the use of machine guns...In this fight two of our comrades lost their lives...we were not prepared for resistance.[60]

Following this shooting, the police began to arrest girijans and seize their arms.[61] By April 12, 1968, *The Statesman* would report that the police had "rounded up 516 Girijans and seized 83 country-made guns, besides scores of battleaxes, spears, bows, and arrows."[62]

*The Times of India Magazine* marked the March 1968 clash with the police as "the point of no return" for the girijans, whose communist leaders retreated to the hills "to streamline their plans and regroup their forces...With meticulous care they organized a courier system, built hideouts and arsenals and gave intensive training to the guerilla bands."[63] The preparation for long-term armed struggle had begun in earnest.

In the later acquittal of six girijans accused in the Parvathipuram Conspiracy Case, the Sessions Judge noted the desperate straits of the girijans because of the private exploitation to which they had long been subjected. He noted, too, the government's collaboration in that exploitation. The Judge ruled that given these circumstances, the violent actions of the girijans were understandable:

> ...No government agency approached the Agency areas except for exploitation purposes. The landlords of the areas sucked their blood and bled them white. The people at the top of the administration do not seem to have evinced any interest to know the real state of affairs prevailing in the areas. In those circumstances *the only alternative course left open to the girijans* in the agency area of Srikakulam District was to take the aid of the party which penetrated into the areas so eagerly as a person in distress, thrown into a wide wild sea, clutches at a piece of straw to help himself reach the shore.[64]

The Judge ruled that the girijan actions must be viewed in the context of "their resistance to the exploitation by the landlords, moneylenders, and Government agencies." With that in mind, the Judge ruled that the girijans were innocent *because they believed they were upholding the law*:

> According to Section 79 [of the Indian Penal Code] "nothing is an offence which is done by a person who is justified by law or who by reason of mistake of fact and not by reason of mistake of law in good faith believes himself to be justified by law, in doing it. Under this section, if there is bonafide intention to advance the law manifested by the circumstances attending the act which is a subject of charge and when the accused have a good motive and when they believe in good faith that they are bound by law to do what they did, it must be said that they acted to the best of their judgment exerted in good faith."[65]

## *The Early Girijan Movement*

In the judgment of the Sessions Judge, the illegal violence of the landlords, and the collaboration of the government in that violence through the actions of corrupt forest officials, corrupt officials of the Andhra Pradesh Scheduled Tribes Co-operative Finance and Development Corporation, a completely unresponsive system of justice, and a police department clearly biased to the protection of the landlords' interests, made the violence of the girijans understandable and forgivable. It thus seems evident that government's failure to uphold the law bears considerable responsibility for creating the conditions leading to the Naxalite revolt in Srikakulam. The revolt seems clearly to have stemmed not only from the impoverishment that is an everyday part of life in much of India, but from the particularly blatant refusal of government to act lawfully and responsibly, even in the face of legal and militant demands by an organized local movement. Government intractability in upholding the status quo, even when that necessitated the ignoring of illegal violence, was the spark, in conjunction with a violent ideology and increasing numbers of revolutionary-minded outsiders, that led to armed revolt.

## NOTES

1. The story was told by Lakshminarayana, Interview, March 31, 1980. Lakshminarayana had arranged the interview between the anthropologist and Satyanarayana's wife.

2. C. Subba Rao, "Srikakulam: The Bullet Beats the Bow," *The Times Weekly*, March 21, 1971, p. 3.

3. Sinha, p. 214.

4. Naidu, p. 2343.

5. C. Subba Rao, "Srikakulam: The Bullet Beats the Bow," p. 3, states that three societies were formed in 1958: Mondemkhallu Labour Contract Co-operative Society; Forest Contract Co-operative; and Parvathipuram Harijan, Girijan Labour Cooperative Society.

6. Ibid., p. 3.

7. C. Subba Rao, "Revolt in Srikakulam," *The Times of India Magazine*, January 4, 1970.

8. Interview with Lakshminarayana, March 31, 1980.

9. Interview with a former official in Srikakulam, who wishes to remain anonymous, March 26, 1980.

10. The exact date of the formation of the Girijan Sangham is unclear. Shanta Sinha, "Andhra Maoist Movement" in *State Government and Politics in Andhra Pradesh*, ed. G. Ram Reddy and B.A.V. Sharma (New Delhi: Sterling Publishers, 1979), p. 533, gives 1957 as the date. Manoranjan Mohanty, *Revolutionary Violence: A Study of the Maoist Movement in India* (New Delhi: Sterling Publishers, 1977), p. 51, gives 1959 as the date. Organization for the Protection of Democratic Rights, Andhra Pradesh, Fact Finding Committee, *Srikakulam Movement: A Report to the Nation* (O.P.D.R., April 1978), p. 52, cites 1958. But all sources seem to agree that by the time the Sangham was formed, Satyanarayana was identified as a Communist.

11. *Judgement, Parvathipuram Conspiracy Case*, August 30, 1976, p. 150.

12. Subba Rao, "Revolt in Srikakulam"; *Naxalite Activities and the Police*, unpublished paper written for the Law and Order Seminar of the 19th Senior National Police Academy Officers' Course, October 1969 - March 1970, p. 15.

13. Sinha, "Maoists in Andhra Pradesh," p. 211, citing Vempatapu Satyam, *Srikakulam Zilla Girijanodhyama Sankshipta Charitra* (Vijayawada: Socialist Publications), p. 16.

14. Ibid., p. 213.

15. Ibid., pp. 213-215.

16. Ibid., pp. 214-216.

17. Subba Rao, "The Bullet Beats the Bow," p. 3.

18. Subba Rao, "Revolt in Srikakulam."

19. Mohanty, p. 51. Emphasis added.

20. Sinha, "Maoists in Andhra Pradesh," pp. 216-217, citing Ryotu Karya Karta, *Amara Veerula Jeevita Charitralu* (Pilupu Publications, 1973), p. 148.

21. Ibid., p. 217, citing Satyam, p. 20.

22. Ibid., p. 222; Subba Rao, "Srikakulam: The Bullet Beats the Bow"; and T. Nagi Reddy, "Genesis of Violence in Srikakulam: A Viewpoint," *How*, August 1978, p. 9.

23. "A Report on the Girijan Struggle," *Liberation*, December 1968, p. 35.

24. Sinha, "Maoists in Andhra Pradesh," pp. 222-223, citing Satyam, pp. 21-22.

25. The workers who struck were yearly servants, rather than day laborers.

26. Sinha, "Maoists in Andhra Pradesh," pp. 224-225, citing Court Statement of V. Ramalingachari in Naxalite Conspiracy Case (Cr. No. 3/70 of Parvathipuram Taluq, P.S. Srikakulam District).

*The Early Girijan Movement*

27. Sinha, "Maoists in Andhra Pradesh," p. 218. "A Report on the Girijan Struggle," *Liberation*, December 1968, p. 36, claimed the girijans had gained 5,000 acres. *Liberation*, a Naxalite publication, also claimed that by 1967, the landlords' share of the crop on land leased to sharecroppers dropped from two-thirds to one-third, and between 1500 and 2000 acres of previously mortgaged land was wrested back from the landlords. It claimed further than in 1967 alone, loans worth Rs. 3 lakhs were annulled. But I could find no collaborative evidence for any of this. Biplab Dasgupta, "Naxalite Armed Struggles and Annihilation Campaign in Rural Areas," *Economic and Political Weekly*, February 1973, p. 177, cites these figures, with no footnote, but the language is taken almost word for word from *Liberation*. Haridwar Rai and K.M. Prasad, "Naxalism: A Challenge to the Proposition of Peaceful Transition to Socialism," *Indian Journal of Political Science*, October-December 1972, p. 465, also state, without citing a source, that the Sanghams "had occupied five thousand acres of government land and seized some two thousand acres from the landlords and distributed them before the end of 1967."
28. Sinha, "Maoists in Andhra Pradesh," pp. 217-219.
29. See *ibid*., pp. 225-227.
30. According to the testimony of Prosecution Witness #41 in the *Judgement, Parvathipuram Conspiracy Case*, issued August 30, 1976, p. 92, "Because of the struggle led by Vempatapu Satyanarayana the cooly rates were raised [from an average of 4 annas per day] to Rs. 2/50 a day to Rs. 3/ a day. Before the establishment of our Sanghams, a servant used to be paid 5 or 6 putties per year, whereas it became 25 to 30 putties per year by 1967."
31. Interview, April 3, 1980.
32. V.M. Nair, "Girijan Revolt: Marxists Organise Armed Action by Andhra Tribes," *The Statesman*, April 12, 1968.
33. *Judgement, Parvathipuram Conspiracy Case*, p. 92. The Witness, Prosecution Witness #41, was Kumburuku Apanna, Sarpanch of Marripili of Gottivada village of Parvathipuram Taluk; he is a member of Congress.
34. Ibid.
35. *Srikakulam Movement: A Report to the Nation*, p. 53. Sinha, "Maoists in Andhra Pradesh," p. 229, also records that in the early 1960s "there was a sudden spurt of police stations. Many police outposts were set up in areas like Nilakantapuram and Mondemkhal where the Sangham was strong....camps of special armed police were opened at harvest times."
36. Interview, April 2, 1980. The two were Kailasam and Panchadi Krishnamurty; the police had charged them with burglary, dacoity, and violation of section 144 (unlawful assembly).
37. Sinha, "Maoists in Andhra Pradesh," p. 227, citing document U-24, *Naxalite Conspiracy Case*.
38. Interview with Chandramowli, April 3, 1980. *Srikakulam Movement: A Report to the Nation*, p. 51, also noted that "labour contract societies...failed in the face of organised competition from contractors and corrupt officials. V.M. Nair, "Time Yet to Wean Girijans from the Naxalites," *The Statesman*, December 11, 1970, stated, "A tribal labour co-operative found itself without any work although the Andhra Pradesh Government had issued instructions to give preferences to such cooperatives in awarding of contracts." Satyanarayana's efforts, according to *The Statesman*, were frustrated by "the local landlords, many of them Congressmen."
39. Sinha, "Maoists in Andhra Pradesh," p. 220.
40. V.M. Nair, "Girijan Revolt: Marxists Organise Armed Action by Andhra Tribes," *The Statesmen*, April 12, 1968.
41. This paragraph from Sinha, "Maoists in Andhra Pradesh," pp. 220-221.

*The Early Girijan Movement*

42. Ibid., p. 227.
43. The above account from Ibid., pp. 227-229; Sinha drew her information from the Court Statement of V. Ramalingachari, and Document U-24, both of the *Naxalite Conspiracy Case*.
44. Sinha, "Maoists in Andhra Pradesh," p. 223, writes: "Though they were functioning within the broad framework of legality, they have always had one foot steeped in illegality. Their agitational politics led them into increasing number of confrontations with law. Even as early as 1964, six hundred of their cadre was involved in cases. [sic] This meant enormous problems of finance, retaining morale of their cadre and continuing their struggles. Their top leaders like district party member Panchadi Krishnamurty and Vempatapu Satyam were more or less functioning underground since 1964 (in the sense that they were dodging warrants). Added to this was the problem of harassment by local landlords. There were several plots to kill Vempatapu and Adhibatla Kailasam, and whenever Vempatapu went into hiding, away from the agency area, the landlords took advantage of the situation to beat and insult his followers."
45. *Judgement, Parvathipuram Conspiracy Case*, p. 26. Emphasis added.
46. Ibid., 97.
47. Nagi Reddy, p. 10. Under Section 144 of the Indian Penal Code, punishment of two years imprisonment and/or fine is imposed on those joining an unlawful assembly when armed with a deadly weapon.
48. Nagi Reddy, p. 10.
49. This incident is recounted in a number of sources including V.M. Nair, "Girijan Revolt: Marxists Organise Armed Action by Andhra Tribes," *The Statesman*, April 12, 1968; C. Subba Rao, "Revolt in Srikakulam," *The Times of India Magazine*, January 4, 1970. The account given in the *Judgement, Parvathipuram Conspiracy Case*, p. 403, names the primary culprit: "On 31-10-67 one such [Communist] meeting was held at Mondemkhal attended by a large number of tribals and a party of tribals was intercepted at Levidi by landlords headed by Medida Satyanaryana who opened fire and killed two tribals." *Naxalite Activities and the Police*, a document prepared for the police, describes those who opened fire as "the prominent Congress landlords led by Meditha Sathyam..." p. 16. "Satyanarayana" and "Sathyam" are the same person.
50. C. Subba Rao, "Revolt in Srikakulam."
51. Interview with Chandramowli, April 2, 1980.
52. The judgement was announced on September 28, 1968. Naidu, p. 2344. Prosecution witness #41 in the *Judgement, Parvathipuram Conspiracy Case*, p. 92, recounted the intimidation of witnesses and the police's refusal to take corrective measures: "During the pendency of the Levidi murder case the landlords used to hold out threats to the witnesses and thus they used to prevent the witnesses from deposing without fear. In spite of our reports to the police in that regard, nothing was done to us." Here, again, it appears that the police were collaborating with landlord violence.
53. *Naxalite Activities and the Police*, p. 16, contends that the dalams were first organized before this. But the charge sheet cited in the *Judgement, Parvathipuram Conspiracy Case*, p. 9, seems to indicate that the bands were not formed until after the shooting at Levidi. In either case, the dalams became *active* only after Levidi.
54. *Naxalite Activities and the Police*, p. 16.
55. Testimony of Prosecution Witness, *Judgement, Parvathipuram Conspiracy Case*, p. 92.
56. *Naxalite Activities and the Police*, p. 16.
57. Ibid. The incident was reported also in the charge sheet cited in *Judgement, Parvathipuram Conspiracy Case*, p. 9, and in Subba Rao, "Revolt in Srikakulam."
58. *Srikakulam Movement: A Report to the Nation*, p. 54.
59. Ibid., p. 32.

## The Early Girijan Movement

60. District Communist Committee, Srikakulam, "Report on Srikakulam," *Liberation*, May 1969, p. 62.
61. *Naxalite Activities and the Police*, p. 17.
62. Nair, "Girijan Revolt: Marxists Organise Armed Action by Andhra Tribes."
63. Subba Rao, "Revolt in Srikakulam."
64. *Judgement, Parvathipuram Conspiracy Case*, p. 424.
65. Ibid., p. 421.

# 4
# THE NAXALITE MOVEMENT IN SRIKAKULAM

The previous chapter demonstrated the failure of local government to adequately enforce the laws protecting girijans' rights. Government failed to uphold girijans' economic rights—with regard to land, forests, wages, indebtedness—and also failed, most crucially, to protect the girijans from the swift violence of murderous armed landlords. A militant, but generally non-violent, movement which was local in nature failed to make any headway in persuading local officials to uphold the law. Even as conservative a source as the Andhra Pradesh Inspector General of Police had to conclude that

> In Srikakulam District...the local issues like podo cultivation, occupation of lands by plainsmen in the tribal areas, money lending by plains people to these illiterate tribals, inaccessibility of the areas and the absence of an effective administration and political machinery to redress their grievance in accordance with law and the policy of the Government have provided a ready-made and explosive ground for the Naxalites to exploit.[1]

This chapter will focus on the ideology and tactics of the radicalized movement in Srikakulam District which, because of its connections with the leaders of the 1967 Naxalbari revolt, can also be called "Naxalite." This chapter will examine how the local leader Satyanaryana brought his movement into the Naxalite fold and how the movement ceased to be a local movement aimed at the redress of local grievances; instead it took on an all-India target: the movement ultimately came to be aimed at the overthrow of Indian state power. The organization and tactics of the movement were woefully inadequate to its ultimate goals, and we will examine the nature of its deficiencies. Since the emphasis here will be on the government response to the movement, we must also look at the proclaimed ideology of the movement and its connections to other movements in India, for the government did not view the Srikakulam Naxalite movement as a local problem, but as part of a larger threat to state power.

## The Naxalite Movement In Srikakulam

Once the movement adopted the violent tactics it did, including assassinations of landowners and those it named as "police informants," the government was compelled to suppress it as vigorously as possible. This would have been true even if the movement had not aimed at the overthrow of the Indian government, but had remained at the local level, aimed at local authority. Even had it been confined to the local level, the most basic authority and legitimacy of government—its ability to exercise a monopoly of the legitimate use of violence—would have been threatened. Furthermore, the interests of that segment of the population which was most supportive of government, and which government had the greatest interest in defending—the powerful class of landlords—would also have been threatened.

But the fact that the ideological pronouncements of the movement quite specifically called for the overthrow of government by armed force, and the fact that the movement ceased to be localized, called forth the full force available to government. Not only the legitimacy but the power of government was targeted, and government responded vigorously. Unfortunately for the revolutionaries, their capacities in no sense approximated their vision.

There are other movements in India, such as the tribal movements in Maharashtra that will be examined below in Part II, that have learned from the mistakes of the Srikakulam Naxalites, and have not attempted violent overthrow of state power. Instead, they have sought a broader forum for the questioning of government's legitimacy by pointing up the failure of government to uphold the laws. As we shall see in the Maharashtra cases, the Maharashtra government also appears to have learned from the Naxalite experience, and has been far more responsive to organized demands than the Andhra government of the 1960s had been. In Andhra, the intractability of government led to violent outburst, but, as will be shown in this chapter, the physical power available to government was sufficient for government to maintain itself in power. As we will see in Chapter Six below, its next task was to set about re-legitimizing itself in the face of its obvious failure to have provided the rule of law.

### The Local Movement Becomes Naxalite

As was recounted in Chapter Three, T. Nagi Reddy and other Andhra Communist leaders had convinced Satyanarayana to join the Communist Party in the late 1950s; in 1960, Satyanarayana and Adibhatla Kailasam, the other school teacher involved with organizing the girijans in the Agency area, were elected to the Communist Party Srikakulam District Committee. Thus, although their activities were confined to the Agency area, they were in contact with party leaders, activists, and with Communist thinking in a broader region, and were affected by organizational and ideological changes in the all-India context. One such relevant change occurred in 1964, when the Communist Party of India split into two groups: a "rightist" Communist Party of India, which leaned toward the Soviet Union, and a "leftist" Communist Party of India (Marxist) which had ideological affinities with the Chinese Communist Party. The Andhra Communists also split into two parties, and sixty percent of the rank and file membership joined the CPI(M).[2] Among those joining were T. Nagi Reddy and, in Srikakulam, Satyanarayana and Kailasam.[3]

The 1967 elections saw the CPI(M) emerge as the largest party in the legislatures of two Indian states, Kerala and West Bengal; the CPI(M) was committed to a peaceful transition to socialism through parliamentarianism. But it was also in 1967, beginning in May, that a peasant revolt erupted in Naxalbari, in Darjeeling District of West Bengal, led by CPI(M) members Charu Mazumdar and Kanu Sanyal. The Naxalbari revolt was put down with armed force by the CPI(M) government of West Bengal. Mazumdar and Sanyal were expelled from the CPI(M) and along with others formed a new "Maoist" group, the All India Coordination Committee of Communist Revolutionaries (AICCCR) in November 1967.[4]

The Andhra section of the CPI(M) was also experiencing ideological splits, with the leftists there increasingly unwilling to engage in electoral activity which it now saw as "revisionist." The Andhra leftists did not urge immediate armed revolt as did the West Bengal extremists; they did not think that the time was yet ripe. But they did want the party to turn its attention to preparations for organizing armed struggle, and to end its strategy of a peaceful, parliamentary path to socialism.[5] The Andhra group pressed this point of view at the all-India plenum of the CPI(M) in April 1968, but without success; indeed, the Andhra leadership of CPI(M) was expelled from the party. In June 1968, four leaders of the leftists—D. Venkateswara Rao, C. Pulla Reddy, T. Nagi Reddy and Kolla Venkaiah—formed the Andhra Pradesh Coordination Committee of Communist Revolutionaries (APCCCR), and brought more than half the members of the CPI(M) in Andhra along with them.[6]

In terms of the struggle in Srikakulam, there were now three important factions of leftists. On the national level, there was the AICCCR, led by the West Bengalis, Mazumdar and Sanyal, which urged immediate armed struggle for the seizure of state power.[7] On the state level, there was T. Nagi Reddy's APCCCR. The strategy of this group was to slowly build toward armed struggle against the state by first organizing mass seizures of land and other intermediate steps; they felt the development of strong mass movements was a necessary prerequisite to the seizure of power.[8] On the district level, the Srikakulam District Committee was engaged in the ongoing struggle in Srikakulam; in March 1968, after the police firings which killed two activists, the leaders of the movement had taken to the hills and were engaged in a period of training and strategizing. They felt that the time was ripe for armed struggle, although they were urged by the state group, the APCCCR, that there were not yet sufficient signs of mass upsurge to warrant such a struggle.[9] The Srikakulam District Committee began to circumvent the APCCCR and to communicate directly with the AICCCR.

In October 1968, Panchadi Krisnamurthy and Chowdary Tejeswara Rao of the Srikakulam District Committee traveled to Calcutta to confer with Charu Mazumdar, who advised them to start armed action immediately against the landlords and the government that defended them.[10] They returned to Srikakulam and in the last week of October 1968, held a meeting in Boddapadu village with about forty other activists, and there decided to undertake immediate armed struggle for the overthrow of state power.[11] The Srikakulam Committee then asked the APCCCR for permission to attack police stations. This permission was refused by the APCCCR with the argument that more efforts to mobilize the people were necessary before a successful armed struggle could begin.[12] Nagi Reddy's insistence on the build up of mass organizations prior to armed struggle was side-stepped by the Srikakulam Committee which instead looked to the AICCCR as the authoritative revolutionary leadership.

Nagi Reddy's group, the APCCCR, which considered itself to be truly Maoist, continued its own pattern of revolutionary activity, selecting Warangal and Khamman Districts of Andhra Pradesh as the center of its own struggle.[13] On August 2, 1968, T. Nagi Reddy had declared to the press that he had lost faith in parliamentary methods, and that he intended to pursue a Maoist course of bringing about armed revolution; on March 11, 1969, he resigned his seat in the Andhra Pradesh Assembly and again proclaimed his intention to organize armed people's revolution.[14] But, he declared that the Srikakulam movement was engaged in sheer adventurism,[15] and set about creating a different model. As will be seen below, however, the activities in Warangal and Khamman also degenerated into the lootings and murders by small numbers of committed activists that Nagi Reddy argued against, rather than achieving sustained political organization of the masses.[16]

The movement in Srikakulam had no outward, violent manifestations until November 1968; March 1968 through November 1968 was a time of ideological assessment and political maneuvering. When the movement again broke forth violently in November, there were several layers of leadership. Nagi Reddy and the state leaders who had been in contact with Satyanarayana since his early years in the Agency, and who had been closely tied to the movement during 1967, were no longer significant. The movement was increasingly directed ideologically by Charu Mazumdar and Kanu Sanyal, both of whom paid several visits to Srikakulam over the next few years, but who mainly issued ideological directives from afar.

## The Naxalite Movement In Srikakulam

On the scene, there were two types of leaders.[17] On the one hand, there were the local leaders, Vempatapu Satyanarayana and Adibhatla Kailasam, both of peasant origin, both elementary school teachers with little formal education, who had been organizing, living among and working with the tribals for over ten years.

On the other hand were increasing numbers of college-educated ideologues: Panchadi Krishnamurthy, an honors B.A. in economics and politics who was to become the primary link between Mazumdar and the Srikakulam Naxalites, and the major on-the-scene theoretician;[18] C. Tejeswara Rao; Subba Rao Panigrahi, "a famous writer of Andhra";[19] and Dr. Chaganti Bhaskara Rao, a "brilliant surgeon" who "left a flourishing practice to join the guerrilla bands in the Srikakulam hills"[20] were among those "bourgeois intellectuals" who joined and came to dominate the movement. It was commonly reported that a number of students "from the Medical, Engineering and Arts Colleges and from high schools where the Marxist students' wing was once active,"[21] left school to join in the armed struggle. These educated people were primarily from Andhra Pradesh, but from the plains, not the Agency areas; they were often from districts other than Srikakulam.[22]

As the movement grew in Srikakulam with the addition of these outsiders, it seems that Satyanarayana, the original leader, lost control over the movement to those with more intellectual sophistication, but considerably less practical experience and understanding. His own popularity and influence were crucial in bringing the tribals into the movement; their respect, even reverence for him is apparent in numerous accounts.[23] But his own leadership seems to have been subsumed under the ideological pursuasions of those from outside the Agency. C. Subba Rao portrays Satyanarayana as a man who, once the CPI(M-L) came to dominate the movement, had "ceased to be master of himself," and had become "a mere actor in a Greek tragedy."[24] The same writer had earlier noted that *Liberation*, the Naxalite publication that recorded Srikakulam events in detail, seemed to regard a November 1968 raid on the house of a rich merchant as the starting point of the revolution:

> ...the magazine's account of the struggle month by month rarely mentions Vempatapu Satyanarayana and his pioneering work. It has always regarded the leaders in Sompeta taluk—Panchadi Krishnamurty, Tamada Ganapati...Chaganti Bhaskara Rao...and Tejeswara Rao...as the real heroes of the revolt.[25]

Although he was actively engaged in the armed struggle until his death in an encounter with the police in July 1970, there seems to be a clear split between the movement Satyanarayana led prior to 1968, and the movement that emerged under Naxalite direction in late 1968. Local leadership, local struggle had failed. The movement entered a phase of far more ambitious goals but, as we are about to see, unrealized organizational capacity; the ability to overthrow the government through armed force was never even approached, and the gap between ideological hopes and practical reality is striking.

*Naxalite Strategy*

Naxalite ideology, as articulated primarily by Charu Mazumdar,[26] was fatally flawed in two essential respects. First, in attempting to emulate the Chinese Communist example, the Naxalites ignored a key difference. In likening the situation in India to that which had existed in the Yenan period in China, they ignored the differences in state power, in the state's capacity to use force. The Yenan experience of building up a revolutionary base and a parallel government occurred at a time when the Chinese government under Chiang Kai-shek was incapable of completely penetrating and controlling all the regions of China, and when the country was under seige from a foreign enemy. The Indian government, however, was firmly in place, enjoying not only widespread legitimacy but also controlling available resources of force: police, army, weaponry. Consequently, it was in excellent shape to suppress and punish local violent uprisings.

In addition to underestimating the power of the state, the second, related error was in assuming that the poor and exploited of India would rise up like a "prairie fire" after an initial "spark" of terrorist activity against landlord power. Biplab Dasgupta has written, "The principal weakness of the movement was its belief that the people of India would rise in revolt as soon as a call for armed struggle was given."[27] Although claiming to be doctrinaire Maoists, the Naxalites in fact disdained the mass organizations and agrarian revolution that were fundamental aspects of the Chinese revolutionary experience.

In China, poor and middle peasants became enthusiasts of revolution because the revolutionaries offered them specific, concrete benefits; the most important of these were land, protection against retaliatory landlord violence, and guns with which to fight the Japanese invaders. The struggles for land were localized struggles, with little interference from a central or even regional authority, for these authorities were lacking sufficient physical power to back up the landlord/usurer class. Thus, the first struggles were not to seize state power, but to seize and redistribute land. Mass organizations were formed to organize and govern these efforts; these organizations were equally vehicles for politicizing the poor. The Chinese Communists were able through agrarian reforms to give the formerly landless peasants an economic stake in the revolution. Through mass organizations—peasant organizations, women's organizations, the army—the Communists gave the peasants a political education and

## The Naxalite Movement In Srikakulam

a mode of organized political action.[28]

The Naxalites, although claiming to follow the Chinese path, in fact developed a theory that was closer to the *foco* theory of Che Guevara;[29] they argued that the annihilation of the class enemy—landlords and their police protectors—by small groups of secretly organized guerrilla squads would so inflame the hatred of the masses that they would spontaneously arise.[30] Mass organizations would not only be unnecessary, they would be "obstacles in the way of development and expansion of guerrilla warfare."[31] This strategy found its most thorough laboratory in the Srikakulam District.

The Srikakulam rebellion was not a completely isolated occurrence. The revolt in Naxalbari in 1967 preceded it; a revolt in Debra and Gopiballavapur in Midnapore District of West Bengal took place between August 1969 and March 1970;[32] Naxalites were engaged in revolutionary activity in the Mushahari Block of Muzaffarpur District of Bihar from August 1968 until they were crushed in 1970;[33] and a "microscopic" Naxalite movement was formed in 1968 in Lakhimpur Kheri of Uttar Pradesh.[34] A Maoist movement also emerged in the Wynad Hills of Cannanore District of Kerala in early 1968, but it suffered from factionalism and, after an attack on a police station in November 1968, "the police mopped up in the Wynad forests and in the process arrested all the important leaders of the movement."[35] In Andhra Pradesh, the Nagi Reddy group, the APCCCR, was engaged in revolutionary organizing in a less violent way in several districts, particularly Warangal, Khamman, Karimnagar and East Godavari.[36]

But these are relatively tiny dots on the landscape of India; although West Bengal and Andhra Pradesh were the two states that had the most violent activity with which to contend, there is no indication that the states' resources were strained by battling these rural Naxalite movements;[37] add to these resources the power of the Central Reserve Police, which was called in to Srikakulam, and the fire power of the State was overwhelming. This was so without the Indian Army being at all involved; the "revolts" were quite adequately put down with mere police power. While the rebels in Srikakulam did have the advantage of hilly, forested terrain, they had little sophisticated weaponry; in addition to axes, bows and arrows, and spears, they fought with muzzle-loading guns and homemade explosives.[38] This was not an arsenal that gave the police much trouble.

Given what appear to be these unequal odds, how did the Naxalites hope to succeed? The strategy rested on the spontaneous rise of the masses throughout the country as a result of the hatreds unleased through the annihilation of local, hated landlords and usurers by small bands of guerrillas. Anything less than massive spontaneous participation, given the force available to the state, would seem doomed to failure. Yet that unlikely event, evidently, is what the

### The Naxalite Movement In Srikakulam

Naxalites counted on. Biplab Dasgupta writes:

> A puzzling aspect of the Naxalite activities in Naxalbari, Debra, Gopiballavapore, Mushahari, Srikakulam and other places was that these were not properly coordinated and were not parts of a strategic plan for the seizure of power in the whole country. In fact in none of these areas could there ever be any hope of sustained struggle for an indefinite period of time. Naxalbari, for example, is well-connected with the national highway system, and is accessible to one of the largest military concentrations in North Bengal, while in terms of political support its neighboring areas were among the worst in the state. One reason for this was the Naxalite faith that the people of India were ready for revolution, and that what was needed was a "spark" to begin a "prairie fire." [Documents written by Charu Mazumdar during 1965-1967] show Mazumdar's faith in "locally based struggles," which would eventually spread to the rest of the country. [In a document published in April 1967] Mazumdar spoke of the need to destroy the state machinery and to work for agrarian revolution, and stated, "if this cannot be done in the whole country, it should be done locally."[39]

The Naxalite strategy called for the immediate seizure of state power; Mazumdar wrote, "militant struggle must be carried on not for land, crops, etc., but for seizure of state power."[40] Naxalites disdained the idea of building mass organizations around economic issues closest to the people. It was this ideological belief, in fact, that caused the rift between the APCCCR on the one hand, and the AICCCR (later the CPI[M-L]) and the Srikakulam District Committee, on the other. A report written in February 1969 by the District Communist Committee of Srikakulam articulated the differences thus:

> [We, the Srikakulam comrades thought] training is possible only through waging war against the enemy. [The methods of Nagi Reddy and Pulla Reddy] are unrelated to struggle. They suggested such things as mobilising the masses on issues like wage-rates, problems of farm-labourers, food, etc. We replied that any programme of action must include resistance to the police. We mean by this that resistance war must be started on guerrilla lines....Our struggle should be...aimed at seizing political power; it should be an armed struggle....Comrade Mazumdar suggested to us that we "build up guerrilla squads and start struggle immediately." He also suggested to us that we concentrate our actions on annihilating the class enemies and

in that context destroy police forces. Comrade Mazumdar's views coincided with those of ours.[41]

Thus, the Naxalite strategy included three related essentials: 1) mass organization is unnecessary; 2) the class enemy can and should be annihilated through terrorist tactics; and 3) any agrarian programs must wait until after the seizure of political power.[42] Mazumdar wrote in June 1969,

> the revolutionary initiative of the wide sections of the peasant masses can be released through annihilation of class enemies by guerrilla methods, and neither mass organization nor mass movement is indispensable for starting guerrilla war.[43]

Unlike in the Maoist experience, agrarian programs, such as the seizure of land, were not to be a part of mobilizing the masses for armed struggle against the state; instead, guerrilla actions by small numbers of revolutionaries against state power would mobilize the peasants and landless to join in the struggle. Agrarian programs would be initiated only *after* state power was seized.

Although, as Dasgupta has pointed out,[44] Mazumdar had conceived of the importance of the annihilation tactic even before Naxalbari, it seems evident that the development of an ideology that utterly negated the importance of mass organization and that glorified secretive, terrorist activity was a response to the difficulties being encountered in practice. Although there had not been a sustained period of organizing in Naxalbari, the revolt there did include "large scale participation of peasants." The activists there "conducted economic campaigns like seizure of land and crops, and converted them into political campaigns by setting up revolutionary peasant committees to administer the new allocation and defend their gains by armed struggle."[45] Yet this revolt was easily crushed by state force.

In Srikakulam, even more dramatically, there was a significant level of mass organization because of the efforts of Satyanarayana and Kailasam over the period of a decade. As has been shown above, by 1967 the movement had achieved some successes, but was also facing severe frustrations, as the landlords engaged in passive tactics such as hoarding their grain and leaving their fields fallow. The landlords appeared to have the economic power to outlast the workers' demands.[46] At the same time that their economic efforts seemed stalemated, the landlords also murdered two tribals at Levidi, and were plainly backed by the police. Non-violent mass organization appeared to the Srikakulam activists to have reached its limits, and they were in search of a new method. This method was provided by Mazumdar's strategy of the seizure of state power through armed struggle.

## The Naxalite Movement In Srikakulam

In the initial stages of violent confrontation in Srikakulam, because of the previous decade of organizing, the guerrilla actions had mass participation.[47] But as the police repression increased in intensity, the tactics shifted to terrorist strikes undertaken by increasingly small numbers of guerrillas. As Shanta Sinha sees it, "the movement started with a mass phase of series of attacks on landlords and money-lenders and later on turned first into limited guerrilla actions, and later still to individual annihilation combined with mere squadism."[48] The ideological justifications put forward by Mazumdar for the annihilation line—in which small guerrilla units formed in complete secrecy would annihilate those enemies whom the party intellectuals deemed most hated by the people[49]—seemed merely to be an adaptation to the impossibility of doing anything else, given the police power in the area. Mass organization had become impossible; only conspiratorial squad actions remained possible, even if purposeless.

By late 1970, when the Srikakulam Naxalites had been thoroughly defeated, a document was circulated within CPI(M-L) circles citing criticisms purportedly made by the Chinese Communist Party.[50] This critique made clear the divergence between Mazumdar's annihilation tactic and the Chinese model. Among the criticisms leveled were the following:

—Regarding the formulation that the open Trade Union, open mass organizations and mass movements [are] out of date and taking to *secret assassination as the only way: This idea needs rethinking*.

—You have applied Lin Piao's People's War Theory in a mechanical way. Lin's Guerilla War theory is a military affair. During the anti-Japanese resistance war...some comrades in the army raised a slogan that positional warfare and mobile warfare are the way to mobilise the people. In reply to this wrong theory, Comrade Lin said that guerrilla war is the only way to mobilise the people. *This military theory has no relation with political and organisational questions*.

—Regarding the forumlation that if a revolutionary does not make his hand red with the blood of class enemies, then he is not a Communist: *If this be the yardstick of a Communist then the Communist Party cannot remain a Communist party*.

—No stress has been given on agrarian revolution and the slogan for the seizure of the state power is counterposed to the land problem. *There is no agrarian programme*.

—Without *mass struggle and mass organization*, the peasants' armed struggle cannot be sustained.[51]

Mazumdar and the Naxalites claimed throughout their revolutionary efforts to be Maoists,[52] and had indeed received early support from China.[53] However, as the annihilation tactic developed, and the masses were left behind, the similarity between Mazumdar's thought and Mao's thought grew almost imperceivable;[54] the results were equally dissimilar. The next section will discuss the course of the armed activity in Srikakulam, and its defeat by police forces.

### *Naxalite Tactics: The Armed Struggle*

> The accused persons...became members to conspiracy to secure arms, attack and kill citizens and public servants, loot properties and to bring about an armed revolt by securing arms and explosive substances, openly and secretly, and to wage war against the Government and to bring about disaffection towards the Government lawfully established. In pursuance of the said conspiracy they secured the stored arms, used fire arms and other weapons, committed murders and dacoities and started armed revolution against the lawfully established Government and its authority from November 1968. Hence the charge sheet...
> —summary of charge sheet of
> Naxalite Conspiracy Case[55]

The period from March to November 1968 in Srikakulam was spent in ideological discussion and preparation for armed struggle. The preparations included creating a network of hideouts, organizing elaborate courier systems through which instructions and information could be passed secretly, collecting and manufacturing arms and training party cadres in guerrilla tactics.[56] In late October about forty district leaders of the Srikakulam District Coordination Committee resolved to launch armed struggle immediately.[57]

The first organized act of violence by the Naxalites was a dacoity, or armed robbery, committed on November 24, 1968; in this action, standing paddy crop was cut and removed.[58] In the next two days, two additional robberies were committed by large mobs of armed girijans:

> The...lightening offence...was committed on 25-11-68 night by about 400 tribals armed with guns, bows, arrows, sticks and spears led by the top leaders. They raided the house of Theegala Narsimhulu of Pedagottili. They inflicted minor injuries on Narsimhulu and threatened his wife and daughter and looted gold jewels, silver articles,

vessels, clothes and grains worth Rs. 20,000/-. In less than 48 hours, on 27-11-68 they crossed over one range of hills and attacked the house of "shahukar" Ramanoorthy of Doddukhallu village and committed similar dacoity carrying away property worth Rs. 27,400/-.[59]

These initial actions of the Naxalites seemed aimed at obtaining funds for the purchase of arms.[60]

In this first stage of armed struggle, the movement in the Agency area had a distinctly mass character. Naxalite actions—which in addition to dacoities soon included murders of landlords and attacks on police—generally had the participation of hundreds of girijans.[61] *Naxalite Activities and the Police*, a police document, cites an incident on December 12, 1968, in which 500 tribals "armed with sticks, stones, knives and spears and raising communist slogans...swooped suddenly on [a] police party shouting that it should be annihilated. The furious mob injured the Deputy Superintendent of Police and nine other police officers." The police opened fire, killing two tribals. From December 20 through December 23, three successive police parties "were attacked by hundreds and hundreds of tribals armed with deadly weapons..."[62] Two national newspapers reported that on December 29, 1968, about a thousand armed tribals committed three dacoities and exchanged fire with the police in Mondemkhal village in Srikakulam.[63]

Another characteristic of this first phase is that it seemed designed not to eliminate the landlord class by killing all landlords, but instead to seize their economic assets and redistribute them to the poor. The intent, also, was to intimidate the landlords so that they would flee, leaving control of the area completely in the hands of the Naxalites. According to the charge sheet in the Naxalite Conspiracy Case, between November 1968 and April 1969, there were fifteen cases of seizure of property and five killings.[64] Journalist C. Subba Rao argued that the dacoities helped to build increased support for the Naxalites:

> For some time the Naxalites' methods endeared them to the local people. They would make it a point to burn the promissory notes in the merchants' houses, thus wiping out all loans at one stroke. Also, after every attack, they would heap all looted property in a central place and invite the villagers to take away whatever they like. This Robin Hood touch helped them win the sympathy of the poor people.[65]

One newspaper reported in June 1969 that since November 1968 the Naxalites had seized and destroyed Rs. 500,000 worth of promissory notes;[66] to the girijans so long enslaved by indebtedness, this must indeed have represented a dramatic liberation.

However, while the mass struggle in the Agency area had considerable success, and the police were unable to capture Satyanarayana despite intensive efforts to do so,[67] the struggle in the plains areas was easily thwarted by the police. A new police station was opened in Bobbili Taluk, and police issued warrants for the arrest of many party members and their sympathizers. These people were forced to flee to the hilly, forested Agency area of Parvathipuram Taluk, where it was still possible to evade the police.[68] In the Agency areas, although "intensive combing operations" were conducted by the police, "police always met with armed resistance from the tribals."[69] Thus, although police repression was intensifying, there continued to be mass support for the Naxalites in those Agency areas in which the girijan movement had existed for some time. Indeed, one newspaper report argued that the police operations "not only failed to check the revolt, but seem to have helped the Marxists to further alienate the tribesmen from the government."[70]

In late January 1969, Charu Mazumdar visited the area and met with local leaders. At this meeting, at a state-wide meeting of AICCCR supporters held in February, and at a Srikakulam District Committee meeting held immediately afterward on February 11 through 14, important decisions were made to extend the geographic area of struggle to the plains and to other districts of Andhra Pradesh, and also to prepare for increased violence. Arms and ammunition were to be snatched from the police, and moneylenders and landlords were to be killed.[71]

Increased emphasis was put on the formation of guerrilla squads. Each squad was to be organized with seven or eight members. The squads were to be in the forefront of resistance and also to be active in mass mobilization programs. Local governing organizations known as Ryotanga Sangrama Samities were to be formed at the village level; these would also serve to convey information about police movements, to make class analyses of their villages in order to identify the worst class enemies, and to aid the resistance.[72]

Once again, however, the struggles in the Plains areas were thwarted by a combination of police strength and lack of enthusiasm on the part of the local poor peasants and landless who, unlike the girijans of the Agency, had no history of organization. Between December 1968 and February 1969, the police sent in nine additional platoons of Andhra Pradesh Special Armed Police and sanctioned one new post of Additional Inspector of Police and two new Inspector posts; three new police stations and a police outpost on the border with Orissa were opened.[73] Because of this police strength, the Naxalites had to recede further and further into the hills.[74] The Naxalites in the plains received little help from the plains peasants, who appear to have weighed the coercive power of the Naxalites against that of the police, and decided they would

## The Naxalite Movement In Srikakulam

rather be allied to the police:

> When the police came and beat up the local peasants of the area, the peasants instead of rising up and helping the maoists to ambush the police as expected (and as happened in the agency areas) instead refused to help the maoists in any way and gave the police information concerning the whereabouts of Maoists. The maoist action squads became disorganized and dispersed...Of the left-over cadres some...retreated into the mountains.[75]

In April, the AICCCR met in Calcutta and formed a new political party, the Communist Party of India (Marxist-Leninist). The announcement of the new party was made (on May 1, 1969) by Kanu Sanyal, who predicted that the formation of the party would usher in an armed revolution that would overthrow the present government.[76] In mid-May, the Naxalite leaders in Andhra Pradesh met and reconstituted themselves as part of the new CPI(M-L).[77] In this meeting, the decision was also made to annihilate landlords, police personnel, and informers.

> This meeting can be regarded as a turning point in the history of the Srikakulam movement. Organizationally it involved a shift from the emphasis on mass activity to the emphasis on guerrilla squads. Programmatically annihilation overshadowed all other activities.[78]

Under conditions of increasing police repression, the movement relied increasingly not on mass participation, which in the plains areas had succumbed to police power, but on terrorist strikes on individual landlords: the annihilation tactic. The annihilation of a hated landlord, the Naxalites believed, would have two effects. In the plains areas, where there was little mass organization, the murder of a landlord would offer an opportunity for propagandizing about the Naxalite cause and firing the people with enthusiasm.[79] The murder of the class enemy would precede mass organization, not follow it. For the murder of the class enemy would also create a liberated zone in which the guerrillas could more easily organize the now-enlightened poor peasants. In a code of instructions originally circulated in November 1970, Charu Mazumdar emphasized both the small secretive nature of the guerrilla squad which would carry out the annihilations and the benefits of annihilation:

> The unit should be kept secret from those among the local people whose vigilance has not yet reached the required level...The method of forming a guerrilla unit has to be wholly conspiratorial....This

### The Naxalite Movement In Srikakulam

> conspiracy should be between individuals, and on a person-to-person basis. The petty bourgeois intellectual comrade must take the initiative...He should approach the poor peasant who, in his opinion, has the most revolutionary potentiality, and whisper in his ear: "Don't you think it a good thing to finish off such and such a jotedar?"
>
> ...it would be wrong to put too much stress on the importance of carrying on intensive propaganda before starting the guerrilla attacks....we must begin by eliminating the local class enemies. Once an area is liberated from...class enemies (some are annihilated while some others flee) the repressive State machinery is deprived of its eyes and ears, making it impossible for the police to know who is a guerrilla and who is not, and who is tilling his own land and who tills that of the jotedars...[81]

However, once again, in areas in which there was no prior organization, the annihilation tactic failed to hold the support of the people; at the first sign of strong police action, the Naxalite support dissolved. In areas with a history of organization, the annihilation tactic was not initially the work of tiny squads, as hundreds of girijans continued to participate in brutal murders.[82]

The Andhra government, which had been relying on the Special Armed Police, began in May 1969 to take stronger action. In early May a top level committee headed by Andhra Chief Secretary M.T. Raju and including Home Secretary A. Krishnaswami and Inspector General of Police Atma Jayaram visited Parvathipuram Agency and suggested that strong measures were needed to curb the Naxalites.[83] On June 7, 1969, the pressure increased as the Andhra government declared the Agency areas in Parvathipuram, Palakonda and Pathapatnam Taluks of Srikakulam District to be "disturbed areas" under the Andhra Pradesh Suppression of Disturbances Act of 1948. An emergency police headquarters was established in Srikakulam in early August to coordinate government efforts.[84] On August 20, the entire taluk of Pathapatnam as well as the taluks of Sompeta, Tekkali, Itchapuram and all of Palakonda, and the agency area of Kurupam Sub-Taluk in Parvathipuram Taluk were also declared disturbed areas;[85] this put most of Srikakulam under the Andhra Pradesh Suppression of Disturbances Act, and gave the police tremendous discretionary power to use lethal violence against suspected revolutionaries. Section 5 of the Act reads:

> Any Magistrate, and any police Officer not below the rank of Sub-Inspector, may if in his opinion it is necessary to do so for restoring or maintaining public order, after giving such warning, if any, as

he may consider necessary, fire upon, order fire to be opened or otherwise use force, even to the causing of death, against any person who in a disturbed area is acting in contravention of any law or order for the time being in force in such an area, prohibiting the assembly of five or more persons or the carrying of weapons or of things capable of being used as weapons.[86]

In effect, the police were allowed to shoot on sight any suspicious persons, and they did so. They were later accused by the press of "a deplorable tendency to be trigger happy,"[87] and of being "ruthless in their operations. On the slightest suspicion they open fire and in the process take many innocent lives."[88] In fact, the police claim that a number of Naxalites were killed in "encounters" with the police was later questioned by several private organizations and a government commission; the accusation was made that the police had in reality "liquidated in cold blood" a number of "Naxalites" whom they had in custody.[89]

Prior to the declaration of much of Srikakulam as a "disturbed" area, the police had had some success in killing or imprisoning Naxalites. *The Times of India* reported on May 27, 1969 that twelve Naxalites had so far been killed by the police; 1,824 had been arrested, and 253 guns had been recovered from them.[90] On March 25, 1970, the Andhra Pradesh Home Minister, J. Vengal Rao reported in the Assembly that since June 1969 sixty-nine Naxalites had been killed and 793 arrested.[91] There seems, however, to be some element of wishful thinking in these figures; since only seventy-five people were eventually brought to trial in the Naxalite Conspiracy Case, one wonders how many of those arrested were in any way responsible for Naxalite actions.

On the night of May 26-27, prior to the declaration of the "disturbed" areas, the police had shot to death Panchadi Krishnamurthy, one of the most important Srikakulam Naxalite leaders, and six others with him. While the police claimed that the seven were shot in an "encounter" begun when thirty armed Naxalites attacked a police party,[92] accusations were later made that the seven were captured by the police at the Sompeta Railway station, taken into the hills, and there "brutally murdered" by the police.[93] In either case, the death of Krishnamurthy was a demoralizing blow for the Naxalites.

With the declaration of "disturbed" areas, and with an obvious commitment from both the Andhra and the Union Government to end the Naxalite rebellion, police power intensified; in mid-July, two battalions of Central Reserve Police were posted to Srikakulam.[94] They were joined, at the height of the tensions, by three battalions of the Andhra Pradesh Special Armed Police and six platoons of the District Armed Reserves, in addition to the regular District Police; eighty Armed Outposts were added to the three police stations that had been created in January and February.[95] In early August an emergency police headquarters was established in Srikakulam to coordinate governmental efforts.[96] Some 3,500 police were combing the Agency Hills.[97] In contrast, the guerrillas claimed that in June 1969 there were 300 guerrillas in the Central squads, sixty in the women's squad, and about 1,200 in the village defense squads.[98] Not only did the police have vastly greater numbers, they also had superior arms: Naxalite guns were usually primitive, and there was considerable reliance on axes, bows and arrows, and spears which, while useful for murdering landlords, could not stand up to police fire power. In his "A Few Words About Guerrilla Actions," Mazumdar tried to portray this evident deficiency as a matter of choice: "We should not use any kind of firearms at this stage," he wrote. "The guerrilla unit must rely wholly on choppers, spears, javelins, and sickles..." Guns, he stated, would almost inevitably fall into the hands of the police. Furthermore, Naxalites should place their reliance on people, not on weapons.[99] The author of the annihilation tactic seems desperately here to be making a virtue of terrorist actions by a few people rather than the mass actions of hundreds that could no longer take place because of successful police repression.

In addition to the repressive actions of the police, the Naxalites seem, in some measure, to have defeated themselves by alienating portions of the population through their violence. Not only landlords but also girijans whom the Naxalites believed to be police informants were routinely murdered; one journalist argues that this so alienated many girijans that "but for the hold Satyanarayana exercised over them, the revolution would have been a non-event."[100] However, even this loyalty had its limits; *The Hindu* of October 31, 1969, reported two instances in which hundreds of tribals "openly expressing that they would not tolerate the acts of violence which the Naxalites were provoking," helped police to search for Naxalites. The tip given to the police that resulted in Satyanarayana's July 10, 1970 death in the hills came from two tribals whose brother had been killed by the Naxalites;[101] Satyanarayana's long time associate Adibhatla Kailasam was killed in the same police attack. The Home Minister, J. Vengal Rao, announced these deaths to the press and told newsmen that the Naxalite menace could now be considered over.[102] Although a few incidents followed, he was essentially correct.

At the height of their power, the Naxalites claimed to have controlled three hundred villages in the agency area;[103] in the one hundred square miles they controlled, they collected taxes and organized "people's courts" which tried, convicted and punished offenders.[104] During the revolt, they committed eighty-three dacoities, taking property worth Rs. 5,65,952/50.[105] They killed approximately forty landlords, moneylenders, and alleged police informants.[106] Approximately one hundred Naxalites were killed by the police.[107]

## The Naxalite Movement In Srikakulam

Accounts of the number of police killed varies absurdly, depending on the source. As of November 1969, the Naxalites claimed to have killed eighty-four policemen;[108] but the Inspector General of Police, whose accuracy regarding the number of his own men killed is probably more reliable, reported that only four policemen throughout the entire state had been killed by Naxalite violence.[109] *The Statesman* reported that two policemen had been killed by 1969 in Srikakulam, and ascribed these low casualty figures to the poor weapons of the Naxalites.[110] The police, also, attributed the limited casualties and superior performance of the police to their "superior training, resources, and fire power."[111]

It seems evident that only in those areas in which Satyanarayana and Kailasam had been organizing for years did the Naxalites enjoy the participation and protection of masses of people. The annihilation tactic in the absence of prior organizing was a failure. The guerrillas were too easily isolated and destroyed by the police. Even in the Agency, the area of their greatest strength, the power available to the police of the district, state, and center was simply too overwhelming for an isolated movement.[112]

The governments both of Andhra and the center were, however, severely shaken by these events. Members of the government and the press made the criticism that the conditions that had led the tribals to have sympathy for the Naxalites were the fault, in substantial part, of government's failure. At best, the government had neglected to govern the area; and it had ignored the legitimate demands of an organized group. At worst, government officials were willing collaborators with the rich in the exploitation of the poor. While government retained its power in the face of violence, its legitimacy in the eyes of many observers in the national scene was shaken. The government realized, too, that if it was to wrest the loyalty of the girijans away from the Naxalites, it was going to have to legitimate itself in their eyes. While this chapter has described the armed struggle between the Naxalites and the state, this struggle represents only half the response of the state. Public opinion widely supported the violent suppression of the terrorist Naxalites; but public opinion also demanded that government correct the conditions that had led to that terrorism. Beginning in 1968, in conjunction with its armed force, government also began an economic program in Srikakulam District, aimed at capturing the hearts and minds of the people. Chapter Six will discuss government's attempts to re-establish its legitimacy. But first, Chapter Five will analyze government's continuing use of force in the years after the initial period of armed struggle.

## The Naxalite Movement In Srikakulam

### NOTES

1. *Statement Filed by the Inspector General of Police on Behalf of the Police Department of Andhra Pradesh*, 1977, p. 14. This *Statement* was presented to a state-created commission, the Bhargava Commission, that was instituted to investigate allegations of police excesses during the struggle against the Naxalites. The Bhargava Commission will be discussed in Chapter 5.

2. M.V. Ramamurty, "Extremism in Andhra Pradesh," *Radical Humanist*, July 1970, p. 12.

3. *Naxalite Activities and the Police*, p. 15; Subba Rao, "Revolt in Srikakulam."

4. *Naxalite Activities and the Police*, p. 5.

5. Mohan Ram, "The Communist Movement in Andhra Pradesh," in *Radical Politics in South Asia*, ed. Paul R. Brass and Marcus F. Franda (Cambridge, Mass.: MIT Press, 1973), p. 312.

6. Ibid., p. 312; *Naxalite Activities and the Police*, p. 5; and Ramamurty, p. 12.

7. Mohan Ram, p. 313; Sinha, "Andhra Maoist Movement," p. 535.

8. Ramamurty, pp. 12-13.

9. Mohan Ram, p. 314.

10. Sinha, "Maoists in Andhra Pradesh," p. 244, citing Charge Sheet of Cr. No. 13/14, Hyderabad, p. 2.

11. *Judgement, Parvathipuram Conspiracy Case*, p. 9; *Statement Filed by the Inspector General of Police...*, pp. 14-15.

12. Sinha, "Maoists in Andhra Pradesh," p. 244, citing document C-28 of Naxalite Conspiracy Case.

13. Ramamurty, p. 13.

14. *Statement Filed by the Inspector General of Police...*, p. 15; *Judgement, T. Nagi Reddy Conspiracy Case* (In the Court of the Additional Chief Judge-Cum-Additional Sessions Judge (Temporary) City Civil Court, Hyderabad. Sri K. Vankata Ramana, Additional Sessions Judge. Sessions Case No. 106 of 1970 and Sessions Case No. 6 of 1971.) Dated April 10, 1972, pp. 4-5.

15. *Naxalite Activities and the Police*, p. 17.

16. Ramamurty, p. 13.

17. The following is drawn from Mohanty, p. 128.

18. *Naxalite Activities and the Police*, p. 18.

19. Biplab Dasgupta, "Naxalite Armed Struggles and the Annihilation Campaign in Rural Areas," *Economic and Political Weekly*, February 1973, p. 179.

20. Subba Rao, "Revolt in Srikakulam."

21. The quote is from *The Hindu*, August 18, 1969. This was also reported in Subba Rao, "Revolt in Srikakulam," and in *Naxalite Activities and the Police*, p. 18.

22. The descriptions of the activists in *Naxalite Activities and the Police*, p. 18, and in Mohanty, pp. 128-129, make this apparent.

23. V.M. Nair, "Extent of Naxalite Revolt in Andhra Pradesh," *The Statesman*, December 10, 1969; Subba Rao, "The Bullet Beats the Bow;" and Chandramowli, interview, April 3, 1980. Mr. Chandramowli tells an anecdote which illustrates Satyanarayana's genuine concern for the tribal people among whom he had lived for so many years. In late 1969, Chandramowli was appointed to set up food distribution depots throughout the Naxalite-controlled areas, as the government began its efforts to buy back tribal loyalties. One of Chandramowli's officials approached Satyanarayana with the request that he be allowed to open a government depot. Satyanarayana allowed it. Chandramowli argues, "This proves the bona fide emotional involvement of Satyanarayana in the welfare of the tribals. He was more interested in the welfare of the tribals than in propagating the party line." Interview, April 2, 1980.

24. Subba Rao, "The Bullet Beats the Bow," p. 3.

25. Subba Rao, "Revolt in Srikakulam."

26. According to Mohanty, pp. 112-113, Mazumdar emerged as the undisputed ideological leader of the Naxalites for a number of reasons. First, the activists of the Naxalbari revolt publicly acknowledged him as their mentor. Secondly, he was a prolific writer, publishing in Bengali in the weekly *Deshabrati* and in English in the monthly *Liberation*, and soon outshone other communist theoreticians. Mohanty also stresses that because the CPI(ML) was relatively unstructured as a result of government repression, there was not a well-defined chain of command, with many intermediate leaders; there were the activists engaged in armed struggle, and, in Calcutta, the intellectual leadership, dominated by Mazumdar. That the Chinese press reported favorably on his activities also added to his prestige, as did the fact that the Indians were searching for a "helmsman" for their movement comparable to Chairman Mao.

27. Dasgupta, *The Naxalite Movement*, p. 63.

28. For further discussion of these points, see Mark Selden, *The Yenan Way in Revolutionary China* (Cambridge, Mass.: Harvard University Press, 1971); Maurice Meisner, *Mao's China: A History of the People's Republic* (New York: The Free Press, 1977); and William Hinton, *Fanshen* (New York: Vintage, 1966).

29. Subba Rao, "Revolt in Srikakulam" makes this point.

30. This is described in Mohanty, pp. 154-155, and in Mohan Ram, "Five Years after Naxalbari," *Economic and Political Weekly*, Special number, August 1972, p. 1473.

31. Charu Mazumdar, "March Forward by Summing Up the Experience of the Peasant Revolutionary Struggle in India," *Liberation*, December 1969, p. 11; cited in Mohanty, p. 154.

32. According to Dasgupta, *The Naxalite Movement*, pp. 52-54, this Naxalite revolt, led by students from outside the area, had the good fortune to take place under West Bengal's CPI(M) government, which "was unwilling to do everything possible to suppress the revolt...the police action in Debra and Gopiballavpore did not go beyond containing the activities of the Naxalites and throwing a cordon round the affected villages. But after the fall of the government in March 1970 and the assumption of power by the Governor, the police force walked into the 'liberated areas' in massive strength and crushed the revolt within a short period. Almost the entire leadership was captured, along with many activists."

33. Ibid., p. 55.

34. Ibid., p. 56.

35. Mohanty, pp. 164-165.

36. Although the Nagi Reddy group's activities were much more widespread than the Naxalites' base in Srikakulam, and caused the government to declare parts of the three Districts of Warangal, Karimnagar, and Khamman "disturbed areas" under the Andhra Pradesh Suppression of Disturbances Act, 1948, the amount of violence used was much less. In the *Judgement, T. Nagi Reddy Conspiracy Case*, it is recorded that there were a total of seven murders; the judge determined that these murders were not committed in "pursuance of any conspiracy among the accused. If murders were committed by some of the Revolutionary Communists they were stray incidents..." (p. 94). Twenty-three of the forty-seven defendants in the case, including T. Nagi Reddy, were found guilty, however, of conspiring to commit dacoities and to commit criminal trespass, and were sentenced to four years and three months of rigorous imprisonment (pp. 1, 95, 98).

37. When the Naxalite movement in West Bengal moved into Calcutta, the battles between police and the mostly student Naxalites grew more troublesome for the police. For a brief account, see Mohanty, pp. 168-172.

38. *Judgement, Parvathipuram Conspiracy Case*, p. 24. Part of the charge sheet against the Naxalite conspirators recorded: "One rifle, 2 SBBL guns [single barrel, barrel loading], 49 SBML guns [single barrel, muzzle loading], 3 pipe guns, 2 revolvers, 3 pistols, a large quantity of country bombs, explosives, blasting materials...a large number of indigenous weapons, like spears, bows and arrows and battle axes were seized in several encounters..."

39. Biplab Dasgupta, "The Naxalite Movement: An Epilogue," *Social Scientist*, July 1978, p. 9. The documents cited were written by Mazumdar under a pseudonym within the CPI(M) during 1965-67, before Naxalbari.

40. "Undertake the Work of Building a Revolutionary Party," *Liberation*, October 1968, p. 9; quoted in Sinha, "Andhra Maoist Movement," p. 535.

41. District Communist Committee, Srikakulam, "Report on Srikakulam," *Liberation*, May 1969, pp. 66-68.

42. For further discussion of these points, see Mohan Ram, "Five Years After Naxalbari," pp. 1473, 1475; Mohan Ram, "The Communist Movement in India," in Kathleen Gough and Hari P. Sharma, eds., *Imperialism and Revolution in South Asia* (New York: Monthly Review Press, 1973), pp. 350-352; Mohan Ram, "The Communist Movement in Andhra Pradesh," p. 315; Mohanty, pp. 154-155; Sinha, "Maoists in Andhra Pradesh," pp. 316-331.

43. *Deshabrati*, June 23, 1969; quoted in Mohan Ram, "The Communist Movement in Andhra Pradesh," p. 315.

44. Dasgupta, "The Naxalite Movement: An Epilogue," pp. 8-9.

45. Mohanty, p. 147.

46. The point about the frustrations of the movement is made in Sinha, "Andhra Maoist Movement," p. 534.

47. Ibid., p. 534; Mohanty, p. 147; Mohan Ram, "Five Years After Naxalbari," p. 1473; Mohan Ram, "The Communist Movement in India," p. 351.

48. Sinha, "Andhra Maoist Movement," p. 535. Mohanty, p. 147, also saw the period of "armed mass campaigns" shifting to "armed squad actions," or the "annihilation line."

49. These tactics were included in Mazumdar's article in *Liberation*, February 1970, "A Few Words About Guerilla Actions." Cited in Mohanty, pp. 154-55. This document, called "Mazumdar's murder manual" by the press, was first circulated in November 1969.

50. Mohan Ram, "Annihilating a Tactic," *Economic and Political Weekly*, November 3, 1973, p. 1954.

51. Kanu Sanyal, et al., "Open Letter to Party Comrades," originally published in *Mainstream*, October 21, 1972; reprinted in Mohanty, pp. 239-243. The quoted material is from pp. 240-241, emphasis added.

52. In "Srikakulam—Will it be the Yenan of India?" *Liberation*, March 1969, pp. 66-67, Mazumdar wrote: "The events of Srikakulam have made the conviction firmer than ever that India will create her own Yenan in no distant future....[The young revolutionaries in Srikakulam] have resolved to build up a revolutionary Party in the whole of Andhra—a Party that bases itself on the thought of Chairman Mao Tse-tung. They have declared that everything that is happening in Srikakulam today is based solely and entirely on the thought of Chairman Mao."

53. The most famous example of this was the article published in *People's Daily*, July 5, 1967, "Spring Thunder Over India," in which the Chinese wrote, "the torch of armed struggle lighted by the revolutionaries of the Indian Communist Party and the revolutionary peasants in Darjeeling will not be put out. 'A single spark can start a prairie fire.' The spark in Darjeeling will start a prairie fire and will certainly keep the vast expanses of India ablaze." Reprinted in Mohanty, p. 228.

54. For further discussion of the divergence between Mazumdar's and Mao's thought, see Rai and Prasad, pp. 472-479.
55. *Judgement, Parvathipuram Conspiracy Case*, p. 25.
56. Rai and Prasad, p. 466, and *Statement Filed by the Inspector General of Police...*, pp. 21-26. In "Report on Srikakulam," *Liberation*, May 1969, the District Communist Committee recalled, "we formed guerrilla squads with militant cadres. We conducted training camps for guerrilla squads...in the handling of a gun...After giving training we prepared the guerrilla squads to help the people's initiative in seizing the properties of the landlords, to help intensify the people's desire to annihilate the class enemies..." pp. 71-72.
57. The meeting was held in Boddapadu from October 23-25, 1968. *Judgement, Parvathipuram Conspiracy Case*, p. 9.
58. Ibid., p. 10.
59. *Naxalite Activities and the Police*, p. 17.
60. *Judgement, Parvathipuram Conspiracy Case*, p. 10.
61. The mass character of the movement at this time is pointed out by Mohanty, pp. 149-150, and Sinha, "Andhra Maoist Movement," p. 536.
62. *Naxalite Activities and the Police*, p. 18.
63. *Indian Express*, December 30, 1968, and *Hindustan Times*, December 30, 1968.
64. Cited in Mohanty, p. 150.
65. Subba Rao, "Revolt in Srikakulam"; the Robin Hood analogy is also made in *The Hindu*, August 5, 1969.
66. *The National Herald*, June 15, 1969; cited in Mohanty, p. 150.
67. *The Statesman*, December 14, 1968.
68. Sinha, "Maoists in Andhra Pradesh," p. 261.
69. *Naxalite Activities and the Police*, p. 18. *The Hindu*, December 19, 1968, reported that nine platoons of Special Armed Police were at this time operating in Srikakulam District, in cooperation with the Orissa government. Cited in Sinha, "Maoists in Andhra Pradesh," p. 262. This is a state police force; the Central Reserve Police had not yet been called in.
70. *The Statesman*, December 14, 1968.
71. Document A-4 of Naxalite Conspiracy Case, Panchadi Krishnamurty's diary, cited in Sinha, "Andhra Maoist Movement," p. 536; Sinha, "Maoists in Andhra Pradesh," pp. 266-267; *Judgement, Parvathipuram Conspiracy Case*, p. 10.
72. Charge sheet of Naxalite Conspiracy Case, p. 17, cited in Sinha, "Maoists in Andhra Pradesh," pp. 267-268; and *Judgement, Parvathipuram Conspiracy Case*, p. 10.
73. *Deccan Chronicle*, December 30, 1968.
74. *Naxalite Activities and the Police*, pp. 31-32. The inability of the police to capture the leaders of the movement had come in for considerable criticism in the press, which blamed government's insufficient commitment of funds; see *Indian Express*, December 21, 1968, and *The Statesman*, December 14, 1968.
75. Document U-9 of the Naxalite Conspiracy Case, cited in Sinha, "Maoists in Andhra Pradesh," p. 271. The events described occurred in the Bobbili plains area in March 1969.
76. Cited in *Statement Filed by the Inspector of Police*, p. 3.
77. Sinha, "Maoists in Andhra Pradesh," p. 274.
78. Ibid., pp. 274-275.
79. Ibid., pp. 277-278. Moham Ram, "The Communist Movement in India," p. 351, describes the prescribed sequence as "guerrilla terror—political propaganda—guerrilla terror."
80. According to Mohanty, p. 154.

81. Charu Mazumdar, "A Few Words About Guerrilla Actions," *Liberation*, February 1970; quoted in *The Statesman*, March 10, 1970.
82. Sinha, "Maoists in Andhra Pradesh," p. 279, based on document D-1 of the Naxalite Conspiracy Case.
83. Mohanty, p. 151; *The Indian Express*, May 20, 1969.
84. *The Hindu*, August 4, 1969.
85. *Judgement, Parvathipuram Conspiracy Case*, p. 25.
86. The Andhra Pradesh Suppression of Disturbances Act, 1948 (Act III of 1948), section 5. Mr. K.G. Kannabiran, attorney for T. Nagi Reddy in his appeal of the Nagi Reddy Conspiracy Case, has written that the Suppression of Disturbances Act "was obviously passed by the then Madras Provincial Legislature to contain Communist activities which had taken hold in the Telengana area." "Who is Responsible for Explosive Situation in Srikakulam Area," unpublished manuscript, 1976.
87. V.M. Nair, "Time Yet to Wean Girijans from the Naxalites," *The Statesman*, December 11, 1969.
88. Subba Rao, "Revolt in Srikakulam." Subba Rao went on to state that, given the situation, perhaps "a certain amount of trigger happiness on the part of the police is inevitable."
89. See V.M. Tarkunde, et al., *First Interim Report of Civil Rights Committee on Alleged Naxalite Encounters and Related Evidence* (Hyderabad: cyclostyled document, May 16, 1977); and Organization for the Protection of Democratic Rights, Andhra Pradesh, Fact Finding Committee, *Srikakulam Movement: A Report to the Nation* (Hyderabad: OPDR, April 1978). The accusations and the government's response to them will be discussed in Chapter Five below.
90. Figures vary widely; *The Hindustan Times*, May 21, 1970, later reported that by the end of 1969, 1,380 rebels had been arrested. Cited in Mohanty, p. 53.
91. *The Indian Express*, March 26, 1979.
92. *Naxalite Activities and the Police*, p. 20; and *The Times of India*, May 29, 1969.
93. *Srikakulam Movement: A Report to the Nation*, pp. 10-12.
94. Sinha, "Maoists in Andhra Pradesh," p. 292.
95. *Statement Filed by the Inspector General of Police...*, p. 106; and *Naxalite Activities and the Police*, p. 32.
96. *The Hindu*, August 4, 1969.
97. Mohanty, p. 53, states there were 12,000 police in Srikakulam.
98. Sinha, "Maoists in Andhra Pradesh," p. 291.
99. *Liberation*, February 1970; quoted in *The Statesman*, March 10, 1970.
100. Subba Rao, "The Bullet Beats the Bow," p. 2.
101. Ibid., p. 3, and interview with Chandramowli, April 2, 1980.
102. *The Indian Express*, July 12, 1970; and *The Times of India*, July 12, 1970.
103. "Red Area of Revolutionary Struggle Expands in Andhra Despite Campaign of Suppression," *Liberation*, July 1969, p. 72.
104. V.M. Nair, "Extent of Naxalite Revolt in Andhra Pradesh," *The Statesmen*, December 10, 1969; *Judgement, Parvathipuram Conspiracy Case*, p. 24.
105. This remarkably precise figure is from *Judgement, Parvathipuram Conspiracy Case*, p. 24.
106. Ibid., p. 24, states that from November 24, 1968, to March 30, 1970, there were 34 murders; since March 30, 1970, 14 additional murders had been committed by Naxalites throughout the state (p. 25); Subba Rao, "The Bullet Beats the Bow," reported 41 murders committed by Naxalites in Srikakulam.
107. Subba Rao, "The Bullet Beats the Bow," cites 102.
108. "One Year of Revolutionary Struggle in Srikakulam," *Liberation*, December 1969, p. 86.

109. *Statement Filed by the Inspector General of Police...*, p. 118.
110. V.M. Nair, "Extent of Naxalite Revolt in Andhra Pradesh."
111. *Statement Filed by the Inspector General of Police...*, p. 118.
112. As discussed briefly above, there were also Naxalite activities in rural areas of Bihar, West Bengal, U.P. and Kerala. While collectively these posed a challenge to the political legitimacy of the central government, none of them posed a significant threat to the government's power.

# 5
# AFTER THE ARMED STRUGGLE: CONTINUING SUPPRESSION OF THE NAXALITES

The previous chapter examined the armed struggle between the Naxalites and the police. Once that struggle was completed, and the police had imprisoned or killed the active Naxalites, there were still legal issues to be resolved, and continued steps to be taken to insure that the revolt would not again erupt. The following chapter will examine the positive inducements, primarily economic, that the government introduced to wean the tribals away from Naxalite sympathies. This chapter discusses various measures the state took to punish the offenders, and also examines government efforts to retain its legitimacy in the face of numerous charges that it had abused its authority during the armed struggle. The last section of this chapter will examine the "re-grouped villages" established by the government in the Agency area; tribals were moved into these villages to keep them "safe" from the Naxalites, and to make the guerrilla war against the Naxalites easier for the police to fight. Many critics of this policy have suggested that the camps represented the forceful imprisonment of innocent people.[1]

Throughout, we will be attentive to the question of government's use of legitimate force; although the government in a democracy does indeed enjoy a monopoly of the legitimate use of force, its continued authority rests in part on the legal use of that force. If force is used illegally, the authority of the state is weakened. Therefore, as political attacks on the government's use of force increased in the years during and after Srikakulam violence, the government had to pay heed.

## *The Conspiracy Trials*

Hundreds of cases were brought against individuals during the Naxalite struggle in Srikakulam for such crimes as dacoities, attacks on police stations, murders, and snatching of weapons.[2] In addition to these cases, the govern-

## Continuing Suppression Of The Naxalites

ment brought to trial several conspiracy cases, of which the two most important in terms of the number and leadership responsibility of the accused were the Parvathipuram Conspiracy Case,[3] also known as the Naxalite Conspiracy Case, and the Nagi Reddy Conspiracy Case.[4]

The Parvathipuram Conspiracy Case charged seventy-five defendants with the seven following crimes:

1) Criminal conspiracy to commit murder, dacoity or robbery with attempt to cause death or grievous hurt; kidnapping or abducting in order to murder; wrongfully concealing or abetting confinement of a kidnapped or abducted person; extortion by putting a person in fear of death or grievous hurt; and making preparation to commit dacoity.

2) Criminal conspiracy to collect arms, etc. with intention to wage war against the Government; concealing with intent to facilitate design to wage war and sedition.

3) Waging or attempting to wage war or abetting waging of war against Government.

4) Conspiracy to overawe the Central or any State Government by means of criminal force.

5) Collecting arms, etc., with the intention of waging war against Government.

6) Concealing a design to wage war against the Government of India with intent to facilitate waging war.

7) Sedition.[5]

Of the seventy-five defendants, fifty were acquitted of all charges; cases against four had been dropped before the end of the trial; three cases were "separated as absconding"; and one defendant died while the case was pending. A total of seventeen were found guilty of charge number one, and were sentenced to life imprisonment; two others were given sentences of five years' rigorous imprisonment.[6]

The Nagi Reddy Conspiracy Case charged forty-seven defendants who had been involved with APCCCR in Warangal, Khamman, Karimnagar and East Godavari Districts with seven crimes. The first two charges were proved against twenty-three defendants, including Nagi Reddy, all of whom were sentenced to four years and three months of rigorous imprisonment. Twenty-four defendants were acquitted of all charges.

The charges were:

1) Criminal conspiracy to commit dacoity.

2) Criminal conspiracy to commit criminal trespass.

3) Waging or attempting to wage war or abetting waging of war against Government.

4) Conspiracy to wage war or attempt to wage war or to abet waging of war against Government.

5) Collecting arms, etc., with the intention of waging war against Government.

6) Concealing with intent to facilitate design of waging war.

7) Sedition.[7]

These conspiracy cases were brought in addition to the individual charges of murder, dacoity and other criminal offenses that had already been tried in earlier prosecutions, and that now made up the meat of the conspiracy charges.[8] There were several reasons for the government's decision to pursue this judicial course. First, tribal testimony provided a propaganda vehicle for the state;[9] detailed narratives of the history of the Naxalites and of various heinous crimes were made part of the public record. Second, the filing of these additional, and extremely grave, charges was a way of keeping suspected Naxalites behind bars while the trials were pending. During the time the Parvathipuram Conspiracy trial was awaiting settlement, all seventy-five defendants were in jail. Some were serving sentences for individual offenses, but others were not, and were being held without bail.[10] Some of the accused, after having been initially released by order of the High Court from the jails in which they were being held under the Andhra Preventive Detention Act, had been immediately re-arrested and included in the conspiracy cases.[11] Mohan Ram contends:

> The *modus operandi* of the Andhra Pradesh government was clear: to apprehend the accused, file preliminary charge sheets but take a couple of years or more to file the final charge sheets. By the time the trial in the Parvathipuram case—the biggest conspiracy case against the Indian communist movement—began in November 1974, some of the accused had already been in prison for about five years.[12]

The Parvathipuram case took one year and ten months to try; by the time the judgment finding more than two-thirds of the accused to be innocent of all charges was issued, some of the innocent had been imprisoned and away from the scene of Naxalite rebellion for seven years.[13] This surely served the government's interest in pacifying the region.

Another reason for introducing the conspiracy charges was that, under Section 10 of the Indian Evidence Act, some evidence that is normally inadmissible becomes admissible; because of this, people against whom there was no direct evidence could be implicated.[14] In the words of the Organization for the Protection of Democratic Rights, "the aggregate of evidence in the Parvathipuram case related to the Srikakulam movement is the sum total of the evidence in scores of individual cases in which the accused had already been acquitted."[15]

Thus, the introduction of major conspiracy cases allowed the government a public forum in which to vilify the Naxalites and justify its own actions in suppressing the movement. In this respect, the trials were an aid to the government's campaign to maintain its legitimacy. At the same time, the government was able to keep scores of potentially troublesome people under lock and key for the lengthy duration of the preparations for and prosecution of the trials; this was an effective use of government's authority which aided its exercise of force in the troubled Naxalite bases.

### Accusations and Investigations of Police Murders of Suspects

Beginning in 1969, the government of Andhra Pradesh was questioned about the legality of its anti-Naxalite operations in Srikakulam and, later, other parts of Andhra Pradesh. Accusations were made of the police having raped, robbed and forced labor upon innocent girijans; under the Andhra Pradesh Suppression of Disturbances Act, it was alleged, thousands of innocent people were falsely imprisoned. Torture and threats were used to elicit information.[16] The most persistent and damning accusation leveled against police activities was that most of the supposed "encounters" between police and Naxalites were in reality not armed battles; rather, it was alleged, the police would frequently take people into custody, transport them to a secluded place, and shoot them.

During the Srikakulam rebellion, these charges were leveled by leaders of the "right" Communist party, the Communist Party of India. While this party was itself committed to parliamentary methods and had no sympathy with the goals or means of the Naxalites, it nonetheless played the role of gadfly in monitoring the police's actions in Srikakulam. Members of the CPI(M) and others also leveled these charges.

The August 17, 1969 issue of *New Age* (the central organ of the CPI) contained a statement by N. Rajasekhar Reddy, the Secretary of the Andhra Pradesh Council of the CPI, in which he accused the police of shooting suspects, and the government of covering up the crimes:

> No one would believe the government's story that a number of "Naxalites" were shot dead in an "encounter" with the police in Srikakulam district, especially when of late there are no news of any arrests in the area. It is difficult to disbelieve the persistent rumours that the police is arresting the tribals and the people in the villages from their hiding places, if warrants are pending against them; and they are simply being taken to the forest and shot dead...(sic)

## *Continuing Suppression Of The Naxalites*

A few days later, these accusations were made in the Andhra Pradesh Assembly by several opposition members, including one Independent; the Home Ministry "stoutly denied" the charges.[17] In the August 24 issue of *New Age*, CPI General Secretary C. Rajeswara Rao made an argument that was to be repeated over and over in the coming years. Why is it, he asked, that in so-called "major encounters" in which numerous Naxalites were reported killed, "nothing happened to any policemen," even though "the Naxalites were supposed to have attacked the fully armed police with bows and arrows and country-made guns." The answer, he suggested, was that

> it has become a practice in Andhra to shoot people in cold blood and then declare that they were killed in an encounter with the police and that crude bombs, country-made guns and bows and arrows were recovered from them.[18]

These charges were made in the Rajya Sabha in August 1969 by members of the CPI,[19] and in March 1970, the Andhra Home Minister was again asked in the Assembly if it was true that most of the Naxalites killed had "died after the police had arrested them," and if the government would order an inquiry. Mr. Vengal Rao denied the charges, and refused to institute an inquiry.[20]

In the late 1970s, concurrent with the continuing designation of "disturbed areas" throughout several districts of Andhra Pradesh, the conclusions of the conspiracy trials, and the continuing resettlement of thousands of Srikakulam girijans in "re-grouped villages," these charges were again revived. In April 1972, Jayaprakash Narayan, as President of the Citizens for Democracy, set up a committee headed by V.M. Tarkunde to investigate alleged "encounters" that had occurred in Andhra Pradesh from 1975 through 1977, during the Emergency.[21] The Committee enjoyed the prestige of JP's sponsorship, in addition to the prestige that accrued from its members, who included Tarkunde, a retired judge of the High Court, and Nabakrishna Chowdhury, a senior Congressman.[22] Their first report was issued on May 16, 1977. They had collected evidence of three alleged encounters and had concluded:

> two of the alleged encounters in each of which four citizens were killed never took place. Enough circumstantial evidence exists to cast serious doubts about official reports regarding the third alleged encounter also in which two citizens were killed.[23]

On June 11, the Tarkunde Committee released a second report, regarding nine more deaths.

Once again the evidence collected by it leads the Committee to conclude that "no 'encounters' took place at all, that the killings were in cold blood. In brief, each of the nine citizens was murdered." A number of policemen of varying ranks were involved in the torture, killing, and subsequent disposal of the bodies. The Committee has received direct evidence of brutal, "almost unspeakable," torture. It has once again found that, as with the cases covered in its first interim report, no public inquest has been held as is required under section 174 of the Indian Penal Code.[24]

The Committee, which because of time limitations had investigated only some of the most recent cases,[25] recommended to the central government that it order a judicial inquiry into all deaths said to have occurred in "encounters"; the recommendation was made to the central government because "The State government is so heavily involved in the crimes that any inquiry instituted by it cannot be impartial." The Committee expressed the hope that if the murders were proven,

> the principle of ministerial responsibility and the principle of collective responsibility of the cabinet will be fully borne in mind and the murders will not be quietly buried by compelling just a few junior police officers to own the blame for them. On more than one occasion the Chief Minister of Andhra, Mr. Vengal Rao, has claimed that he has "wiped out" the "Naxalites."[26]

Vengal Rao had been Andhra's Home Minister during the Srikakulam rebellion, and thus had been the official primarily responsible for its suppression.

Members of the Tarkunde Committee met with the Prime Minister and the Union Home Minister to acquaint them with the results of their inquiry.[27] As a result of the pressures brought, the central government asked the Andhra government to appoint a commission of inquiry. The Tarkunde Committee had asked that the central government itself appoint a commission, because the Committee had clearly accused the Andhra government of pursuing a policy of murder and cover up. As *Economic and Political Weekly* pointed out, "By asking the AP government to appoint the commission, the central government has shown that in its eyes, it is not the Vengal Rao ministry, but the police personnel who are the 'accused.' "[28]

Nonetheless, members of the Tarkunde Committee decided to cooperate with the one-man commission, because of their faith in the impartiality of Justice V. Bhargava, a retired judge of the Supreme Court of India, and because his name had been suggested by the center.[29] The Bhargava commission was empowered to examine encounters during the period 1968 to 1977.

The Commission, however, never finished its inquiry and never published a report. According to K.G. Kannabiran, a member of the Tarkunde Committee and chief advocate for its position before the Bhargava Commission, the Andhra government found that the evidence was going against it. The first case that had been documented in the first Tarkunde report had been proved again before Bhargava. Then, an official of the Central Bureau of Investigation, appointed by Bhargava, reported that the state had tampered with evidence. At this point, the state insisted that the proceedings of the Commission, which had been open, be instead held *in camera*. Kannabiran and the other advocates for the Tarkunde Commission refused to participate in a closed proceeding, and the Bhargava Commission collapsed.[30]

In April 1978, the Organization for the Protection of Democratic Rights, a group which the police had labeled a "front organization" for the Nagi Reddy group,[31] issued its own report on encounters in Srikakulam during the rebellion.[32] This group had refused from the outset to cooperate with the Bhargava Commission because it found its terms of reference too limited and because of the "hostile circumstances prevailing in the state."[33] The O.P.D.R. Fact Finding Committee was chaired by the journalist Mohan Ram, who has written extensively on the Communist movement in India, and included, among others, Rajani Desai, the Associate Editor of *Economic and Political Weekly*. Its report, based on interviews in the villages where the alleged encounters had occurred, reached conclusions virtually identical to those reached by the Tarkunde Commission about more recent encounters:

> ...the so-called encounters are clear fabrications....in all cases where deaths are said to have been caused as a result of encounters, the persons concerned were taken into custody by the police prior to the date and time of alleged encounter....From the nature of killings of the leaders of the movement and villagers, the Committee has reason to believe that no police officer could have indulged in committing the illegal acts without there being a high political decision of Government.[34]

Although the government's innocence or guilt cannot be conclusively tried in these pages, the uniformity of the accusations made by several groups against the police and the government over a period of nearly ten years is striking. Both the Tarkunde Commission and the Organization for the Protection of Democratic Rights reports include pages and pages of detailed depositions taken from villagers who would indeed seem to have little incentive to falsely accuse the police and thus place themselves in considerable jeopardy. At least some of the CPI accusations made at the time of the revolt were also based on local investigations.[35] The insistence of the Andhra government, headed by the same man who had primary ministerial responsibility for suppressing the Naxalite rebellion, that the Bhargava Commission be held *in camera*, although circumstantial evidence, does seem to indicate that the evidence being publicly revealed would have been damaging to government.

It appears likely that the Andhra government systematically allowed the use of illegal force against suspected Naxalites. That it was able to avoid punishment for this misuse of power reveals the depths of the unpopularity of the Naxalites among most powerful segments of the Indian population and government. And, indeed, there is some irony in a situation in which those pledged to overthrow the state through armed force later complain that government used illegal violence against them. A democratic government that murders etainees without trial should not retain its legitimacy. But this logic appears to have been overcome by fear of the Naxalites and those who appeared to give them support, anger at their ruthless tactics, and support for the government in whatever measures it saw fit to defeat them.

## *Regrouped Villages*

In 1969, the Government of Andhra Pradesh began a program in which girijans from villages in the hills were brought, "not without pressure,"[36] to government-established villages in the plains. The government's stated motives for the regroupment were two: to protect the tribals from Naxalite intimidation, and to extend to them such social and economic benefits as drinking water, electricity, and education.[37] Mr. Lakshminarayana, then a Special Deputy Collector, also points out the obvious benefit that the regrouped villages made it easier for the police to keep watch over the population; they simplified the task of maintaining law and order.[38] When girijans who had been arrested returned from jail, they would return not to their villages in the hills but to the regrouped villages where police surveillance was easier.[39] In addition, the removal of tribals from the Agency served to dry up some of the hospitable "water" that the guerrilla "fish" needed for survival.[40] For example, girijans living in the regrouped villages were not allowed to carry food with them when they left the villages to work in the fields. The police thus hoped to prevent any Naxalites from obtaining food supplies.[41]

Six regrouped centers were formed during the Naxalite movement, with a total population of five to six thousand people.[42] While initially the government provided rice, kerosene, salt, sugar, and clothing free of charge to the inhabitants, this support ceased in 1971 as the government assumed that the villagers would continue to work the land available to them and to collect minor forest produce.[43] But by 1974, *Economic and Political Weekly* was reporting famine conditions in the regrouped villages; villagers were pleading to be able to return to their homes in the hills.[44]

Life in the regrouped centers was strictly controlled. Villagers would leave the centers by day to work in the forests and fields, but had to return by sundown; they were not allowed to carry food with them or to build small shelters in the fields to protect them from the sun, lest they use the shelters as places in which to hide for later escape. Policemen would escort them home from the fields. During their absence at night, crops were frequently damaged by wild animals; but requests to remain in the fields to guard the crops were denied.[45]

Nearly a decade after their establishment, the camps were still in existence,[46] and five taluks of Srikakulam District — Tekkel, Mandasa, Parvathipuram, Kothapeta and Palkonda — were still notified as "disturbed areas."[47] Some three hundred tribal hamlets in these areas had been destroyed by the police, as they were suspected of being Naxalite strongholds.[48] Thus, thousands of tribals remained separated from their homes and lived under the Andhra Pradesh Suppression of Disturbances Act which "arms the police with sweeping and arbitrary powers."[49]

Thus, in the decade following the most dramatic violence of the Naxalite revolt, the government continued to use coercive measures to insure that violence would not erupt again. Some of these measures, such as the conspiracy cases, are more easily defended by a democratic system than others; that there was a "conspiracy" to overthrow the government seems self-evident, and if the wheels of justice turned slowly, that was not unique to these cases.

The regrouped villages, however, while allegedly established for developmental purposes, were plainly initiated and maintained for the purpose of suppressing the Naxalites; those five to six thousand girijans who have been forced to live in the villages have been victims, not beneficiaries, of government's priorities. Government's reluctance to systematically and conscientiously investigate allegations that public servants engaged in illegal activities, including murder, is still less defensible in a democracy.

That government has been able to pursue these courses of action with impunity is indicative of the illegitimacy of the Naxalites themselves, of the fear they inspired, and of the government's own legitimacy. There has been acceptance of government's need to defend itself and to protect citizens from the extraordinary threat of Naxalite violence. Even in those instances in which it appears that government has overstepped legal boundaries, public outcry has been muted. When a government is under armed attack, all but the most naive will acknowledge the inevitability of violent response. Indeed, all but a government's most bitter enemies will probably acknowledge, too, the right of a government to retaliate with both punitive and preventative violence. What in less trying circumstances would appear excessive was legitimized by the violence of the Naxalites.

## NOTES

1. Subba Rao, "The Bullet Beats the Bow," p. 3, referred to them as "concentration camps."
2. *Statement Filed by the Inspector General of Police*, p. 109.
3. Cr. No. 3/70 of Parvathipuram Taluk Police Station of Srikakulam District, registered on January 16, 1970.
4. Cr. No. 57/59, Central Crime Station- Hyderabad, registered on December 17, 1969.
5. *Judgement, Parvathipuram Conspiracy Case*, p. 5.
6. Ibid., p. 5. The precise judgment was as follows: 1) charges 1, 4 and 7 proved against 8 defendants; 2) charge 1 proved against 2 defendants; 3) charges 1, 3, 4 and 7 proved against 2 defendants; 4) charges 1 and 3 proved against 3 defendants; 5) charges 2, 4 and 7 proved against 1 defendant; and 6) charges 4 and 7 proved against 1 defendant.
7. *Judgement, T. Nagi Reddy Conspiracy Case*, p. 1.
8. Mohan Ram, "Where is the Political Approach?" *Economic and Political Weekly*, May 21, 1977, p. 829.
9. Interview with Kannabiran, March 25, 1980.
10. Ibid.
11. *New Age*, March 1, 1970; and Mohan Ram, "Where is the Political Approach?" p. 829.
12. Mohan Ram, "Where is the Political Approach?" p. 830.
13. *Srikakulam Movement: A Report to the Nation*, p. 59.
14. Interview with Kannabiran, March 25, 1980.
15. *Srikakulam Movement: A Report to the Nation*, p. 59; Mohan Ram, "Where Is the Political Approach?" p. 830 makes the same point.
16. Reports of these and other allegations are found in *The Indian Express*, August 22, 1969, and January 9, 1970; *Deccan Chronicle*, August 22, 1969, and January 11, 1970; *New Age*, March 22, 1970; and in two articles by C. Rajeswara Rao in *New Age*: "Police Terror: Main Obstacle Towards Return to Normalcy in Affected Areas," March 29, 1970; and "Stop this Massacre of Naxalites," August 24, 1969.
17. *The Indian Express*, August 22, 1969; and *Deccan Chronicle*, August 22, 1969.
18. C. Rajeswara Rao, "Stop this Massacre of Naxalites," *New Age*, August 24, 1969.
19. *New Age*, September 7, 1969.
20. *The Indian Express*, March 26, 1970.
21. V.M. Tarkunde et al., *First Interim Report of Civil Rights Committee on Alleged Naxalite Encounters and Related Evidence* (Hyderabad, May 16, 1977), p. 1.
22. Kannabiran, interview, January 25, 1980. In addition to representing Nagi Reddy on appeal, Kannabiran was also a member of the committee.
23. Tarkunde, p. 1.
24. "Killings in Guntur: Second Interim Report of Civil Rights Committee," *Economic and Political Weekly*, June 18, 1977, p. 971.
25. "Ominous Silence on Killings," *Economic and Political Weekly*, June 11, 1977, p. 943.
26. Tarkunde, p. 2.
27. "Killings in Guntur...," p. 971.
28. "The Bhargava Commission," *Economic and Political Weekly*, July 23, 1977, p. 1169.
29. Ibid.
30. Interview with Kannabiran, March 25, 1980.
31. *Statement Filed by the Inspector General of Police*, p. 54. The *Statement's* description of the OPDR, pp. 54-56, states that it was founded in 1975 and "took up issues as to free legal aid to extremists apprehended by police...demanded the release of

all extremist prisoners; agitated for the commutation of two death sentences...supported the cause of striking workers and...demanded a judicial enquiry into all 'encounters.' "

32. *Srikakulam Movement: A Report to the Nation.*

33. Ibid., pp. ii-iii. It claimed that the terms of reference did not take into account that "the struggle of the people was solely based on Socio-Economic problems. To brand the peoples' struggle as one of law and order problem would be a deliberate attempt to tamper with facts and truth."

34. Ibid., pp. 24-25.

35. "Police Terror: Main Obstacle Towards Return to Normalcy in Affected Areas," *New Age*, March 29, 1970, was written by Rajeswara Rao after he toured Srikakulam with five Andhra Pradesh CPI leaders.

36. Erhard Haubold, "Srikakulam: Model of a Guerrilla Uprising," *Swiss Review of World Affairs*, March 1971, p. 13.

37. Amrita Rangaswami, "Making a Village: An Andhra Experiment," *Economic and Political Weekly*, September 7, 1974, pp. 1525-1526.

38. Interview with Lakshminarayana, March 31, 1980.

39. Amrita Rangaswami, "And Then There Were None: A Report from Srikakulam," *Economic and Political Weekly*, November 17, 1973, p. 2041.

40. The metaphor is borrowed from Mao Tse-tung, who wrote, "The popular masses are like water, and the army is like a fish. How then can it be said that when there is water, a fish will have difficulty in preserving its existence?" *The Political Thought of Mao Tse-tung*, ed. Stuart R. Schram (New York: Praeger, 1971), pp. 287-288.

41. Rangaswami, "And Then There Were None...," p. 2042; and Mohan Ram, "More Than Legal Aid," *Economic and Political Weekly*, April 27, 1974, p. 666.

42. Rangaswami, "Making a Village...," p. 1524. A former subdivisional magistrate who requested anonymity, interviewed March 16, 1980, recalled that about one thousand families were involved. An official source, Government of Andhra Pradesh, Tribal Welfare Department, Tribal Cultural Research and Training Institute, *Integrated Tribal Development Plan for Tribal Areas of Srikakulam District* (Hyderabad, May 1977), p. 19, reported in 1977 that 1,234 tribal families were living in the regrouped centres. Mohan Ram, "More than Legal Aid," p. 666, wrote in 1974 that "at least 50,000 Girijans are still herded together in Vietnam-type 'strategic hamlets.' " Given that in 1971, there were a total of 74,470 tribals in the Scheduled areas of the District, this figure appears to be either a printing error or a gross distortion. Between five and six thousand people, or between 6.7 and 8 percent of the total tribal population, seems a more accurate figure.

43. Haubold, p. 13; and Rangaswami, "Making a Village...," p. 1524.

44. Rangaswami, "Making a Village...," pp. 1524-25.

45. Ibid.

46. Interview with former subdivisional magistrate who requested anonymity, March 26, 1980; and *Integrated Tribal Development Plan for Tribal Areas of Srikakulam District*, May 1977, p. 19.

47. "Intimidation of Witnesses to Police Atrocities," *Economic and Political Weekly*, September 10, 1977, p. 1603; and *Srikakulam Movement: A Report to the Nation*, p. 57.

48. "Intimidation of Witnesses to Police Atrocities," p. 1603.

49. *Srikakulam Movement: A Report to the Nation*, p. 57.

# 6
# GOVERNMENT RECOGNIZES THE LEGITIMACY CRISIS

In 1969, the Home Ministry of the Government of India issued a report evaluating *The Causes and Nature of Current Agrarian Tensions*.[1] The report noted the rise of agitations throughout the country between 1966 and 1969 "on issues of distribution of land to the landless workers and increase of agricultural wages."[2] The burden of responsibility for the conditions leading to these outbreaks was placed squarely on the failure of post-Independence governments to relieve land hunger. Indeed, the governments' policies, according to the report, had led not to equality in the countryside, but to widening disparities between the rural rich and the rural poor. The authors of the report approvingly cited Gunnar Myrdal's assessment of India's land policies:

> Perhaps the most conspicuous result of post-war policies...has been the strengthening of the upper strata in the villages and a corresponding reduction in the position of sharecroppers and landless laborers...All the significant policy measures for agricultural uplift adopted by the governments—whether technological or institutional—have tended to shift the power balance of the rural structure in favour of the privileged classes.[3]

The report argues that because of insufficient attention to the "social imperatives" of development, "elements of disparity, instability and unrest are becoming conspicuous with the *possibility of increase in tensions*."[4] In the wake of widening incidents of rural unrest, of which Naxalbari and Srikakulam were the most dangerous examples, governmental elites were made aware of potential crisis. In Chalmers Johnson's terminology, there was increased recognition that values and environment were disequilibrated for portions of the population. Government feared that "certain political parties"[5] would seek to exploit that disequilibrium for revolutionary purposes.

Chapters Four and Five described how government used force to end the immediate, violent threat to its power and legitimacy in Srikakulam. This chapter will analyze government's efforts to alter the environmental conditions of those who had turned to the Naxalites for help so that radical groups would have less fertile soil in which to plant the seeds of revolution.

## Government Recognizes The Legitimacy Crisis

*The Causes and Nature of Current Agrarian Tensions* was government's most explicit statement of its understanding both of the problems it faced, and of the fact that it had inadvertently helped to create them. The progressive stance post-independence governments had taken towards uplift of the rural poor was judged in this report to be more apparent than real. There was a large gap between goals and accomplishments:

> Any study of the impact of India's land policy is best conducted at two distinct levels: one, intentions as contained in plans and resolutions, and incorporated in the statutes; and two, implementation and achievements. As regards the former, the pledge to attack the ills afflicting the Indian peasantry — the inequities of the agrarian social structure, the feudal character of landlord-tenant relationship, the burden of rural indebtedness and the stranglehold of the money-lender and existence at near destitution of the vast masses of agricultural labourers — was given a prominent position during the freedom movement and in party manifesto in the General Elections from 1952.[6]

On the level of achievements, however, the detailed evaluations of each state indicated little if any progress. The report on land policy in Andhra Pradesh showed the failure of legal measures to produce significant change in ownership or tenancy patterns.

> In Andhra where substantial areas were cultivated through tenants and share croppers, particularly in the coastal districts, they were generally not recorded. The interim law, i.e., the Andhra Tenancy Act has been ineffective. A tenant holds at the will of the landlord and may not offer any resistance if the landlord desired to dispossess him. The prevailing rent was half the gross produce and in case of fertile lands it was as high as two thirds of the produce. As regards ceilings, no surplus land has yet been taken possession of but it is estimated that the surplus area is likely to be less than 0.2 percent of the cultivated area. The law has thus only a limited significance.[7]

The record in the uplift of agricultural labor was judged by the report to be equally grim; government had failed to assure a guaranteed minimum wage or adequate credit facilities, and had failed to increase opportunities for employment:

> The condition of agricultural labour has not changed materially, and in some respects has worsened, in spite of land reforms. The incidence

of unemployment is as high as 15 percent for agricultural labour households, as compared to 3 percent among the other rural households...

...the Minimum Wages Act remains a dead letter because wages fixed about eight or ten years ago have not been revised....The rural labour is mostly ignorant of the Minimum Wages Act in agriculture and its provisions....There is hardly any machinery for effective implementation of the Minimum Wages Act in agriculture.

The extent of indebtedness of agricultural labour households presents an equally grim picture...it is seen that the percentage of indebted agricultural households for the whole country has increased steeply from 44.5 to 63.9....[8]

Various studies...undertaken by the Planning Commission, the All India Rural Debt and Investment Survey, the National Sample Surveys and most recently the All India Rural Credit Review Committee have convincingly brought out the neglect suffered by the small cultivaters and tenants in the matter of credit facilities.[9]

The report, while intensely critical of all facets of government's agrarian program, called particular attention to government's tribal policies, specifically pointing to the failure of government to implement the numerous laws designed to protect tribals from exploitation and to design programs to improve their particularly grim economic conditions:

The conditions of tribals merits special mention. Laws enacted in the earlier years of the twentieth century to protect the land owned by the tribals from alienation have not been effectively implemented in various states, particularly in Andhra Pradesh, Bihar and Orissa. As a result, a large number of tribals have been deprived of their lands. In addition, the domination of tribal economy by the money-lenders has led to a worsening of the economic condition of the tribals. Inaccessibility of the terrain and the poor state of communications in tribal areas have contributed to their comparative neglect in the programmes of social and economic development launched during Five Year Plans. This has already led to a widespread agitation by the Girijans in the agency areas in Andhra Pradesh.[10]

*The Causes and Nature of Current Agrarian Tensions* argues that the agitations among the landless and the poor peasants, which are "expected to be continued,"[11] had emerged because of the "widening gap"[12] between the relatively few affluent farmers and the landless and poor; that increasing gap was itself a product of active governmental policies or of governmental neglect. The report admonishes government that in order to combat the movements threatening its authority, it must address itself to the underlying causes of discontent:

> It will be unrealistic to seek lasting solutions to a socio-economic problem of this magnitude through coercive measures alone. The problem has to be attacked and solved through proper legislative measures and proper implementation of those measures.[13]

The Naxalite rebellions in Naxalbari and Srikakulam, the agitations that posed the deepest threat to governmental authority, forced government to acknowledge that a situation of crisis existed in pockets throughout the country and that it was essential for government to take measures to re-establish its legitimacy. The government recognized that this could not be done through the use of force alone,[14] although force was seen as the essential first step in curbing the Naxalite threat. The Andhra Home Minister Vengal Rao publicly stated his contention that "Anarchy must be put down first and then only a solution aimed at the socio-economic developments could be considered."[15] In reality, however, the Andhra government took early steps to lure girijan loyalties away from the Naxalites by a quick introduction of material benefits. The immediate task was to convince the girijans that their physical well-being lay with allegiance to the government rather than with loyalty and assistance to the Naxalites. Once this re-alignment toward the government was initiated, government's next step was to systematically re-legitimize itself with the girijans through continuing socio-economic programs. The next section examines government's initial efforts to lure the girijans away from the Naxalites.

## *Establishing the Government's Legitimacy*
## *The Naxalite Years, 1969-70*

With the intensification of agitational activity in Srikakulam in 1968, the government introduced several measures designed to wean the girijans away from the agitators and encourage their loyalty to the government. A first step was the appointment of new district administrators and police officers; this was an implicit recognition of the failings of the officials then in place to pursue their jobs vigorously and honestly. The posting of "young, honest and efficient police officers"[16] and "dynamic, young" and "enthusiastic"[17] district officials was widely heralded in the press.[18] The creation in 1968 of a new position, the Special Deputy Collector for Tribal Welfare, in direct response to the tribals' enthusiasm for Naxalite activity was a further recognition that government's previous unresponsiveness to tribal needs was in substantial part responsible for the Naxalites' successes.[19]

The new officials were mandated to perform three sets of tasks: they were to initiate temporary relief measures designed to immediately transfer girijans' loyalties from the Naxalites to the government; they were to begin the construction of permanent development works, such as roads and irrigation works; and they were to vigorously implement the protective legislation that already existed, but which had largely been ignored. Emergency funding for these projects was provided to the district officials by the state government.[20]

The first task of the new officials was to persuade the girijans that government existed not only to arrest girijans who aided the Naxalites, but also to help the innocent. Lakshminarayana saw his immediate task as creating "rapport" with the girijans and establishing governmental credibility. "They didn't believe we were interested in helping them. They thought we were just interested in booking them." The government began to distribute clothing, food, and money. Virtually every tribal family was given money and rice.[21] On Republic Day, 1970, celebrations were sponsored by district officials, who distributed food and clothes to 9,000 tribals at meetings held throughout the district.[22] Some 600 pairs of bullocks were eventually distributed.[23] By providing these concrete benefits, the government hoped to draw the girijans away from the Naxalites and convince them that their interests could be better served through cooperation with government. While the police forces wielded a heavy stick, the administrative officials offered these various carrots.

The immediate material benefits were accompanied by the initiation of permanent development projects of which the most important were irrigation works and roads.[24] In addition to asking for new pumps and wells, the girijans took the opportunity of the new governmental commitment to request the restoration "of those irrigation tanks which were left unrepaired for the last fifty years."[25] The new roads, although presented to the girijans as necessary for "bringing the benefits of development to the remotest villages,"[26] also served the government's need to introduce more armed power into the inaccessible hill region. The Chief Minister of Andhra, Brahmananda Reddy, told the press "that it was imperative to 'open up' the dense jungles in the Agency areas through a network of roads, if the Naxalite activities were to be curbed. Though adequate police force had been deployed, the inaccessibility of the forests made the combing operations by police difficult."[27]

In 1970-71, the State government allocated an additional Rs. 32.74 lakhs to Srikakulam District "with a view to accelerate the development of the Scheduled Tribes." Of this allotment, Rs. 17.00 lakhs were allocated to

## Government Recognizes The Legitimacy Crisis

"communications"; another Rs. 1.20 lakhs were allocated specifically for forest roads.[28] Thus, more than half of the new allocations, 55.5 percent, went for opening up the area. A 1970 Government of Andhra Pradesh document had noted that

> Development of communications is a prerequisite for throwing open the inaccessible tribal areas in order to facilitate the percolation of development programmes, fostering of cultural contact and growth of trade and commerce. It is also an indispensable requirement for effective maintenance of law and order.[29]

Greater accessibility for development also meant greater accessibility for police supervision. Efforts to re-establish governmental legitimacy continually went hand-in-hand with the immediate task of physically suppressing the Naxalite threat.

As was articulated most forcefully in the Union Home Ministry's document *The Causes and Nature of Agrarian Tensions*, the problem of tribal landlessness, a problem due in substantial part to the illegal alienation of tribal land to non-tribals, was considered the foremost underlying cause of the Naxalite success. As described above in Chapter Two, this problem had been tackled a decade earlier in legislation[30] that was designed to prevent the transfer of land from members of Scheduled Tribes to non-tribals.[31] This law had not, however, been implemented in the Srikakulam Agency area; local officials had completely failed to prevent the illegal alienation of tribal land, or to prosecute offenders after the fact. The foremost task undertaken by the new district administration was to attempt to redress decades of governmental neglect, and restore land to the tribals through the implementation of existing law.

Two new laws were quickly passed to aid them. The Andhra Pradesh Muttas (Abolition and Conversion into Ryotwari) Regulation 1969 (Regulation II of 1969) provided for the abolition of muttas in certain scheduled areas of Andhra. Under the muttadari system, a kind of "mini-zamindari system,"[32] a Muttadar held rights to a village or group of villages, subject to the payment of a fixed amount of land revenue to the government; in return for this privilege, the Muttadar assisted the government in maintaining law and order in the villages.[33] The new regulation legally replaced this system with a conventional ryotwari system, under which tenants who were members of Scheduled Tribes were given ownership rights to the lands they worked.[34] While this law worked to establish legal occupancy rights for the tribals, it was relevant only for those tribals who already had access to and were working the land; as noted above in Chapter Two, by 1971 only about one-third of working girijans were cultivators.[35]

## Government Recognizes The Legitimacy Crisis

More significant for the government's desire to restore land to tribals who had become landless through loss of land to their non-tribal creditors or through other illegal and coercive means was the amendment to the Andhra Pradesh (Scheduled Area) Land Transfer Regulation, 1959: the Andhra Pradesh (Scheduled Areas) Land Transfer (Amendment) Regulation 1970 (Regulation I of 1970). This amendment was intended to make the job of restoration of land to tribals easier by declaring null and void *any* transfer of immovable property in the Agency by *anyone*—tribal or non-tribal—unless the transfer was made to a member of a Scheduled Tribe.[36] Under this regulation, any immovable property in the Agency found in the possession of a non-tribal "shall be presumed to have been acquired by such a person or his predecessor in possession through a transfer made to him by a member of a Scheduled Tribe." As the regulation states that this presumption will be made "until the contrary is proven,"[37] the burden of proof is placed on the non-tribal owner, not on the tribal who claimed the land had been illegally alienated.

Unfortunately for the local officials attempting to implement this amending Regulation, in 1971 the Andhra Pradesh High Court ruled that the Regulation was not retroactive. By stating that the Regulation could not affect transfers which were made by the tribals prior to the passing of the Regulation, the High Court ruling in effect totally nullified the Regulation's purpose.[38]

The 1959 Land Transfer Regulation remained the legal source for the changes the new local officials attempted to initiate. In September 1969, surveys of the land in the Parvathipuram Agency were begun; these were the first surveys ever undertaken in the area.[39] The tehsildars working under the Special Deputy Collector went into the villages, informed the tribals of their rights, and wrote out court applications for the restoration of the lands taken from them.[40] Despite this dramatic commitment by local officials, the restoration of lands did not proceed smoothly. Local landowners worked to prevent the officials from taking depositions and pressured the girijans to declare in court that the land which they had claimed in the applications was not truly theirs.[41] The local officials appointed to implement the legislation complained that the judiciary was the biggest delayer of land restoration.[42] There were, one official noted, "endless stays" granted by the courts to the non-tribal landowners.[43] Thus, even in an emergency situation, the courts worked slowly and to the benefit of those with the resources to move the courts; despite the efforts of local officials, the status quo remained largely unchanged. By January 1970, fifty-seven of the two hundred seventy villages in the area had been surveyed; over a year later, less than half of the total villages, one hundred thirty-one, had been surveyed.[44] *The Times of India* reported in January 1970 that two hundred ten acres had been transferred to tribals from non-tribal owners; in the next year, only six hundred fourteen additional acres were transferred.[45]

## *Government Recognizes The Legitimacy Crisis*

The Andhra Pradesh government, in a *Note on Protective Legislation—Srikakulam District*, acknowledged the severe difficulties it was encountering in returning land to the tribals. Although

> 1172 cases of illegal transfers of land covering an extent of 7434.39 acres were detected in the Scheduled Areas of this district, only 215 cases measuring an extent of 895.70 acres could be restored so far. 630 cases covering an area of 4928.85 acres are covered by Stay Orders of High Court. 205 cases covering an area of 1125.25 acres are under enquiry...The progress is slow because the affected non-tribals are trying to perpetuate the possession of lands by filing innumerable writ petitions from time to time and obtaining stay orders from the high court...unless they are all won by the Government it would not be possible to enforce this regulation on effective lines.[46]

Thus, despite the urgency of the situation, the government, even when it committed substantial resources to the effort to return land to the landless, was unable to quickly alter a status quo that both favored the landed non-tribals and appeared to be in contradiction to the law.[47]

Although the progress under the Land Transfer Regulation was thus inhibited by the vested interests and the slowness of court proceedings, the government could more easily assign government-owned waste lands to the tribals. It was estimated that there were approximately 25,000 acres of wasteland available in the District.[48] By 1971, the government had distributed between eight and nine thousand acres of this land to landless tribals.[49] Thus, tribals received far more land through the distribution of government-owned wasteland, a process which did not directly impinge on the prerogatives of the vested interests in the area, than from implementation of the Land Transfer Regulation, which did harm those interests.

It was widely recognized that the underlying cause of girijan landlessness was indebtedness. Legislation designed, like the Land Transfer Regulation, to protect the girijans against rapacious outsiders had been passed in 1960; like the Land Transfer Regulation, however, the Andhra Pradesh (Scheduled Area) Money-Lenders Regulation, 1960 and the Andhra Pradesh (Scheduled Tribes) Debt Relief Regulation, 1960 had gone unimplemented.[50] And so in 1970 a new Regulation intended to strengthen the 1960 laws was promulgated as the task of alleviating tribal indebtedness took on new urgency.

The government's interest in the introduction of the Andhra Pradesh Scheduled Tribes Debt Relief Regulation (Regulation III of 1970), which came into effect on September 1, 1970, is clearly stated in the preface:

## Government Recognizes The Legitimacy Crisis

> Whereas economic and educational backwardness of the members of Scheduled Tribes in the Scheduled Areas in the State, has led to *wide-scale exploitation* of those members by money-lenders...
>
> And whereas there is reason to believe that there is *large scale contravention and circumvention of the provisions of laws* relating to money-lending and money-lenders...
>
> And *whereas for the peace and good Government of the Scheduled Areas*, it is expedient to relieve indebtedness among the members of the Scheduled Tribes...(emphasis added)

The Regulation represented an effort to provide quick relief to the indebted tribals, and thus show government and legality to be superior to Naxalite violence.

The 1960 Regulations, which had been ineffective, were both strengthened by the new Regulation. Whereas the 1960 Moneylenders Regulation prohibited moneylending without a license, the 1970 Debt Relief Regulation rendered all loans granted by unlicensed moneylenders null and void and unenforceable in any court of law.[51] The Regulation strengthened the provisions of the 1960 Debt Relief Regulation by scaling down all debts incurred by tribals before the commencement of the Regulation to that part of the principal originally advanced that was still outstanding; no interest charges were valid. Furthermore, legal proceedings initiated by moneylenders for the recovery of debts were barred for a two-year period.

This last provision would seem to be the only part of the law that provided much relief to the indebted. For according to data published by the Tribal Cultural Research and Training Institute of the Tribal Welfare Department in *Indebtedness Among Scheduled Tribes of Andhra Pradesh*, it seems that government officials did not, in the wake of the Naxalite rebellion, successfully undertake to reduce the girijans' debts or to prosecute unlicensed moneylenders. In the year 1971-72, 1169 cases were booked under the Andhra Pradesh (Scheduled Areas) Money-Lenders Regulation, 1960 in Srikakulam District; of these, only 84 were disposed of. The delay here, as was the case with many protective legislations, seemed to lie with the courts; quick relief was often not possible when it was contingent on court action. The authors of the government-sponsored study concluded, "In spite of the provisions of this Regulation, Moneylending has been taking place on an unprecedented scale at exorbitant rates of interest in Scheduled Areas."[52]

The 1960 Debt Relief Regulation was to be implemented by Special Deputy Tahsildars appointed to obtain applications from tribals and apply on their behalf

## Government Recognizes The Legitimacy Crisis

to the courts for the scaling down of their debts.[53] During 1971-72, the Tribal Cultural Research and Training Institute found that 2,015 cases were booked; however, in only 153 cases had debts "so far" been scaled down.[54] The study noted a number of problems that prevented a more rigorous prosecution:

> ...most of the moneylenders have not come to the court and the tribal continues to pay the debt because he considers it as his moral responsibility. He also understands that he *has to depend upon the moneylenders for his future credit needs.*
>
> The Special Deputy Tahsildars should have the power to arrest or search-warrant authority to go to creditor in case he fails to attend the court after issuing summons. There is no provision in the present act for the Special Deputy Tahsildars to file a suit or call for attachment when the creditor or debtor fails to attend the court. *If the Creditor fails to attend the court, the case will be kept pending or dismissed.*[55]

Thus, the continuing problem of lack of alternative sources of credit available to the tribal coupled with an apparent government unwillingness to move against illegal moneylenders resulted in a failure of government in the years immediately following the Naxalite rebellion to make any substantial progress towards reducing indebtedness.

In addition to these legal measures aimed at landlessness and indebtedness, government created a new organization, the Girijan Cooperative Corporation, that was given primary responsibility for providing daily food requirements, purchasing the girijans' products at fair price, and providing means of credit. The Girijan Cooperative Corporation was, in its early years, an important factor in the re-establishment of governmental legitimacy; it managed to win the confidence of the tribals.

The Girijan Cooperative Corporation was not the first development agency in Srikakulam. In 1955, the Education and Endowments Department of the Government of Andhra Pradesh established the Andhra Scheduled Tribes Finance and Development Corporation Ltd. In the Order establishing the Corporation, the government noted that

> unless the exploitation of the Tribal people by the plainsmen is put an end to, it will not be possible to achieve their economic uplift. The Government are advised that the establishment of a Finance and Marketing Corporation to provide the tribal people with credit facilities to procure and supply them their domestic requirements and other

necessities of life and to arrange for the marketing of their agricultural produce will to a great extent, solve this problem.[56]

In 1956, the Corporation was changed to a Cooperative Society, and its name was changed to the Andhra Scheduled Tribes Cooperative Finance and Development Corporation Ltd. The Corporation was charged with these responsibilties: to purchase the produce brought by members of the Scheduled Tribes through Primary Marketing Societies and market it to the best advantage; to supply the requirements of the tribals by making bulk purchases; to provide working capital for the affiliated Societies; to borrow funds for the issuance of loans to girijans; and to acquire godowns or sale depots for the storage and sale of produce.[57] In reality, however, the activities of the Corporation were, until 1968, confined essentially to the purchase and sale of minor forest produce.

> It would also appear that the functioning of the Corporation during the period up to 1968...was looked upon as a commercial venture...the pproach during this time was that the Corporation should make profits...In other words, it was the commercial rather than the welfare aspect which dominated the thinking in those early years.[58]

A study undertaken by the Tribal Cultural Research and Training Institute in 1968 found that the Corporation had achieved no tangible results in either freeing tribals from the traditional middlemen or in ensuring a fair deal for them for their forest produce. The Corporation's overhead was found to be so high that "it could not guarantee to tribals even 50 percent of the price prevailing in the market"; private traders continued to operate freely in spite of the monopoly purchasing right belonging to the corporation.[59] The need for the revitalization of the Corporation was evident, particularly in view of the Naxalite threat:

> The Naxalite struggle in Srikakulam and Visakhapatnam Districts, which gave rise to the need for urgent action to the otherwise growing awareness on the part of the Government of the need to undertake comprehensive welfare measures for the Scheduled Tribes in the Agency districts, resulted in a re-orientation of the policies, and expansion and diversification of the activities of the Girijan Cooperative Corporation.[60]

In August 1969, V. Chandramowli, I.A.S., was appointed general manager of the Corporation, and promptly changed its name to the Girijan Cooperative Corporation. "Girijan," or "children of the hills,"

## Government Recognizes The Legitimacy Crisis

had become the popular name for the tribals, and it was the name used by the Naxalites. Chandramowli hoped to symbolically associate the Corporation with this popularization, and gain the trust of the girijans.[61] The Girijan Cooperative Corporation became the government agency most directly, and most successfully, engaged in providing material benefits to the girijans in hopes of dispelling their loyalty to the Naxalites and transferring it to the government.

The Corporation set up nearly two hundred Daily Requirement Depots in remote places throughout the area in which the Naxalites were active. From these depots, essential foodstuffs and other needs were sold to the tribals at fair prices; some commodities, including rice, were subsidized. Several free kitchens distributing rice gruel were set up at market centers. These weekly markets, which had been closed because of Naxalite violence, were re-opened, and the Corporation paid higher prices to the girijans for their produce than was offered by merchants.[62]

The Corporation became the conduit for the government to disburse short and medium-term loans to the tribals; government placed at the disposal of the Corporation a sum of Rs. 25 lakhs for this crucial purpose.[63] These loans, however, were available only to those engaged in settled cultivation,[64] and thus their utility was limited. More important to the effort to wean the tribals away from the Naxalites was the Corporation's creation of projects designed to offer employment to the tribals: young girijan men were taught to drive, and became jeep drivers for government agencies operating in the area. Girijans staffed the Daily Requirement Depots. Tribal women were given jobs de-seeding tamarind. The Corporation also took the unusual step of leasing forest coupes from the state government and directly providing work for the girijans "to save [them] from harassment of forest guards and policemen."[65] The girijans were given the right to freely collect firewood from the coupes and the Corporation would then buy it from them.[66]

These activities brought the Corporation considerable praise in the press. C. Subba Rao, writing in *The Times Weekly,* called the Corporation "the only silver lining in the tribal area."[67] *The Indian Express* cited "the good work done by the Girijan Cooperative Corporation" as one of the important factors leading to the breaking of the Naxalite movement.[68] And the *Free Press Journal* commended the Corporation's "energetic removal of undesirable staff members" and success in rooting out corruption and inefficiency in the Corporation.[69]

As importantly, the girijans themselves, indeed, even the Naxalites, appreciated the services provided by the Corporation. This is evident in the "fact that the Naxalites have not even once molested its staff. There were occasions when the corporation's officials carried thousands of rupees to *shandees* (weekly markets) in the remotest villages with complete immunity."[70] In Chandramowli's words, "no vehicle of the corporation was ever shot at, no depot was raided, no corporation official was ever manhandled; the Naxalites did not oppose us."[71] In the years during and immediately following the Naxalite rebellion, the Girijan Cooperative Corporation was a significant agent in revitalizing government's image and in performing genuine services for the girijans. Unfortunately, as will be seen below, the Corporation was not long able to sustain this fine record.

On the whole, then, the government's efforts during the Naxalite uprising to wean the girijans away through economic means had some successes, notably the Girijan Cooperative Corporation, and some failures, particularly in reducing indebtedness. The local officials had success in distributing land, and very little success in returning illegally alienated lands to the landless.

However, it is evident that the efforts taking place in Srikakulam were only partly aimed at the girijans immediately affected. The publicity gained in the national press was also critical for the re-establishment of government's legitimacy. It was necessary for the government to give the appearance of moving in the right direction.

The importance the government attached to good publicity about its development efforts is made apparent in a news story carried by the English-language *Deccan Chronicle* on August 28, 1972. On the occasion of the inauguration of a new coffee plantation, "Illiterate tribals...were addressed in English by Ministers and Officers....There were about half a dozen speeches of which only two were in Telegu....All those who spoke in English, except the Union Minister, were Telegu-speaking people."[72] Clearly, it was hoped that the creation of a new plantation, and thus new jobs, would bring benefits to government's image with an educated audience at least as great as the benefits it would give to the tribals. It seems reasonable to suppose that immediately following the Naxalite rebellion the wider audience would be attentive to changes in law and government pronouncements of development efforts. It may also be assumed that once the furor had died down, so too would the interest in analysing what benefits were actually accruing to the tribals. The next section will attempt to evaluate the nature of the changes the tribals of Srikakulam experienced once the shooting stopped.

## Ending Tribal Exploitation and Restoring Government Legitimacy in the 1970s

As soon as the Naxalite threat had been disposed of, in the short run at least, with force, the traditional local powers began to re-assert themselves, and with some success. As early as March 1971, *The Times Weekly* reported,

## Government Recognizes The Legitimacy Crisis

> It is freely said in Hyderabad that the powerful landlords' lobby in the ruling Congress is trying desperately to get the district collector transferred. His only fault seems to be that he has taken his job seriously.
>
> In these circumstances, there is every need for the State secretariat to back up the officials on the spot. Sadly enough, however, this is lacking. There are even reports that the bureaucrats sitting in Hyderabad have taken exception to some of the unorthodox projects undertaken by the enthusiastic local officials.[73]

By the middle of 1971, the District Collector had indeed been transferred out of the district "since the local politicians in the Congress Party complained against him to the Chief Minister."[74] A year later, C. Subba Rao, writing in *The Times of India*,[75] indicated that the state government was clearly supporting the local vested interests, and was withdrawing both funding and legal backing from the energetic local officials it had sent to the district when the Naxalites were still active. While the "local vested interests, mainly landlords and money-lenders, had been gunning for the collector for a long time," the opportunity to oblige them arose

> when the collector launched prosecution against a particularly influential political leader in connection with the affairs of the Cooperative Central Bank. The state government went to the extraordinary length of issuing a directive that all inquiries against that particular worthy be dropped. The collector's transfer to an innocuous post followed soon after.

Development work that had been started in the Agency areas, wrote Subba Rao, had come to a standstill; land transfers had stopped "partly because of the administration's inertia and partly because of the stay orders obtained by landlords from the High Court," and road building had "ground to a halt."

> What is worse, the Girijan Cooperative Corporation, which had been doing commendable work, is in the doldrums....[Employees have] not received their salaries. The corporation's kitty is empty and the managing director has had to make a pilgrimage to Hyderabad in search of funds.

Subba Rao warned that if in the future the Naxalites should succeed in winning back the girijans, "the blame will lie largely with the state government."

## Government Recognizes The Legitimacy Crisis

In 1975, *The Times of India* contended in an editorial[76] that Andhra Pradesh's tribal administration was once again "dominated by officials with a colonial approach to tribals...there is growing collusion between unsympathetic tribal officials and landlords and traders who have been traditionally exploiting the tribal people."

It appears that once the most immediate threat posed by the Naxalites was overcome, the state government decided not to alienate their traditional supporters; energetic and relatively autonomous officials were firmly reined in, and dramatic measures designed to wean the tribals away from loyalty to the Naxalites, such as the distribution of free food, were dispensed with. Government's development efforts would henceforth be more systematic, more controlled by the state government in Hyderabad, and less threatening to vested interests. At the same time, the potential threat posed by angry tribespeople was still acknowledged and necessitated continued movement to end the most excessive exploitations.

One of the most important issues repeatedly raised in discussions of the sources of tribal poverty and exploitation has been the alienation of tribal lands to non-tribals. Government, as we have seen, attempted to rectify this through a series of Land Transfer Regulations in 1959, 1970 and 1971. In 1978, the Regulation was again amended to prohibit the registration of documents transferring land to non-tribals; all offenses under the Regulation were made cognizable and punishable with rigorous imprisonment for one year, or a fine up to two thousand rupees, or both.[77]

How much effect did all this legislation have in Srikakulam? By 1978, land survey operations throughout the district were finally complete,[78] and by 1979, 1,519 cases had been tried under these regulations; a total of 5,543.67 acres had been restored to tribals.[79] The total geographic area of the Integrated Tribal Development Agency Project Area of Srikakulam is 527,000 acres. Of this, 328,000 are forest and 60,000 acres are barren and uncultivable. This leaves approximately 139,000 acres of land that is either sown area, fallow land, or cultivable waste land.[80] Thus, the figure of 5,543.67 acres represents 3.9 percent of the total cultivable land. Given the long history of land alienations, and government's understanding that the girijan discontent that fed into the Naxalite rebellion stemmed largely from loss of land due to illegal alienations,[81] this figure does not seem to represent much progress.

The Organization for the Protection of Democratic Rights alleged in their report on the Srikakulam movement that some of the land transferred to tribals "had in fact been taken away from *poor* non-tribals."

> Though these landholdings ranging from two to five acres only had been given benami [in name only] to the poor non-tribals by the

landlords after the Land Alienation Act of 1917, these non-tribals had themselves laboured on and cultivated them ever since....while the government had taken away their lands for redistribution among tribals, the two biggest landlords in the area, holding about 100 acres each, had been spared. The Collector apparently adjudged that those lands had been cleared and settled by the non-tribal landlords and had never belonged to the tribals....by focusing attention on the tribal/non-tribal conflict, without changing the basic pattern of land distribution in the area which makes it possible for the various forms of exploitation to survive and thrive there, government and its officials are diverting attention from the fundamental factors that are responsible for the plight of the tribals. It is the concentration of land and wealth which forms the basis for the real power of the exploiter.[82]

If indeed land was transferred from poor non-tribals to poor tribals, government's recorded accomplishments in reversing illegally alienated lands is even less of a system- legitimizing achievement than it appears.

However, more land was made available to tribals from other sources. The Andhra Pradesh Land Reforms (Ceiling on Agricultural Holdings) Act, 1973, which took effect from January 1975, revised the 1961 Andhra Pradesh Ceiling on Agricultural Holdings Act. Under this new law, some 7,134 acres of land became available for redistribution in Srikakulam; of this amount, 2,466 acres were given to 1,937 Scheduled Tribe members.[83]

Some government-owned cultivable waste lands were also distributed to tribals, adding to the eight to nine thousand acres that had already been distributed by 1971. In 1972, a Centrally financed pilot project, the Girijan Development Agency, was begun in Srikakulam. This Agency was later integrated into the state-financed Integrated Tribal Development Plan. Under these auspices, according to the 1977 *Integrated Tribal Development Plan for Tribal Areas of Srikakulam District*,[84] 1,744 landless tribal families had been settled on 3,020 acres of reclaimed waste land; government provided subsidies to cover one hundred percent of the start-up costs of 1,276 of these families; the others received partial subsidies.[85] In addition, "about 2,247.50 acres of land belonging to 932 tribal families" were "reclaimed" by shaping the land to allow for plough cultivation; the tribals were given a fifty percent subsidy for this work.[86]

From these three combined sources—land retrieved for the tribals through the 1959 Land Transfer Regulation (5,543 acres) and the revised Ceilings Act (2,466 acres), and land formerly designated as government waste land (8,000 to 9,000 acres through 1971, and 3,020 acres in 1972-77)a total of 19,029 to 20,029 acres of land was transferred to tribal ownership. In addition, 2,247 tribal acres not previously unsuitable for cultivation was developed.[87] Thus, a total of 21,276 to 22,276 acres of cultivable land became available for tribal ownership and use.

How much more land the government intends to turn over to tribals is not clear. The *Integrated Tribal Development Plan for Tribal Areas of Srikakulam District*[88] urged in 1977 that because of the "large number of tribals...engaged in agricultural labour, podu cultivation and collection of Minor Forest Produce," 500 more acres of cultivable land be reclaimed through subsidized agricultural inputs, and 250 landless tribal families be settled there. This suggestion, however, would do little to ease the continuing problem of land poverty, as is made evident in the *Annual Plan for 1978-79 (Special Central Assistance Programme)* which urges special steps to curb podu cultivation, including the creation of "Anti Podu Committees" to educate tribals "about the evils of podu." This was felt to be necessary because some 9,253 acres were estimated to be under podu cultivation.[89] The authors of the Plan do not appear very hopeful about finding alternative land to offer the tribals: the Committees were urged to indicate alternative land "if any" for assignment to the tribals, but if, "in the absence of any other source of living and alternative land to cultivate" the tribal was to be allowed to continue podu, the Committees were instructed to provide "inputs needed for mixed forest plantation and intercropping..."[90]

It is not apparent why more land has not been available for distribution. Earlier government sources had cited 25,000 acres as government-owned waste lands.[91] As has been shown above, some 11,000 to 12,000 acres of waste lands had been distributed; there would appear, therefore, to be thirteen to fourteen thousand acres still available. Chandramowli suggests that considerable amounts of government-owned land is in reality being cultivated by wealthier members of the community. This "concealed cultivation" is not reported by the village officers who do land surveys, because "they won't give reports that go against their own interest. And they don't want the landless to get land. So village officers will say that land is not available."[72] Thus, while by the late 1970s, government seemed to be operating on the presumption that nearly all government-owned cultivable land had been distributed, the data seem to indicate otherwise. The beneficiaries of the discrepancy appear to be the vested interests.

While government had made genuine progress in distributing land to the landless and the land poor, more than half the available wasteland remained undistributed, and the amount of land regained through the 1959 Land Transfer Regulation which most directly pits the tribals against wealthier non-tribals seems quite small. The girijans owned considerably more land than they had before the Naxalites; government had moved in a positive direction. But

## Government Recognizes The Legitimacy Crisis

government seems to have been intent on balancing the interests of the wealthier vested interests against the interests of the tribals. Government moved to appease the tribal need for land while not severely threatening the interests of those who already controlled land.

The same evidence of balancing interests was initially apparent in government's prosecution of the Andhra Pradesh Debt Relief Regulation, although by the end of the 1970s, the Union government had taken a much firmer stand against usurious moneylending, and the state government fell in line with that position.

A survey done in 1971-72 by the Tribal Cultural Research and Training Institute established that in the Scheduled Areas of Srikakulam and the neighboring Visakhapatnam District, 70.54 percent of the tribal households were indebted, with the average indebtedness being Rs. 560.[93] The households had borrowed from the following sources:[94]

- Cooperatives (especially the Girijan Cooperative Corporation) ............ 59%
- Private moneylenders ..................... 27.58%
- Taluk office ............................. 14.17%
- Landlords ............................... 8.81%
- Panchayat Samithi ....................... 7.66%
- Relatives ............................... 7.28%
- Banks .................................. 1.15%

Thus, 36.39 percent had borrowed either from landlords or moneylenders.

In 1978, the estimated tribal population in the Srikakulam tribal sub-plan area was 179,000;[95] it is therefore reasonable to assume there were approximately 36,550 tribal families.[96] Of these 36,550 families, some 70.54 percent, or 25,782 families, were indebted. Therefore, one can deduce that 9,382 families (36.39 percent of 25,782) were indebted to landlords or moneylenders.

Through the end of 1976, less than 2,100 instances of tribal indebtedness had been scaled down under the 1960 and 1970 Andhra Pradesh Debt Relief Regulations.[97] Thus, the government had "detected" only twenty-two percent of the probable instances of indebtedness to landlords and moneylenders.

However, in response to Prime Minister Indira Gandhi's announcement on July 1, 1975 of her 20-Point Programme,[98] Andhra Pradesh and other states took dramatic action with regard to rural indebtedness. In August 1975, an Ordinance was issued providing a temporary moratorium on recovery of debts from certain agriculturalists, landless laborers, and rural artisans, including tribals; the Ordinance was replaced in 1976 by the Andhra Pradesh Agricultural Indebtedness Relief Act. Under this Act, no suit for the recovery of a debt could be instituted in any Civil or Criminal Court; as important,

> All debts including interest thereon due by the tribals who are either agricultural labourers, rural artisans or marginal farmers and whose annual household income does not exceed Rs. 2,400 in any two years within three years immediately preceding the commencement of the legislation shall be deemed to be wholly discharged.[99]

This was indeed a step that offered relief to the indebted by automatically ridding them of debt. However, even this victory for the poor raised problems. The Government of India's *Report of the Commissioner for Scheduled Castes and Scheduled Tribes (1975-76 and 1976-77)* noted

> There have...been some reports that the persons belonging to the weaker sections were being denied credit even for their dire needs because money lenders hesitated in advancing them loans and satisfactory alternative sources of credit had not been provided by the Government.[100]

Thus, it was essential for government to offer adequate alternative forms of credit; in Srikakulam this function was performed primarily by the Girijan Cooperative Corporation, the workings of which will be examined shortly.

Before turning to the Corporation, the success of the Andhra Pradesh Moneylenders Regulation should be examined. It was noted above that by 1972, only 84 cases of illegal moneylending had been disposed of, and that illegal and usurious moneylending continued to be rampant. However, by 1979, substantial progress had been made. 2,164 cases had been brought under the Regulation, and 2,163 had been disposed of; debts of Rs. 4.9 lakhs had been discharged.[101]

By the end of the decade, then, the government had significantly reduced tribals' indebtedness to usurious moneylenders. It was now up to the government to take up the slack in the provision of credit that would henceforth be available to the tribals.

All credit to the tribal areas of the state was funneled through the Girijan Cooperative Corporation.[102] While during the years of the Naxalite crisis the Girijan Cooperative Corporation had been effective in meeting the consumption needs of tribals, by the mid-1970s the Corporation had foundered. It was riddled with corruption and mismanagement, and, in the absence of reliable government support, girijans were again turning to private, and exploitative, sources of credit and purchase.

The Girijan Cooperative Corporation was charged with five main func-

## Government Recognizes The Legitimacy Crisis

tions: 1) to procure Minor Forest Produce from tribals; 2) to supply daily domestic requirements through Daily Requirement Depots; 3) to provide credit to tribal cultivators for agricultural purposes; 4) to set up forest-based industries in Agency areas; and 5) to implement welfare schemes for the economic uplift of tribals.[103] However, by 1975, the Corporation's ability to successfully implement these goals had become questionable. In March 1975, because "instances of mismanagement and misappropriation by the employees of the Corporation" had come to the attention of the state government, a Committee of the Andhra Pradesh Legislative Assembly was appointed "to probe into the circumstances leading to the deficits and appropriations and apportion blame and responsibility."[104]

The Report issued by this Committee revealed widespread corruption among employees of the Corporation. "Many Shandy Inspectors" were found to be "in the habit of manipulating the weights" when purchasing agricultural produce from the girijans; the girijans received less money than was due them. The payments to the girijans for their goods were also sometimes "delayed."[105] Evidence of corruption and mismanagement were also found in the Daily Requirement Depots, at which essential commodities were to be sold to the tribals at fair price. The Committee reported that "Spoiled and damaged stocks are...mixed with current stocks in the daily requirement," and that "the prices of commodities sold at daily requirement depots are invariably high when compared to the rates prevailing in the local market." Furthermore, "the allotment of rice to the societies by the Civil Supplies Authorities was found to be very meagre and without any relevance to the tribal population covered by the Society."[106]

Corruption existed not only at the local levels, but also in management. Maintenance of financial accounts was shoddy:

> ...due importance was not given by the Managers and other officers of the Corporation for the maintenance of up-to-date and clear accounts to exhibit the true and correct state of affairs of their respective units. Consequently, one finds it difficult to get any dependable information from such accounts at any time.[107]

Nor were the Corporation's auditing practices adequate: "many irregularities were noted in audit reports" including the "retention of heavy cash balances by the Managers for unduly long periods." Although numerous defects had been uncovered over the years, and directives issued for their correction, the directives were not implemented.[108] Further, the Corporation had failed to submit annual budget reports to the Legislature to justify the grants given to it for the establishment of new Primary Societies (the operating agencies

## Government Recognizes The Legitimacy Crisis

of the corporation) and for forest rentals:

> ...The Committee regret to note that the aforesaid reports of the Corporation were never submitted to the Legislature at any time in the past since the inception of the Corporation. What is revealing is that these reports were also not sent to the Government all these years for scrutiny. The implications of such a situation can [more] easily be imagined than described.[109]

Although the Legislature had, until 1975, continued to supply funding to the Corporation despite these problems, the Reserve Bank of India was more sensitive to the lack of auditing. The Girijan Cooperative Corporation was the vehicle for channelling short- and medium-term loans from the Reserve Bank to the Girijans. However, in 1974-75, the Bank stopped funding the Corporation because it had not received a final audit report for the year 1973-74.[110] This meant that the Corporation had Rs. 25 lakhs less to distribute as credit.[111]

Even prior to this loss of funding, the Committee judged, the Corporation had been "unable to meet the full credit requirements of the tribals due to paucity of funds."[112] The Report also found that despite the fact that the tribals preferred to get loans entirely in cash, loans were being given to tribals in a combination of cash and kind that was not useful. Rs. 70 out of the Rs. 100 per acre loaned to cultivators of dry land were being given in the form of daily requirements or seeds, fertilizers and pesticides. But

> The Committee..learned that tribals are not very enthusiastic [about] the use of chemical fertilisers since they have not yet resorted to improved methods of agriculture. Due to this reluctance, the tribals have not lifted fertilisers fully as a component of credit granted to them. Similarly the daily requirements as part of credit to the tribals was also not fully utilized. In view of this, the tribals could not make full use of the credit facilities sanctioned under "daily requirements and kind components."[113]

Not only were portions of the credit of a useless nature, but "the scale of finance approved by the Corporation per acre is very low and not related to the actual costs of inputs and other requirements." Furthermore, the interest charged on the loans was found by the Committee to be "high" and the interest on overdue loans was deemed "high and exorbitant."[114]

Because of the Girijan Cooperative Corporation's failures, tribals were forced to approach private moneylenders for finances to meet their agricultural

## Government Recognizes The Legitimacy Crisis

needs.[115] A later Legislative Assembly Report (submitted to the Legislature on June 28, 1977) found that because forest produce purchased from tribals by the Corporation was often underweighed, and because private traders could be more relied upon to give the tribal credit when needed, tribals were selling their Minor Forest Produce to private traders despite the Corporation's monopoly designed specifically to protect the tribals from private traders.[116] Thus, the failure to provide adequate credit to agriculturalists and on-going corruption in the purchase of the tribals' produce and the selling of daily requirements had driven the tribals back into the arms of the private moneylenders and traders whose exploitative practices had been the cause of so much misery.

Another deficiency of credit offered through the Girijan Cooperative Corporation is that it offered credit only for agricultural purposes. However, the 1971 census recorded that only thirty-six percent of all Scheduled Tribe workers in Srikakulam were cultivators; the rest were either agricultural laborers or were engaged in the non-agricultural sector. Even with the additional lands granted to tribals during the decade of the seventies, there were many who remained landless. According to the state Medium Term Tribal Sub-Plan issued by the Social Welfare Department of Andhra Pradesh, in 1978 there were 646,802 tribal workers in the tribal sub-plan areas of Andhra Pradesh. Of these, 318,614, or forty-nine percent, were cultivators.[117] This means that *fifty-one percent of all tribals in Andhra Pradesh were landless*. Data included in the Integrated Tribal Development Agency's *Medium Term Tribal Sub-Plan for Srikakulam District, 1978-83*, indicates that *forty-three percent* of all tribals included in the Plan Area *depend* on shifting cultivation.[118] The credit offered by the Corporation, however, was directed entirely to settled cultivators, and did not in any way relieve the burden of lean times for this sizeable part of the population that was landless and worked as laborers and/or at shifting cultivation.

Similarly, although the central and state governments spent increasing sums of money in Srikakulam's tribal areas on development schemes, these projects, too, were geared very heavily towards the improvement of settled agriculture. The Integrated Tribal Development Agency did work to alleviate the poverty of the landless to some degree through the creation of jobs in new occupational areas, such as horticulture. However, on the whole, the emphasis has been much more on the development of agriculture by aid to individual cultivators.

This agency had its start in 1972 as the Girijan Development Agency, when the central government's Co-ordination Committee for Rural Development and Employment decided to establish six pilot projects to aid tribal development.[119] By 1978, there were Integrated Tribal Development

Agencies modeled on the Girijan Development Agency in seven districts in Andhra Pradesh; in 1979 the name of the original Girijan Development Agency was changed to conform to this new title. Although the funding for these Agencies intially came entirely from the central government, since 1978, the major portion of ITDA funding has been taken over by the states.[120] Nationally, under the Fifth Five Year Plan, the tribal development programs were extended to all the Scheduled Areas and to areas with more than fifty percent Scheduled Tribes; the coverage under the scheme is intended to include seventy percent of the total Scheduled Tribe population of the country.[121] Thus, the model first developed in substantial part as a response to Naxalite violence has become the model for tribal development nationwide. The fact that it was begun by the Union government is another indication, apparent too in the study on *The Causes and Nature of Current Agrarian Tensions* that the government recognized the need for substantial reform in the countryside if widespread disruption was to be avoided.

The "main objective" of the Girijan Development Agency Project "is to develop the Agriculture and allied Sectors in tribal areas of Srikakulam";[122] communications, particularly road building, was the second priority.[123] Development efforts aimed at providing jobs for the landless and improving "human resources" through nutritional programs, education and health care did follow, although the emphasis remained on settled cultivation. While advances in all these areas were made, and the government could point to increased irrigation schemes, the creation of coffee plantations and other physical achievements, the conclusion of one research study was that "perceptible impact on the levels of income and also on the levels of living of the tribal households is yet to be achieved."[124] Some critics have argued that the reason for this may well be the focus on settled cultivation rather than on producing forest-related jobs and resources.[125]

Government spending in the agricultural sector of the Andhra Pradesh Scheduled Areas did rise dramatically after the Naxalites. The *Statistical Compendium on Agricultural Sector of Sub Plan Area in Andhra Pradesh* issued by the Tribal Cultural Research and Training Institute lists the following growth in expenditures (see Table 2).

The agricultural development efforts, which included increased irrigation and the provision of high yielding seeds and fertilizers, were plagued with some of the difficulties often attached to local development schemes: insufficient attention by the central planners to the idiosyncratic agricultural conditions in particular areas, difficulty in supplying *all* the needed inputs simultaneously so as to assure success, and insufficient education of the target population in the best methods of using the new facilities made available to them.

**Table 2**
Growth in Agricultural Expenditures

| Plan | Expenditure in Agricultural Sector (Rs. in lakhs) |
| --- | --- |
| First Five Year Plan | 10.46 |
| Second Five Year Plan | 58.41 |
| Third Five Year Plan | 52.02 |
| Annual Plans | 15.81 |
| Fourth Five Year Plan | 120.34 |
| Sub-Plan (1974-78) | 1576.10* |

*Of the Rs. 1,576.10 lakhs, only Rs. 42.05 lakhs were designated for "forests." p. 76

Source: *Statistical Compendium on Agricultural Sector Plan Area in Andhra Pradesh*, pp. 66-67.

---

Thus, government figures of expenditures and even of physical achievements do not reveal the whole story. For example, at the end of the Fourth Five Year Plan, 5.06 percent of the net area sown in Tribal Development Projects throughout Andhra Pradesh was irrigated; by the end of the Fifth Five Year Plan, that figure had risen to 13.60 percent.[126] However, a university study that evaluated the effects of irrigation in the Girijan Development Agency in Srikakulam found that the increase in irrigation did not have as dramatic an effect as had been hoped:

> The farm economy of beneficiary households shows signs of change for the better. The use of modern inputs, percentage area under HYV [High Yielding Varieties], percentage area under commercial crops, marketed percentageall these are found to be distinctly higher on the farms of the beneficiary households....However, some aspects of farm economy of the beneficiary households cause disappointment. Yield levels of paddy even with HYV are no more than 8.36 quintals per acre. Traditional varieties yielded much less and productivity on the farms of beneficiary holdings is no better than on non-beneficiary holdings. Here it may be noted that since the agro-climatic conditions vary considerably within short distances in the tribal areas, the results of general agricultural research appears to be of little benefit in the tribal regions.

> The beneficiary farms provided with wells as a result of the efforts of the GDA show gains mainly through shifts in cropping patterns and high intensity. The response of the tribal farmer...cannot be considered discouraging. With better water management and proper fertilizer application there is scope for more fruitful results. The need for better water management is revealed by the disparity in the expected area and actual area irrigated under well. The expected area irrigated as per the agency was two acres per well while the actual area irrigated in a majority of wells was less than one acre. To get more advantage out of wells, the extension work should be stepped up more vigorously to give the tribals training in water management and judicious use of inputs.[127]

Similarly, a program through which landless laborers were supplied with milch cattle at a fifty percent subsidy, while helpful, did not meet expectations.[128]

> ...wide disparities are noticed between the expected benefits on one hand and observed benefits on the other. It was assumed that a milch animal could yield five litres of milk per day...But the observed yields are on an average only one litre a day.[129]

Another program directed at the landless, in addition to the land reclamations discussed above, was the introduction of horticulture; some 10,000 coconut saplings were distributed to five thousand tribals for growing in homesteads. Banana, mango, lime and pineapple saplings were also distributed.[130] But as government acknowledged, this program "would be a long drawn process requiring heavy initial expenditure without return for five to six years at least."[131]

Another investment in the future to which government devoted considerable resources was education. In 1967-68, there were twenty-two Ashram schools serving all the Scheduled areas of Andhra Pradesh;[132] by the end of 1978, there were sixty-one serving Srikakulam alone. In addition, there were two hundred twenty-seven elementary schools in the Tribal Development Blocks of Srikakulam and seventy elementary schools in tribal villages found in nontribal development blocks.[133] Nonetheless, the government found that

> In spite of all these efforts, the desired results could not be achieved and the literacy level among the tribals continued to be far less than the literacy level of the District. This set back is mainly due to the low economic standards of the tribals and their lack of motivation

to send their children to schools. A tribal generally prefers to utilise his children for grazing cattle or collection of fuel or some other economic pursuit...[134]

Consequently, despite the government's provision of some incentives such as free text books, clothing, and, in some cases, scholarship money, only marginal progress was made in advancing the literacy rate. While in 1971, the literacy level in the area covered by the Girijan Development Agency in Srikakulam had been 8.02 percent, in 1979 it was up to only 10.4 percent and the *Medium Term Tribal Sub-Plan* acknowledged that "much more effort need be taken to bring the tribals on par with the plainsmen in the educational sector."[135]

On the whole, it would appear that in the aftermath of the Naxalite rebellion, the government did recognize a local crisis of legitimacy. By increasing its commitment to improving the economic conditions of tribals and ending the worst exploitative excesses, government hoped to prevent a recurrence of the despair that had made the girijans responsive to extremist appeals. But despite government efforts, a variety of problems ranging from corrupt officials to the poverty and lack of education of the tribals hindered development. The emphasis on aiding those tribals who were already among the better-off, the settled cultivators, neglects the most impoverished, the landless. Some observers have alleged that government programs have been most beneficial not to tribals at all, but to the very traders, usurers and landlords who had customarily exploited the tribals. "After the police came in and made it safe for them to return," Lakshminarayana has said, "they went back. When more money was pumped into the area, when works were taken up, the non-tribal exploiters benefitted the most. *They* became the contractors for the road works, for irrigation."[136]

Development progress, although recognizable, is slow in Srikakulam. In 1976, for example, a government study found that "malnutrition is widespread among the tribals of Srikakulam."[137] Chandramowli, former manager of the Girijan Cooperative Corporation argues that "not even ten percent of the credit needs of the tribals are being met."[138] While government had quickly introduced welfare measures into the area affected by Naxalite violence, such as the distribution of free rice, these emergency measures were not sustained after the Naxalites had been conclusively defeated by force. It has been shown that after years of governmental support, both active and passive, for the exploitative practices of the non-tribal moneylenders and landlords in Srikakulam, force, not authority, was the only tool the government had with which to successfully combat the Naxalites. Its effort to re-establish its legitimacy by protecting the girijans against exploitation and advancing them economically are painfully slow. Furthermore, the economic effects continue to be mixed with repressive measures, such as the regrouped villages.[139] Although government has made a significantly greater effort than it did in the years before the Naxalites, the conditions that led to the outbreak of violence in Srikakulam have not dramatically changed.

## *Government Recognizes The Legitimacy Crisis*

### NOTES

1. Government of India, Ministry of Home Affairs, Research and Policy Division, *The Causes and Nature of Current Agrarian Tensions*, August 1969.
2. Ibid., p. 4. According to the report, "Regular movements in the form of satyagrahas and forcible occupation of land were launched in the States of Assam (5), Andhra Pradesh (5), Bihar (3), Gujarat (1), Kerala (3), Madhya Pradesh (6), Maharashtra (1), Mysore (1), Manipur (1), Orissa (3), Punjab (2), Rajasthan (2), Tamil Nadu (2), Tripura (1) and Uttar Pradesh (5). In West Bengal in 1967 a violent movement for the forcible occupation of the lands of the Jotedars was launched by the extremists in the Naxalbari area."
3. Ibid., p. 30.
4. Ibid., p. 3. Emphasis added.
5. Ibid., p. 3. "Not surprisingly, the consciousness of injustice and wide prevalence of land-hunger have been used by certain political parties to organise agitations."
6. Ibid., p. 12.
7. Ibid., Annexure III, p. 2.
8. This between 1950-51 and 1956-57.
9. *The Causes and Nature of Current Agrarian Tensions*, pp. 23-25.
10. Ibid., pp. 7-8.
11. Ibid., p. 5.
12. Ibid., p. 10.
13. Ibid., p. 34.
14. In addition to the Home Ministry Report, numerous press reports cite statements by Union officials to the effect that "the Naxalites prospered on the genuine grievances in the tribal areas. The causes of discontent of the people had to be removed through social and economic measures." Statement by Union Home Minister Y.B. Chavan, *National Herald*, August 30, 1969. *The Indian Express* of June 14, 1969 contains a similar statement by Phulrenu Guha, Union Minister of State for Social Welfare; and *The Indian Express*, October 2, 1969, reports on the views of the internal affairs committee of the Cabinet. The national press also repeatedly put forward the view that force alone would not be sufficient to deter continued Naxalite agitation. *The Times of India* editorialized on June 2, 1969, "...the administration will make a grievous mistake in treating the Naxalite challenge as a mere law and order problem. In the long run it can contain the mounting violence only by coming to grips with the basic causes of the rebellion. It is not enough to say that the Naxalites are only exploiting tribal discontent. The administration must ask itself *what it is doing* to save the Girijans from the clutches of unscrupulous landlords and moneylenders....The unrest in Srikakulam started almost ten years ago. If a large number of the tribals now look upon the Naxalites as their saviours, it is because they are *utterly disillusioned with the administration*. It is for the Government to end their alienation by seeing to it that no one encroaches on their land and that where they work as tenants they get a fair share of the produce." Emphasis added.
15. *The Indian Express*, May 5, 1970.
16. *The Indian Express*, December 28, 1970.
17. V.M. Nair, "Time Yet to Wean Girijans from Naxalites," *Statesman*, December 11, 1969; and Subba Rao, "The Bullet Beats the Bow."
18. Among those often lauded by the press were the new District Collector, B.N. Yugandhar; the District Revenue Officer, P.V. Rao; the head of the re-organized Girijan Cooperative Corporation, V. Chandramowli; and the Special Deputy Director for Tribal Work, Lakshminarayana. The last two have provided much valuable information to the author.
19. Interview with Lakshminarayana, March 31, 1980.

20. Interview with Lakshminarayana, March 27, 1980.
21. Ibid.
22. *The Hindu*, January 28, 1970.
23. Subba Rao, "Revolt in Srikakulam."
24. Ibid.; and V.M. Nair, "Time Yet to Wean Girijans from the Naxalites."
25. *The Indian Express*, October 1, 1969.
26. Nair, "Time Yet to Wean Girijans from the Naxalites."
27. *The Deccan Chronicle*, November 2, 1969.
28. Government of Andhra Pradesh, Tribal Welfare Department, *Pilot Project for Tribal Development, Srikakulam District: Action Plan* (Hyderabad, 1971), p. 26. The rest of the funds were allocated thusly: Agriculture, 2.44 lakhs; animal husbandry, 0.30; land colonisation schemes, 0.65; drinking water wells, 2.00; irrigation, 2.00; education, 3.95; medical, 3.20.
29. Government of Andhra Pradesh, *Special Program for the Development of Scheduled Areas and Scheduled Tribes of Andhra Pradesh in Fourth Five Year Plan* (Hyderabad, 1970), p. 48.
30. The Andhra Pradesh (Scheduled Area) Land Trasfer Regulation, 1959.
31. This law was itself an amendment to Act I of 1917, which had provided insufficient protection.
32. *The Deccan Chronicle*, November 2, 1969.
33. This is according to Regulation II of 1969, sections 1(2)(g) and 1(2)(h).
34. Regulation II of 1969, section 5.
35. Government of Andhra Pradesh, Tribal Welfare Department, Tribal Cultural Research and Training Institute, *Integrated Tribal Development Plan for Tribal Areas of Srikakulam District* (Hyderabad, May 1977), p. 6.
36. Section 2(1)(a). The 1959 Regulation had allowed for *non*-tribals to transfer land to non-tribals.
37. Section 2(1)(b).
38. Koka Raghava Rao, *The Law Relating to Scheduled Areas in Andhra Pradesh* (Hyderabad: Andhra Pradesh Law Publishers, 1972), p. 15; and *Srikakulam Movement: A Report to the Nation*, p. 50.
39. *The Hindu*, September 26, 1969; and Subba Rao, "Revolt in Srikakulam."
40. Interview with Lakshminarayana, March 31, 1980; and Subba Rao, "Revolt in Srikakulam."
41. Ibid.
42. Interviews with Lakshminarayana, March 31, 1980; Chandramowli, April 2, 1980; and Anonymous former subdivisional magistrate, March 26, 1980.
43. Interview with Anonymous former subdivisional magistrate, March 26, 1980.
44. Subba Rao, "Revolt in Srikakulam," and Subba Rao, "Srikakulam: The Bullet Beats the Bow."
45. Ibid.
46. Cyclostyled, no date. quoted in Sinha, "Maoists in Andhra Pradesh," pp. 198-99.
47. In January 1971, a further amendment to the 1959 Regulation was issued; this was the Andhra Pradesh Scheduled Areas Land Transfer (Amendment) Regulation, 1971. This amendment provided for the mortgaging of immoveable property in the Agency tracts by a tribal or non-tribal to cooperative societies, commercial banks, or other financial institutions approved by State Government. In the event of such property being brought to sale in default of payment it shall be sold only to a member of a Scheduled Tribe or society registered or deemed to be registered under the Andhra Pradesh Cooperative Societies Act, 1964 (Act 7 of 1964), which is composed solely of members of the Scheduled Tribes. [Section 3(2)]. According to Raghava Rao, p. 16, this regulation "failed to solve the real problem in this regard."

*Government Recognizes The Legitimacy Crisis*

48. *Pilot Project for Tribal Development, Srikakulam District: Action Plan*, p. 46; and Government of Andhra Pradesh, Tribal Cultural Research and Training Institute, *Statistical Compendium on Agricultural Sector of Sub Plan Area in Andhra Pradesh* (Hyderabad, October 1978), p. 35.

49. *Pilot Project for Tribal Development, Srikakulam District: Action Plan*, p. 46, states that 8,000 acres were given; information in Subba Rao, "Revolt in Srikakulam," and Subba Rao, "Srikakulam: The Bullet Beats the Bow," would indicate the number to be over 9,000; an anonymous former subdivisional magistrate, interview, March 25, 1980, recalls seven to eight thousand acres distributed.

50. See Chapter Two above.

51. Raghava Rao, p. 18.

52. Government of Andhra Pradesh, Tribal Welfare Department, Tribal Cultural Research and Training Institute, *Indebtedness Among Scheduled Tribes of Andhra Pradesh*. (The data for the study was gathered in 1971-72, but no publication date is given.) p. 113. As will be seen below, by the end of the decade, substantial progress had been made under the Andhra Pradesh Moneylenders Regulation.

53. Ibid., p. 114.

54. Ibid., p. 115.

55. Ibid., p. 116. Emphasis added.

56. G.O. Ms. No. 2551, dated December 14, 1955; reprinted as Annexure III in Government of Andhra Pradesh, Revenue Department, *Report of the Committee on the Girijan Cooperative Corporation* (1971).

57. Ibid., pp. 3-4.

58. Ibid., p. 5.

59. The TCRTI study is cited in *The Deccan Chronicle*, September 13, 1968.

60. *Report of the Committee on the Girijan Cooperative Corporation*, p. 5. In June 1969, the Union Minister of State for Social Welfare commented that the working of the Andhra Pradesh Tribal Development Corporation must be improved. After a two-day tour of the Naxalite-dominated areas of Srikakulam, she said that if tribals were not exploited, "they would surely dissociate themselves with the Naxalites." *The Indian Express*, June 16, 1969.

61. Interview with Chandramowli, April 2, 1980.

62. *Report of the Committee on the Girijan Cooperative Corporation*, p. 6; V. Chandramowli, *A Conspectus of the Corporation for the Girijans* (cyclostyled, 1970), pp. 2-3; *The Indian Express*, December 28, 1970; *Free Press Journal*, December 26, 1970.

63. *Report of the Committee on t;he Girijan Cooperative Corporation*, p. 6.

64. *Indebtedness Among Scheduled Tribes of Andhra Pradesh*, p. 98.

65. *The Free Press Journal*, December 26, 1970; see also *Report of the Committee on the Girijan Cooperative Corporation*, pp. 6-7; and *A Conspectus of the Corporation for the Girijans*, pp. 1-4.

66. *A Conspectus of the Corporation for the Girijans*, p. 4.

67. Subba Rao, "Srikakulam: The Bullet Beats the Bow."

68. *The Indian Express*, December 28, 1970.

69. *Free Press Journal*, December 26, 1970.

70. Subba Rao, "Srikakulam: The Bullet Beats the Bow."

71. Interview with Chandramowli, April 2, 1980.

72. The editorializing title of the news story is "Blah, Blah, Blah."

73. Subba Rao, "Srikakulam: The Bullet Beats the Bow."

74. Mohanty, p. 173.

75. C. Subba Rao, "Naxalite Threat in Andhra: Government's Indifference to Girijan Woes," *Times of India*, July 19, 1972.

76. *The Times of India*, June 4, 1975.

## Government Recognizes The Legitimacy Crisis

77. Government of Andhra Pradesh, Social Welfare Department, *Medium Term Tribal Sub-Plan 1978-83 (revised)* (Hyderabad, June 1979), pp. 36-37.

78. Government of Andhra Pradesh, Social Welfare Department, *Notes for Review Meeting on Implementation of Tribal Development Programme* (held: Chambers of Minister of State for Home, New Delhi, June 23, 1978), p. 51.

79. Government of Andhra Pradesh, Integrated Tribal Development Agency, Srikakulam, *Medium-Term Tribal Sub-Plan, 1978-83, Srikakulam District*, p. 35.

80. *Statistical Compendium on Agricultural Sector of Sub Plan Area in Andhra Pradesh*, p. 32. The total land use is listed as follows (in lakhs): total geographic area, 5.27; forests, 3.28; barren and uncultivable land, 0.60; miscellaneous — tree crops and groves, 0.04; cultivable waste land, 0.25; other fallow land, 0.17; net area sown, 0.93.

81. *The Causes and Nature of Current Agrarian Tensions*, pp. 7-8.

82. *Srikakulam Movement: A Report to the Nation*, pp. 37-38.

83. Government of Andhra Pradesh, Information and Public Relations Department, *Land Reforms in Andhra Pradesh* (September 1979), Annexure III. The rest of the land was divided among members of Scheduled Castes (3,024 acres), backward classes (1,609 acres) and others (35 acres).

84. *Integrated Tribal Development Plan for Tribal Areas of Srikakulam*, p. 26.

85. The 1,276 families "have been provided plough bullocks, agricultural implements, seed, fertilisers, etc." Ibid., p. 26.

86. Ibid., p. 25. The figures cited here are not too far off the figures cited in A.G. Prasada Rao and N. Gopala Rao, *Tribal Development in Andhra Pradesh — With Special Emphasis on Girijan Development Agency, Srikakulam* (Waltair: Occasional Paper ff13, Agro-Economic Research Centre, Andhra University, undated) (the content would indicate the publishing date was either 1976 or 1977). This paper lists 1,700 acres shaped under a 50 percent subsidy, and 2,537 acres developed for the landless on 100 percent subsidy as of August 31, 1976. Appendix 2.

87. *Integrated Tribal Development Plan for Tribal Areas of Srikakulam District*, p. 25.

88. Ibid., p. 59.

89. Government of Andhra Pradesh, Social Welfare Department, *Annual Plan for 1978-79 (Special Central Assistance Programmes)*, p. 189.

90. Ibid., p. 190.

91. *Pilot Project for Tribal Development, Srikakulam District: Action Plan*, p. 46; and *Statistical Compendium on Agricultural Sector of Sub Plan Area in Andhra Pradesh*, p. 35.

92. Interview with Chandramowli, April 3, 1980.

93. *Indebtedness Among Scheduled Tribes of Andhra Pradesh*, p. 30.

94. Ibid., p. 48.

95. *Statistical Compendium on Agricultural Sector of Sub Plan Area in Andhra Pradesh*, p. 8.

96. *Indebtedness Among Scheduled Tribes of Andhra Pradesh*, p. 56, states there are an average of 4.9 people in a tribal family in the Scheduled areas of Andhra Pradesh.

97. *Integrated Tribal Development Plan for Tribal Areas of Srikakulam District*, p. 18, states, "2,065 tribals were detected to be indebted"; *Medium Term Tribal Sub-Plan, 1978-83, Srikakulam District*, p. 36, gives the figure as 2,085.

98. Government of India, *Report of the Commissioner for Scheduled Castes and Scheduled Tribes, 1975-76 and 1976-77*, p. 127.

99. *Notes for Review Meeting on Implementation of Tribal Development Programme*, pp. 38-39. The above paragraph derived also from Government of Andhra Pradesh, Social Welfare Department, *Medium Term Tribal Sub-Plan: Annual Plan for 1979-1980* (Hyderabad, 1979), p. 31.

100. *Report of the Commissioner for Scheduled Castes and Scheduled Tribes, 1975-76 and 1976-77*, p. 139.
101. *Medium-Term Tribal Sub-Plan, 1978-83, Srikakulam District*, p. 35.
102. *Integrated Tribal Development Plan for Tribal Areas of Srikakulam District*, p. 42.
103. Government of Andhra Pradesh, Andhra Pradesh Legislative Assembly, *Report of the Committee of the House to Enquire into Matters Relating to Deficits and Misappropriations Etc. in Girijan Cooperative Corporation* (Hyderabad, 1976), p. 21.
104. Ibid., p. 1.
105. Ibid., p. 23.
106. Ibid., pp. 26-27.
107. Ibid., p. 50.
108. Ibid., pp. 55-56.
109. Ibid., p. 43.
110. Ibid., p. 31.
111. Ibid., pp. 30-31.
112. Ibid., p. 33.
113. Ibid., pp. 30-31.
114. Ibid., p. 33.
115. Ibid., p. 32.
116. Government of Andhra Pradesh, Andhra Pradesh Legislature (Assembly Secretariat), Committee on Welfare of Scheduled Tribes, 1976-77, *First Report on Educational Facilities, Representation in Services, Medical Facilities and other Socio-Economic Schemes Implemented for the Welfare of Scheduled Tribes* (Hyderabad, presented to the legislature on June 28, 1977), pp. 109, 129.
117. *Medium Term Tribal Sub-Plan 1978-83 (revised)*, p. 107.
118. *Medium Term Tribal Sub-Plan 1978-83, Srikakulam District*, p. 41, states that 164,090 tribals are covered by the Srikakulam ITDA. Page 44 indicated that 14,593 families depend on shifting cultivation. With an average of 4.9 persons per family, this means 71,505 people, or 43 percent of the tribals, are dependent on shifting cultivation.
119. Prasada Rao and Gopala Rao, p. 19. That decision was made in August 1970. Srikakulam was chosen as the site for one of these projects "since it has the highest density of tribal population [in Andhra Pradesh] and was also the scene of terrorist activities." p. 20.
120. *Medium Term Tribal Sub-Plan, 1978-83, Srikakulam District*, p. 3.
121. Government of India, *Report of the Commissioner for Scheduled Castes and Scheduled Tribes, 1975-76 and 1976-77*, p. 117. Tribal development blocks have been integrated into these new projects.
122. *Medium Term Tribal Sub-Plan, 1978-83, Srikakulam District*, p. 1.
123. Ibid., and *Integrated Tribal Development Plan for Tribal Areas of Srikakulam District*, p. 1.
124. Prasada Rao and Gopala Rao, p. 30.
125. This point is made by Ibid., p. 31, and Chandramowli, interview, April 3, 1980, who argues that what is most needed, and has been most neglected, is the regeneration of minor forest produce.
126. *Notes for Review Meeting on Implementation of Tribal Development Programme*, p. 3.
127. Prasada Rao and Gopala Rao, pp. 28-29.
128. By 1979, 1,773 milch cattle were supplied to 1,773 tribal families. *Medium Term Tribal Sub-Plan, 1978-83, Srikakulam District*, p. 23.
129. Prasada Rao and Gopala Rao, p. 29.

130. *Medium Term Tribal Sub-Plan, 1978-83, Srikakulam District*, p. 19; and *Integrated Tribal Development Plan for Tribal Areas of Srikakulam District*, p. 24.

131. *Annual Plan for 1978-79 (Special Central Assistance Programmes)*, p. 313.

132. Government of Andhra Pradesh, Tribal Welfare Department, Tribal Cultural Research and Training Institute, *Study of Ashram Schools in Tribal Areas of Andhra Pradesh*, p. 14.

133. *Medium Term Tribal Sub-Plan, 1978-83, Srikakulam District*, p. 27.

134. Ibid., p. 28.

135. Ibid., p. 29.

136. Interview with Lakshminarayana, March 31, 1980.

137. Government of Andhra Pradesh, Tribal Welfare Department, Tribal Cultural Research and Training Institute, *Impact of Supplementary Feeding on the Tribals of Srikakulam District* (Hyderabad, 1976), p. 14.

138. Interview with Chandramowli, April 3, 1980.

139. It is also significant that in the *Medium Term Tribal Sub-Plan, 1978-83, Srikakulam District*, the largest single expenditure, Rs. 256.752 lakhs out of a total of Rs. 845.061 lakhs, was to be for "communications," an expenditure vital for the police as well as the economy. p. 127.

# CONCLUSION TO PART 1

The Naxalite movement in Srikakulam was the result of a disequilibrium that went uncorrected by the governmental elites. Since the nineteenth century, as people from the plains moved into the Agency areas, the objective economic condition of the tribals—the "environment"—was in a state of continual decline. Despite some attention to the matter, demonstrated by the passage of many protective laws, government failed to stop the decline; the legislation, although passed, was never implemented.

Not only did the environment change for the worse, but in the 1950s, Vempatapu Satyanarayana began to introduce new values; he attempted to organize the tribals to demand what was rightfully, legally, theirs. This process of organizing people to make demands includes what the Maharashtra movements we are about to discuss call "conscientization"; Americans would recognize the process as "consciousness raising." The act of politically organizing a group of people involves changing values; it teaches passive individuals that they have rights, that they should make demands, that they should not remain quiescent. Chalmers Johnson's model of disequilibrium calls for change in either environment or values; in Srikakulam there was a change in both environment *and* values in a way that led to their intense clash.

The government not only failed to recognize that this disequilibrium had taken place; through its support of the illegal and violent acts of landlords and usurers, it deepened the crisis. Government became, in the eyes of those aroused by the disequilibrium, completely illegitimate. But this degree of illegitimacy could not bring down a government. The governments of Andhra Pradesh and of India survived the violent attack of the Naxalites with no difficulty for two reasons: the government had far greater resources of force than were available to the Naxalites, and the government had widespread legitimacy outside of the affected region even if it was seen as illegitimate in several localities. It was force that defeated the Naxalites; but it was widespread legitimacy that gave the government such power.

## Conclusion To Part 1

While the government's first response to the Naxalites was violence, the government also recognized that its own failures had led to the disequilibrium. Acknowledging the need both to calm the girijans' anger and to maintain its legitimacy with the wider audience of Indian public opinion, the government set about instituting economic reform in the area where Naxalite violence had occurred.

Thus, government has initiated a number of development schemes in the area affected by the Naxalites, and in areas throughout India that are similar to it. These efforts, so far, have had some significant concrete results, but have not made changes that fundamentally alter the status quo. But the effort itself is important for establishing government's credibility. And, for the present, government continues to have sufficient resources of force to guarantee its survival.

The next part of this discussion analyzes two movements in Maharashtra that have concentrated their efforts not on immediately attacking the force available to government, but on more slowly undermining the government's legitimacy. The first step in this process is the politicization and organization of the poor, a strategy born of the Naxalite failure. The Maharashtra movements hope to create a mass movement that will first question government's capabilities and later, when these capabilities are demonstrated to be inadequate, question government's very legitimacy and attack its right to rule.

# PART 2

# THE MAHARASHTRA MOVEMENTS: SHRAMIK SANGHATANA AND BHOOMI SENA

# INTRODUCTION TO PART 2

The Naxalite experience demonstrated the futility of undertaking immediate violent action to overthrow the Indian government. Others who would like to see systemic changes in the Indian polity—including the two movements, Shramik Sanghatana and Bhoomi Sena, examined here—seem to have learned two key lessons from the Naxalites' mistakes.

First, the state and union governments of India command considerable coercive power. Unlike in China at the time of the Maoist revolution the Naxalites claimed to emulate, there is no vacuum of power in India, no weakness to be easily exploited. The military and police strength of the Indian government is sizable and there is certainly no lack of will to use that power in defense of its authority.

Second, the rural poor, no matter how objectively "oppressed," do not spontaneously arise like a "prairie fire" after an initial violent revolutionary "spark." When the Naxalites, who disdained organization, instead took to annihilating landlords, the local tribals they had hoped would join with them instead seem to have determined that their life expectancy would be longer if they cooperated with the more powerful police rather than with the less powerful Naxalites. They made a rational, and conservative, choice. For these reasons, it has become apparent in the wake of Naxalite defeat that quick violence in the absence of painstaking organization is fruitless.

Two movements in Maharashtra—Shramik Sanghatana in Dhule District and Bhoomi Sena in Thane[1]—have begun to develop a new strategy for forcing change. Rather than focusing on government's resources of coercion, these movements have become attentive to the other factor in government's power: its legitimacy. The movements are using the government's need to maintain its legitimacy as a tool with which to mobilize the poor and move government in a progressive direction. The hope of some of the movements' leaders is that in time so many of the poor will have become politicized that they will be able to force radical systemic change. But that future possibility is not confused with current reality. For the present, the tactic of the movements' leaders is to organize grassroots movements to demand legal changes and/or the implementation of existing laws.

The strategy appears to have two aspects. The first goal is the political

## The Maharashtra Movements

education and mobilization of the poor, a step which was largely, and disastrously, ignored by the Naxalites. Shramik Sanghatana and Bhoomi Sena, in contrast, view mass organization as central to any strategy for forcing political change.

These movements, like the Naxalites in Srikakulam, are organized among a largely tribal population, the "adivasis." Some of the issues important to Shramik Sanghatana and Bhoomi Sena have been of particular relevance to tribals, such as the alienation of tribal land to non-tribals. This may have improved their chances of gaining a sympathetic response from government, since Scheduled Tribes are one of the categories of people recognized in India as being in particular need of assistance.

But the grievances the Maharashtra movements raise may be heard throughout India: the need for access to land, adequate employment, and a living wage for agricultural labor. Thus while the Maharashtra movements have thus far centered on a tribal population that is among the poorest of the poor, the issues are of all-India significance, and the tactics utilized are potentially transferable to other populations. Using similar appeals and organizing tactics, it might be possible to transform the tribal movement into a movement of the rural poor. This is the long-term goal of the movements: to politicize the poor so that they can become India's most powerful political force.

The other aspect of the strategy is to hold government to its legal and moral responsibilities by non-violently demanding the rule of law. In the immediate future, the movements hope to gain small victories that will nonetheless make a positive difference in the lives of their supporters. For example, demanding that the Maharashtra government *actually* provide jobs under its Employment Guarantee Scheme is not a system-threatening goal; but victory in this effort confers a real benefit on people who would not otherwise have jobs. The movements hope that such small victories will add to the popularity and thus the power of the movements. In the short run, then, the tactics are reformist, not revolutionary.

But the long range strategy has more radical potential. Numerous demands that government implement laws may put an impossible strain on government's ability to do so. Government at present simply does not have the financial or administrative capacity to execute all the progressive legislation it has passed. Shramik Sanghatana, with its Marxist-influenced perspective, believes this incapacity is caused by government's ties to the landed and the wealthy. The movements hope, by demanding the rule of law, to deepen the contradiction between what democratically elected government *promises* it will do for India's poor, and what, given its class configuration, it actually *can* do. Eventually, the hope is, an increasingly politicized poor will aggressively demand social and economic improvements, causing the system to collapse because of its own incapacity.

Indian governments are elected democratically and must therefore give, at the minimum, the appearance of working for the uplift of the poor who are the majority of India's population and electorate. Since independence, Indian governments at state and union levels have indeed passed an extremely progressive body of legislation that, if fully implemented, would mean profound changes for India's poor. Not only an individual government's popularity, but the very legitimacy of the system as a whole rests in part on the moral commitment represented by this legislation to work for improvements in the lives of the people.

The continuing legitimacy of democratic government rests too, perhaps most fundamentally, on the rule of law. A government that does not obey its own laws lessens its claim to legitimacy. By pressing for the passage and implementation of more progressive legislation the movements hope in the short run to politicize the poor and gain local victories; but in the long run, they hope to create a crisis wherein politicized masses first recognize that in the absence of profound systemic change government will always be unable to implement progressive laws, and then force that change.

What has been the impact of the movements thus far? The Maharashtra movements that will be analyzed below are presently extremely modest in size and power. They have, however, attracted the attention of the Bombay intelligentsia and media, and have thus been able to draw the sympathetic attention of Maharashtra's largely liberal constituency.[2] They have been able to make their local concerns, particularly tribal concerns, matters of statewide interest.

The Maharashtra government has evolved a tribal policy that, on paper, is extremely impressive; in addition to the issues of land, wages and work that will be discussed fully in the chapters below, the government has also created legislation to relieve indebtedness, provide consumption loans for poor tribals, and institute monopoly purchase by government agencies of the adivasis' produce.[3] In part, the impetus for the tribal program has come from pressures exerted by the central government. But it is apparent that the impact of the adivasi-based movements has been substantial both in the creation of legislation at the state level and, locally, in the area of implementation.

Discussions with two Maharashtra officials—one a Collector in a heavily tribal district in the early 1960s, and one a former high ranking official associated with tribal policy at the state level—illustrate the importance of the movements for creating a tribal agenda. The former Collector stated that in the early 1960s, there simply was no governmental consciousness of tribals in his district; no special thought was given to them, no special programs developed for them.[4] That situation, of course, has changed dramatically, and the cause, according to the state official, rests primarily with the political movements. But for these groups, he said, none of the legislation, none of the programs, would have been initiated.[5]

The passage of legislation that has occurred in part because of the statewide interest generated by the movements has transformed the movements from agitators to defenders of the legal system; when the movements demand the rule of law, their position becomes the legal position. Thus, their demands cannot be legitimately suppressed. As Professor Niranjan Mehta put it, the laws "neutralize the repressive apparatus of the state."[6]

Following the passage of legislation at the state level, the movements pursue its enforcement locally. Even state bureaucrats who are deeply suspicious of the broader motives of the movements acknowledge the local impact the movements have had in pushing government to do its job correctly. One official of the Social Welfare Department who complains that Shramik Sanghatana's interests are "agitational,"[7] nonetheless acknowledges that the adivasi movements "have put local bureaucracy and landlords on the defensive: they now know they can't take the adivasis for granted. This is a large achievement—to put the local bureaucracy on the defensive. They will think twice before making errors."[8] The same official also allows that the passing of a law "gives people a powerful political tool," for "pressure can be put on government."[9]

The adivasi movements are doing what government itself is pledged to do—working to uphold the law and the progressive spirit of the constitution. Thus, government's own legitimacy becomes tied to its responsiveness to the demands of the movements. The easiest way to meet its obligations is by improving the laws, and that is the most common response. It is much more difficult to actually enforce the laws; not only the financial and administrative means but also the political will to override the wishes of landed elites must be strengthened. By pushing slow legal change and enforcement, the movements can embarrass government into finding the requisite political will. The government, by giving a positive response, aids the growth of the movements, and further legitimizes the style of confrontation.

Indian governments' desire to appear to be on the side of the downtrodden is reflected in rhetorical support for the political organization of the poor. In its *Draft Five Year Plan* for 1978-1983, for example, the Government of India contends:

> The poor and dispossessed will not come into their own only by plans and programmes, however well-conceived, by declaration of interest or by exortations to thrift and labour. If the Plan is to succeed, they have to be helped to organise themselves to claim as a right

the benefits that should flow to them, so that in turn they may make due contribution to society.[10]

The Government of Maharashtra has also acknowledged the utility of local organizing. Government has repeatedly stressed the necessity to reduce the exploitation the tribals suffer at the hands of local landlords, moneylenders, and traders. The *Draft Sixth Five-Year Tribal Sub-Plan* seems to recognize the impact local organizations can make in fighting local exploitation:

> Elimination of exploitation of all forms, speeding of process of socio-economic development, building inner strength of the people and improving organizational capabilities are some of the immediate objectives of the 6th Tribal Sub-Plan.[11]

The Naxalites in Srikakulam violently challenged the power of the state and were easily crushed by a government whose legitimate claim to the monopoly of force was widely recognized and upheld. The adivasi movements of Maharashtra, by pushing government to achieve its own stated goals in a non-violent and legitimate manner, have not been crushed by government nor, legitimately, can they be. Their small successes in moving government provide them with additional tools for continued progress; government becomes a collaborator in their success, albeit often, and particularly at local levels, a reluctant one.

The next two chapters will analyze the development of tribal poverty in the districts where Shramik Sanghatana and Bhoomi Sena work, and the founding and early struggles of the two movements. Chapters 9 and 10 analyze the interaction between the movements and the government as the movements have organized protest around several issues. Chapter 9 addresses the efforts to gain land, while Chapter 10 focuses on issues of work and wages. A concluding section will evaluate the movements' achievements and potential.

## The Maharashtra Movements

### NOTES

1. In recent years, the spellings of these two district names have changed. The present text will use the contemporary spellings of "Thane" and "Dhule," but a number of the quotations will utilize the former spellings of "Thana" and "Dhulia."

2. The author is indebted to S.D. Kulkarni and Harsh Sethi for this insight. Interviews, February 13, 1980, and October 4, 1979.

3. The first Sub-Plan for adivasi development came into effect in April 1976. Under the aegis of these sub-plans, laws relating to adivasis have been administered and a number of programs designed to end exploitation and improve the adivasi's economic condition have been introduced. The sub-plan is directed toward "bringing the level of development in the Sub-plan area on par with that of adjoining areas as quickly as possible" through the "establishment of infra-structural facilities at the identified centres; increase in productions and employment through various schemes suited for tribal areas; removal of exploitative elements from Tribal areas." Government of Maharashtra, *Draft Sixth Five Year Tribal Sub-Plan, 1978-83*, p. 5.

In addition to the issues that will be discussed in the chapters that follow, the government has passed other laws that have had, or potentially may have, an impact on tribal development. The Maharashtra Debt Relief Act (Act III of 1976) provided a dramatic outright cancellation of the debts of certain categories of small farmers, rural laborers, rural artisans and urban workers. All members of Scheduled Tribes were automatically included under the provisions of the act. According to one Shramik Sanghatana activist, the law was immediately implemented in Dhule by the Shramik Sanghatana activists themselves: "As soon as the law was announced, the people, by this time organized by Shramik Sanghatana, immediately went to the moneylenders and took back their pawned goods." Interview with "K," January 29, 1980. (Please see Appendix I for explanation of the interview coding.)

In 1978, the government began to offer "consumption loans" to tribals who are either small landholders or landless. The government has not, however, distributed the total amount of funds that are allocated to the program because of problems in recovering the loans. Landless tribals were to pay back their loans with money earned through the Employment Guarantee Scheme. But as will be shown below, the gap between the *reality* and the *guarantee* given by EGS is wide; when the landless did not get EGS jobs, they could not repay their loans. However, the Tribal Development Corporation which administers the loans and a high government official both have expressed optimism that the recovery of loans will improve and the program expand. The Maharashtra State Co-operative Tribal Development Corporation, Ltd., *Annual Report for the Year 1978-79*, p. 10; Interview with "A," February 19, 1980.

An evidently successful program initiated by the government under the Maharashtra Tribals Economic Condition (Improvement) Act (Act 5 of 1977) has been the monopoly purchase scheme. According to S.D. Kulkarni, generally a critic of government inaction, monopoly purchase by the Tribal Development Corporation of adivasis' produce "has done much to reduce the exploitation of tribals by the traders." S.D. Kulkarni, "Problems of Tribal Development in Maharashtra," *Economic and Political Weekly*, September 20, 1980, p. 1600.

4. Interview with "G," February 21, 1980.

5. Interview with "B," February 28, 1980. A former Assistant Collector in Thane, citing the importance particularly of Godavari Parulekar's CPI(M), claimed that the government in Bombay "can't make a decision that affects Thane without having her movement at the back, at least, of their minds." Interview with "E," February 8, 1980.

6. Interview, February 6, 1980.

7. Interview with "A," February 22, 1980.

8. Interview with "A," February 19, 1980.
9. Interview with "A," February 22, 1980.
10. Government of India, Planning Commission, *Draft Five Year Plan, 1978-83* (New Delhi: Government of India Press, 1978), p. 32.
11. Government of Maharashtra, *Draft Sixth Five-Year Tribal Sub-Plan*, p. 6.

# 7
# THE DEVELOPMENT OF TRIBAL POVERTY IN MAHARASHTRA

Maharashtra incorporates, in the Bombay area, some of the greatest wealth of India and, in the countryside, some of its most severe poverty. Sulabha Brahme writes that

> Maharashtra is considered the most advanced state in India. Industrially it is highly developed...It is the leading Indian state in terms of per capita industrial production, electricity consumption, bank credit disbursement, number of motor vehicles, and such other indices of development.[1]

In their study of "Poverty in India," however, Dandekar and Rath discovered that 61.04 percent of the rural population of Maharashtra suffered from an inadequate intake of calories.[2]

Among the poorest people in Maharashtra are the 2,954,000 members of the Scheduled Tribes, or "adivasis," as they are known in Maharashtra. Although the adivasis comprise only six percent of the total population of Maharasthra, their numbers are significantly higher in some districts. Thirty-seven percent of the population of Dhule District in northwest Maharasthra are tribals, and tribals comprise twenty-five percent of the population of Thane District, located next to Bombay.[3] These two districts have fostered the most prominent political movements to improve the economic, social and political standing of the adivasis.

The tribals of Maharashtra, like the tribals in Srikakulam, have a long history of exploitation at the hands of outsiders who took advantage of their poverty and their naivete. This chapter outlines the development of tribal poverty in Dhule and Thane Districts. The pattern described here is not, however, unique to these districts;[4] indeed, a similar development had occurred in Srikakulam. As the problems of the Maharashtra tribals are replicated throughout India, it is conceivable that the solutions put forward by Maharashtra's movements are also transferable.

In 1937, a Congress government was elected under the 1935 Government of India Act to govern the Bombay Presidency. This Congress government commissioned D. Symington to write a *Report on the Aboriginal Hill Tribes*[5] that would analyze the economic and social conditions of tribal life and make suggestions for their improvement.

Symington found the tribals to be "degraded, timid and exploited," "chronically victimized by moneylenders," and insufficiently fed and clothed.[6] His analysis of the cause of their depressed economic and social condition placed the blame squarely on the actions of more worldly, exploitative outsiders:

> ...the problem of aboriginal and hill tribes lies not in their isolation from but in their contacts with the main body of the community. Where their geographical position keeps them beyond the reach of the outside world...they are happy and independent; but in the places, now all too many, where they are in constant contact with more educated people, they are degraded, timid and exploited...[7]

In more contemporary parlance, the adivasis were the victims of modernization and the spreading commercialization and capitalization of agriculture.

The influx of outsiders occurred in Dhule before it did in Thane. In the early nineteenth century, Gujars (a section of Gujarati Kunbis, a cultivator caste) began to settle in increasing numbers in the fertile lands of the Tapti River valley of West Khandesh District, which encompassed present day Dhule District. Their settlement increased in the 1830s as the British began to actively encourage cotton cultivation. As of 1837, West Khandesh "was still 'miserably populated,' large tracts being held by Bhils." (Bhil is the name of the predominant tribe in the area.) But by 1852, the population had increased by 40 percent, and "with the rise of produce prices (1856), the introduction of a lighter and more even assessment (1860-66), and the opening of the railway (1863)" the population increased over the next twenty years by nearly 50 percent.[8]

The Gujars acted as cultivators, and in time, as moneylenders, village Patils, and revenue collectors. According to Maria Mies,

> They used to raise higher rates of rent than fixed by the British, and kept a proportion to themselves. Thus, in the course of time they were able to give loans to the Adivasi peasants...When the Adivasis were

> unable to repay their debts their land was taken by the Gujar Patils..."[9]

In the mid-nineteenth century the incentives for aggregation of land were great. "The Government made systematic efforts to encourage the cultivation of cotton between 1830 and 1880. ...New varieties were introduced. Cotton gins were established."[10] Between 1861 and 1865 the Great Indian Peninsula Railway opened into the Khandesh District, connecting it to the center of the cotton trade in Bombay.[11] With the cessation of the United States' export of cotton because of its civil war, the Indian cotton trade boomed. The 1880 *Gazetteer of the Bombay Presidency* noted that in northwest Khandesh, the area which includes Shahada Taluka, the primary site of Shramik Sanghatana's activities, "the land holders are mostly Guzar capitalists, not peasant proprietors."[12] The stage for exploitation of the Adivasis' land through usurious moneylending had been set.

Government inadvertently aided the development of tribal poverty; British-made laws and the British courts gave the Gujars key tools for their own advancement at the expense of the ignorant adivasis. Gujars who had acquired land would hire adivasis as *saldars* (or *awtyas*), laborers on contract for one year. As the pay he received in this position was insufficient to maintain himself, the adivasi also had to accept loans from the Gujar. These loans, which the adivasi had no means to repay, became the instrument of his enslavement. The Government of India Act of 1859 (Civil Procedure) made non-payment of a loan punishable by attachment of property or "by imprisonment of the party against whom the decree is made."[13] By 1870, the pattern of exploitation was clear to a local British official, who reported

> Every Guzar has a bond on stamped paper purporting to be executed by his servant, acknowledging the loan of a sum of money the man can never by any chance repay. Directly an Awtya shows a disposition to leave a Guzar's service, his master files a suit against him in the civil court for the amount set forth in the bond. The Bhil, knowing he has no chances of success, does not appear to defend the suit. The Court accordingly decrees against him, and a distress warrant follows: the poor wretch's few household goods are seized, and any little ornament his wife may possess is taken from her, and he himself is arrested and carried off a prisoner to the Munsif's Court. There *his master, having reduced him to a state of utter helplessness, offers him his choice of returning to work or going to Dhulia jail.* He returns to service with his liabilities increased by the costs of the suit, his own arrest, etc., and with no proper arrangement with his master.

## The Development Of Tribal Poverty In Maharashtra

> It is no part of the duty of the Court even then to see that his master is bound to treat him fairly. He serves on for a few more months, or perhaps years, on a pittance of grain and the smallest quantity of clothing that will cover him, until tired out, he again strikes work; again his master rushes off to the civil court, and this time the Bhil is not even invited to have his say; the former decree is still unsatisfied, and another distress warrant is issued without further enquiry....What is this man but a slave? What hope has he? What redress is there for him?...He is mere chattel to be disposed of whenever his master wants money. *It is a common occurrence for one Guzar to sell his Awtya to another under the pretence of a transfer of the Awtya's debts.*[14]

In a similar manner those adivasis who worked as sharecroppers rather than saldars were cheated, and enslaved by debt. The sharecropper would be advanced money for the purchase of bullocks; for the first year he would be fed and minimally clothed by the Gujar landlord. A bond would be drawn up, to which the uneducated adivasi would accede. At harvest, the entire crop would be taken by the landlord, on the ground that the sharecropper was still in debt because of the bullocks and other goods.

> After struggling for a year or two he decides to leave. Then he finds that his partner, or master, has his acceptance for twenty or more; that the bullock he had toiled for is not his, and that he and all he has are at his master's mercy. A decree is made and the Bhil's goods are seized and sold. Then his master offers him a chance of return, and he serves for some more time...Thus things go on from year to year.[15]

Thus did newly passed British law, and, as important, the better understanding of and access to the legal system by the more educated, worldly non-adivasi landed class, aid in the adivasis' loss of land and virtual enslavement through indebtedness in Dhule District.[16]

In Thane District, further to the south, the expropriation of land began in the late nineteenth century when the nearby urban areas became increasingly developed and the produce of the area, including grains, timber, and grass, acquired increased commercial value. Non-Maharashtrians who came to the area as moneylenders, traders and forest contractors gradually amassed land through usurious lending and cheating of the adivasis.[17] A British civil servant, Mr. Orr, recorded in 1885:

## The Development Of Tribal Foverty In Maharashtra

> The Mahalkari of Umbergaon [a taluka of Thane] who is thoroughly acquainted with the land and the people, assures me that not ten percent of the Warlis and Kolis [adivasi tribes of the area] whom he knew as holding large estates two decades back, can claim a single acre as their own today...[18]

By 1938, when Mr. Symington issued his report, the situation for adivasis in both districts had not improved. It is important to examine Symington's report in some detail, for many of the problems he outlines and suggestions for corrective action he makes are strikingly similar to those presented throughout the 1970s. While a number of Symington's suggestions did find their way into legislation, implementation has been woefully inadequate, and conditions have remained largely unchanged.

In analyzing the adivasis, Symington divides his report into geographic and problematic areas. In his section on the agricultural and general economic conditions of West Khandesh, Symington first discusses the difficulties faced by those adivasis owning land. Many had been dispossessed but had recently acquired new holdings under Government Resolutions No. R.D.4702/24 of February 1926, January 1927 and January 1928, which gave preference to Bhils in the granting of government waste lands, and which granted them lands on terms of inalienable tenure.[19] However, even those Bhils who owned land were not able to enjoy the fruits of it, because of their chronic victimization by moneylenders:

> I have seen and spoken to hundreds in my enquiry and it would hardly be an exaggeration to say that there is *not one*...who is not in debt to sowcars, and not only in debt but hopelessly involved so that, unless special measures are taken, neither he nor his heirs have any prospect of extrication.[20]

The Bhil would fall into debt at the beginning of his first cultivating season; in order to plant and to eat until the harvest, he would borrow the cost of cultivation as well as food, clothing, drink, and land revenue.

> At harvest time the sowcar or his agent comes and takes the whole of the money crops away, if necessary by force, measures it roughly, and credits the Bhil's account with the value—as calculated by the sowcar....Needless to say, the market rate is rarely allowed....If his debt is large, or his sowcar particularly grasping, his food crops go as well....The Bhils then have to begin to beg or borrow immediately after the harvest...as a usual thing the Bhil's debts go on

increasing on paper even when repaid in full in fact.[21]

Symington notes the ironic condition that those Bhils who received land under the 1926-1928 resolutions and who had thus "been saved from becoming landless labourers have become instead a kind of serf, working their own fields on a bare maintenance for the profits of others."[22]

While he considers unscrupulous moneylenders to be a major cause of the adivasis' poverty, Symington nevertheless harshly criticizes government for its inadequate protection and urges both stringent measures to control moneylending by private individuals and alternative institutional methods of supplying agricultural credit. He documents the methods of the sowcars, which include, 1) rates of interest above 25 percent per year, or part of a year; 2) promissory notes taken for double the amount actually lent; 3) recoveries of loans taken in kind, with the result that the Bhil is cheated both in the measurement of the crop and in the price he receives for it; 4) the use of force to collect produce from a reluctant Bhil; 5) the use of hired bullies to terrorize the Bhil into meekness; and 6) the use of intimidation to force the Bhil to bear the responsibility for the debts of deceased relatives.[23]

Symington, wondering at the evident complacency of the Bhil "in the face of outrageous injustice," comments that the extreme dependence of the Bhils on the sowcars make them loath to antagonize them in any way, and that the Bhil, who for so long has lived on a bare subsistence, "is now prepared to put up with anything, provided the sowcar continues to support him with doles." By temperament, too, the Bhil is "extremely law abiding, peaceful, and averse from violence."[24]

These reasons may account for why the Bhil "does not protect himself by extra-legal methods," a fact at which Symington marvels. As to legal means, the Bhil "is too ignorant and poor to avail himself of legal redress...Moreover the sowcar is often able to corrupt officials of all departments."[25] Later in his report, Symington again turns to the issue of official corruption at the local level, but regrets that he "cannot suggest a means of preventing this."[26] All three of these issues—usurious and violent moneylenders, inadequate alternative sources of credit for cultivation and consumption, and the collusion of local officials with the local powerful—have remained on the adivasis' agenda through the 1970s.

Turning then to the problems of the landless of West Khandesh, Symington, after reviewing the difficulty procuring work on a regular basis, and the inadequacy of wages, notes that the Bhils have some access to fishing and to the collection of honey. But a combination of wages, some fish, and honey is still gravely inadequate.

## The Development Of Tribal Poverty In Maharashtra

> For the rest, they must beg, go hungry or eat *ambadi* (hemp), *waskhand* (a semi-poisonous root that requires soaking before it can be safely taken) or other such articles usually regarded as inedible. In a word it seems to me to be almost a miracle that they keep alive at all.[27]

In his discussion of Thane District, Symington points out that the vast majority of the adivasis had been landowners, but have become tenants whose land has passed "into the hands of sowcars who are now their landlords."[28] The loss of land leads to extreme impoverishment because of the exorbitant rents exacted in kind. Symington finds "that rentals are now far too high and it is certain that they do not leave the cultivator sufficient for his livelihood even for half the year."[29] The cultivator is then forced to borrow for the second half of the year; "the bulk of the aboriginal population" finds itself facing inescapable debt and servitude through the *veth* system of forced labour, described by Symington as "hardly distinguishable from slavery."[30] Under this system, those tenants who pay a fixed rent in kind are liable to be called upon by their landlord to work his fields or, if the landlord is also a forest contractor, to do forest work. "Thus at the critical period of the agricultural season...cultivators are forced to be present on their landlords' fields. Work on their own rented fields is postponed and their crops suffer substantial damage." The usual pay for a day's *veth* labor is a quantity of rice "barely sufficient for one man for one meal." Yet if the adviasis "refuse or procrastinate, they are liable to assaults and beatings. These are of common occurrence." Symington notes the rumors that men have also been killed; he neither verifies nor denies them. Both men and women are called upon to do domestic labor for their landlords, and rape is commonplace: "Landlords will not scruple to use their power in fulfillment of other purposes—for instance the use of their tenants' womenfolk for the gratification of their lust."[31]

Given the terms of loans agreed to by the ignorant and illiterate adivasis, they would be enslaved for life. Symington offers a number of illustrations of actual loan transactions in Thane. In one typical contract

> A...boy this year borrowed Rs. 140 from his landlord for his marriage. Interest one anna per rupee per month. [An anna is one-sixteenth of a rupee.] The loan is to be worked off by carting work every fair season. On these terms he will still be carting for his landlord at the time of his death and will then owe about Rs. 1500![32]

As a result of the extreme impoverishment of the adivasis at the hands of the sowcars, during the final weeks of the rainy season "many of them...have to live on semi-poisonous roots."[33]

Having documented the adivasis' impoverishment, semi-starvation and enslavement, Symington challenges the government to take corrective action.

> The condition under which the jungle tribespeople work and live are wretched in the extreme, and the abuses to which they are subject...constitute a blot on the administration.[34]

Symington's final recommendations include proposals "for very stringent restrictions on sowcars, for the composition of debts, for a new system of agricultural credit, for regulations concerning tenancy and certain kinds of wages" and for "compulsory education."[35]

In 1939, the Congress Government did enact two pieces of legislation which reflected Symington's concerns.[36] However, neither the Bombay Agricultural Debtor's Relief Act (Bombay Act No. XXVIII of 1939) nor the Bombay Tenancy Act (Bombay Act No. XXIX of 1939) had much positive effect. The 1939 Tenancy Act was ambitious; according to a 1974 government study, it

> defined and created a class of protected tenants, gave them fixity of tenure and protection against eviction except for some specified circumstances, laid down a procedure for the determination of "reasonable rent" payable by these tenants, fixed the duration of lease of ordinary tenants and prohibited the levy by landlords of any cess, rate, tax or service of any kind....[This] law was not made operative until 1941, and then too it was applied to only two districts, Thana and Dhulia.[37]

Tenants could be evicted, however, if the landlord wanted the land for personal cultivation or for any non-agricultural use. In the 1939 law and in its 1946 amendment, no ceiling was placed on the amount of land the landlord could resume.[38] This loophole was large enough to negate all the other provisions of the Bill and render it meaningless.[39]

By the 1970s, when Shramik Sanghatana emerged in Dhule and Bhoomi Sena was organized in Thane, there had been no improvement in the economic condition of tribals in these districts. In Dhule, according to Maria Mies, the systematic expropriation of adivasi land reached its peak in the early 1970s when the Gujars began to expand their sugar cultivation into a flourishing agroindustry.[40] Two non-tribal castes, the Levapatils (originally tradesmen from neighboring areas of Maharashtra) and the Gujars, constitute about 20 percent of the population of Dhule, but own 80 percent of the land.[41] In the

## The Development Of Tribal Poverty In Maharashtra

Shahada Taluka, the base of Shramik Sanghatana, about 58 percent of the male adivasi workers and 92 percent of the female adivasi workers are agricultural laborers.[42] An article published in a Marathi journal in June 1972 documented the contemporary condition of agricultural laborers:

> ...the agricultural labourers fall mainly into two groups. The first group are the saldars who have to work on a yearly contract. Their "sal" means yearly pay, usually 400 to 800 rupees. They have to do various types of work from four in the morning to nine at night. In a year they have a day's vacation, and if they are absent they lose two days of pay. But however sad the year laborer's condition is, still it is much better than the condition of the unskilled laborers who get work only seasonally. A man gets two rupees for twelve hours of unskilled (hard) labor and a woman gets seventy-five paise for eight hours of work. They are also perplexed as to whether they will get work and something to eat on the second day or not.[43]

Shahada Taluka has experienced aspects of the "green revolution" since the 1950s; and, as in the green revolution elsewhere in India,[44] the "trickle down" effect for which Indian planners have hoped has not been in evidence. A number of key economic and social indicators show that life for the poor of the district remained at least as desperate, if not more so, in the early 1970s as in the years preceding independence. The following is a brief introduction to three important economic factors affecting the lives of Dhule's poor: landlessness, insufficient wages, and indebtedness. All of these problems have been addressed by Shranik Sanghatana and are important issues at the state level.

Throughout Maharashtra, the introduction of irrigation and water supply projects, necessary for increased production, has raised the incomes of larger landlords but has deprived a number of poor cultivators and sharecroppers of land. Frequently, because the government-sponsored irrigation schemes are located in mountainous areas, it is adivasis who are uprooted and who then join the ranks of landless laborers.[45] According to the Marathi journal *Magowa*, in 1970-71 4,540 tribal families in Maharashtra lost 20,060 acres to government projects. Of these, only 1,398 families received compensation in the form of land; these families received a total of 3,577 acres.[46] The green revolution has an even greater impact as the amount of income it is possible to generate from farming increases because of irrigation, fertilizers, double cropping, etc. When such inputs are available, wealthier farmers who can afford them seek more land; tenants and sharecroppers are pushed off and poor peasants indebted to large landholders lose their land.[47] Brahme and Upadhyaya found that in the period from 1951 to 1971, as the wealthier farmers resumed land for their own cultivation, the percentage of landless agricultural labor in Shahada increased, while the percentage of cultivators correspondingly decreased:

### Table 3

#### Distribution of Male Workers by Occupation

| Year | % Cultivators | % Agricultural Labourers | % Other |
|---|---|---|---|
| 1951 | 45.3 | 36.6 | 18.1 |
| 1961 | 41.6 | 40.8 | 17.6 |
| 1971 | 33.9 | 48.4 | 17.7 |

Source: Brahme and Upadhyaya, p. 53.

This issue of increasing landlessness was the very first raised by the Shramik Sanghatana in Shahada. Another, related, issue raised early on was that of wages; despite the increased prosperity of agriculture in Shahada, here too there has been no "trickle down" of benefits from the green revolution. The *Study of Economic Conditions of Agricultural Labour in Dhulia District, Maharashtra*, completed by Sulabha Brahme and Ashok Upadhyaya in 1975, demonstrates that, since the 1950s, *real* wages for agricultural workers have actually *declined*.[48]

The problem of low wages is compounded by underemployment. In Shahada Taluka, a male worker can find employment for approximately 170 days per year, while a female worker is employed only about 125 days.[49] Public works projects begun during the drought year of 1972-73 provided some additional work for 30 percent of the agricultural workers of Shahada during that year. Another important source of supplemental income comes from the collection and sale of grass and wood from the forest.[50] Despite these extra sources of income:

> The average family income at the taluka level for the rural labour families worked to Rs. 1,510 and the per capita income came to Rs. 294 (for the period November 1973-October 1974). This works to about a third of the per capita income for Maharashtra State....78 percent of the families had annual per adult income below Rs. 500 which can be considered as the poverty line at 1973-74 prices.[51]

Comparing these statistics to those of the 1880 *Gazetteer*, Brahme finds "some deterioration in the level of consumption of the rural labour families."[52] The poverty is especially severe for these families in the months preceding the monsoon; during this period, more than half of the labour families were able to obtain only one meal a day.[53]

It is also at this time of the year that the poor must borrow — generally at very high rates — from the *maldars*, or large landowners. In addition to the loans for personal consumption, the adivasis sometimes need loans for ceremonial purposes, such as a wedding, or because of illness. The difficult procedures for obtaining an institutional loan — the filling in of forms, the travel to the proper office, the red tape — are time consuming and near-impossible for the illiterate adivasis. Consequently, they turn more frequently to their maldar. In a survey of Shahada Taluka in the mid-1970s, 47 percent of the laboring families reported being in debt; the average outstanding debt per family was Rs. 230.[54] The interest charged on these loans is extremely high, and the borrower frequently becomes permanently indebted to the maldar as a result.

> The *saldars* draw small amounts of cash and receive some quantity of grain during the year and at the end of the year when the accounts are finalised, they often find some outstanding. They usually continue to work with the same *maldar* because of debt obligation.[55]

> The agricultural labourers...approach the *maldars* for small loans particularly when they do not get any work during the lean season and agree to work with the *maldar* at the harvest time at wage rates 40 to 50 percent below the market rates. In effect, they are burdened with very heavy interest charges on the small amount borrowed. The consumption needs in the lean season thus land the agricultural labourers into the mire of debt; their earnings get depressed due to the debt obligations. Consequently they have little opportunity to improve their lot.[56]

Thus, in addition to the issues of landlessness and inadequate wages, indebtedness became an additional focus for organizing by the Shramik Sanghatana.

Although political organizing among the adivasis did not begin in Dhule until the 1950s, Dahanu and Talasari taluks of Thane District had experienced a significant Communist-led revolt in 1945-47.[57] The movement was organized by the Kisan Sabha of the Communist Party; the primary leader of the movement was a young woman named Godavari Parulekar. The Communists agitated for a number of the same social and economic improvements, such as increased wages and an end to forced labor, that had also been championed by the Congress Party under British rule. However, once Congress was elected to the Bombay government in 1946, during the period of transition to Indian independence, it came down violently on the Communists.[58] The newly emerging Congress government, seeking to establish its own legitimacy, refused to encourage any local demands, no matter how valid, that would aid the broader cause of Communist popularity and legitimacy. The Communists had sided with the British imperialists against Congress during the Quit India movement; they did not support the parliamentary structures for which Congress fought. At this stage of the Indian independence movement, the infant Congress government was simply too insecure to allow a serious threat to its authority; this was not yet the deeply legitimated and powerful national government of present day India.

Thus, Congress used the coercion necessary to destroy the movement, even though the movement's tactics, while militant, were largely peaceful. A State of Emergency was declared in Thane,[59] and orders were issued expelling the leading Communists from the district. The Government of Bombay explained that the orders were "aimed solely at curbing the undesirable activities of those who advocated violence to bring about political change, namely, the ushering of a Communist state in India."[60] Eventually, approximately one thousand police officers and a division of the Maratha Light Infantry were brought into the area,[61] and the movement was overcome.

The movement had very little lasting effect. It did succeed in frightening away many of the largest landowners, but their lands were purchased in smaller parcels by other non-tribals[62] who proceeded, in their turn, to replicate the exploitative relations the former landholders had had with the adivasis:

> Thirty years after the historic revolt, the next generation of the adivasis today remains illiterate, ignorant, half-starving and oppressed by a new class of sawkars, perhaps less brutal than the feudal lords, but equally exploitative through processes economic and where necessary through means extra-legal and physically coercive.[63]

Thus, despite the existence of a political movement in the 1940s, neither the economic conditions nor the political consciousness of the adivasis in Thane had been altered: "The sons and daughters of the adivasis who were declared by Godavaribai [Godavari Parulekar] as class-conscious have again been reduced to passive acquiescence."[64]

By the 1970s, the impoverished condition of tribals in Maharashtra described by Symington in 1938 remained fundamentally unaltered. As will be seen below, Maharashtra governments after independence had passed a number of laws designed to uplift the adivasis, but many had remained unimplemented. The next chapter examines the development of two movements aimed at raising the consciousness of the adivasis, particularly their sense of political efficacy, as they organize legal demands against government and the landed who have benefitted most from government inaction.

## The Development Of Tribal Poverty In Maharashtra

**NOTES**

1. Sulabha Brahme, "Drought in Maharashtra," *Social Scientist*, July 1973, p. 47.

2. V.M. Dandekar and Nilakantha Rath, "Poverty in India, I: Dimensions and Trends," *Economic and Political Weekly*, January 2, 1971, p. 29. Only Kerala, with 90.75 percent of the rural population receiving inadequate calories, and Andhra Pradesh, with 62.14 percent, have higher percentages than Maharashtra. These data are based on figures for 1961-62.

3. There are 616,000 tribals out of a total population of 1,662,000 in Dhule; Thane has 580,000 tribals in a total population of 2,281,000. The data are from the 1971 census, quoted in Government of Maharashtra, Department of Social Welfare, Cultural Affairs, Sports and Tourism, *Draft Annual Tribal Sub-Plan, 1980-81*, p. 1; and Government of Maharashtra, Tribal Research and Training Institute, "Statistics on Scheduled Tribes," *Tribal Research Bulletin*, March 1979, p. 13.

4. Similar patterns throughout India have been noted by Kathleen Gough, "Indian Peasant Uprisings," *Economic and Political Weekly*, Special Number, 1974, p. 1393: "During and since British rule, there has been increasing encroachment on tribal hill territories and oppression of tribes people by European and Indian planters, by government usurpation of forest areas, by landlords, merchants, and moneylenders from the plains, and by government agents. To the loss of large tribal areas was added exploitation in such forms as rack-renting, unequal terms of trade, usury, corvee and even slave labour, and the obligation to grow cash crops for little or no return."

5. D. Symington, *Report on the Aboriginal Hill Tribes* (Bombay: Government of Bombay, 1938).

6. Ibid., pp. 1, 6 and 7.

7. Ibid., p. 1.

8. Government of Maharashtra, *Maharashtra State Gazetteers: Dhulia District (revised edition)* (Bombay: Government of Bombay Gazetteers Department, 1974), p. 186.

9. Maria Mies, "The Shahada Movement: A Peasant Movement in Maharashtra (India): Its Development and Its Perspectives," *Journal of Peasant Studies*, July 1976, p. 474.

10. S.D. Kulkarni, "Over a Century of Tyranny," *Economic and Political Weekly*, March 9, 1974, p. 389.

11. *Dhulia District Gazetteer*, p. 567.

12. Quoted in Kulkarni, p. 389.

13. Ibid., p. 390.

14. Report by Pritchard, First Assistant Collector, Khandesh, dated July 1, 1870; quoted in *Deccan Riots Commission Report*, Bombay, 1876, Appendix B, p. 166. Emphasis in the original. Cited in Kulkarni, p. 390.

15. Pritchard in the *Deccan Riots Commission Report*, pp. 197-198. Cited in Kulkarni, p. 390.

16. In 1875, increasing indebtedness led to rioting in the Poona and Ahmednagar Districts of the Bombay Presidency. In response to these outbreaks, the Government instituted the Deccan Agriculturalist's Relief Act of 1878, designed to reduce indebtedness through court investigation of claims. The new law, according to Sulabha Brahme and Ashok Upadhyaya, "did not really prove beneficial to the ryot. As the court went into the past history of each transaction and often reduced the amount of interest mentioned in the bond, the money-lenders took from the debtors bonds for much higher amounts than were actually advanced. They refused to give loans on merely personal security and began to insist on the debtor passing a sale deed, the oral agreement being that the land was to be returned when the debt was repaid." *Study of Economic Conditions of Agricultural Labour in Dhule District, Maharashtra* (Poona: Shankar Brahme

Samajvidnyana Granthalaya, 1975), unpublished cyclostyled paper, p. 31. Government efforts to provide better credit facilities through the Land Improvement Loans Act of 1883 and the Agriculturalists' Loans Act of 1884 also largely failed due to inadequate implementation. Brahme and Upadhyaya, p. 34.

A considerable amount of the data gathered in the unpublished study by Brahme and Upadhyaya cited here was later included in a shorter published article by Brahme, "Economic Conditions of Agricultural Labour: A Study in Shahada Taluka of Dhule District," *ICSSR Research Abstracts Quarterly*, January-June 1976, pp. 1-14. The unpublished study is in the library of the Gokhale Institute of Politics and Economics in Pune, with which Brahme is associated.

17. See Nitish R. De, "India's Agrarian Situation: Some Aspects of Changing the Context," in *Agrarian Relations in India*, ed. Arvind N. Das and V. Nilakant (New Delhi: Manohar, 1979), p. 250; and G.V.S. de Silva, Niranjan Mehta, Anisur Rahman and Ponna Wignaraja, *Bhoomi Sena: A Struggle for People's Power* (Bombay: National Institute of Bank Management, 1978) (pre-publication draft), pp. 7-11.

18. Quoted in Symington, p. 47, and in de Silva, et al., p. 10.

19. Cited in Symington, p. 4.

20. Symington, p. 6. Emphasis in the original. "Sowcars" may be defined as "traders cum money lenders who...have also become landowners through a process of usurious moneylending and cheating of the illiterate adivasis." The definition is offered in G.V.S. de Silva, et al., *Bhoomi Sena: A Struggle for People's Power*, p. 7.

21. Symington, pp. 6-7.

22. Ibid., p. 8.

23. Ibid., p. 11.

24. Ibid., pp. 12, 13.

25. Ibid., p. 12.

26. Ibid., p. 98.

27. Ibid., p. 25. The number of landless leading such a tenuous existence was greatest in the Shahada Taluka, where Shramik Sanghatana was organized in the 1970s.

28. Ibid., p. 29.

29. Ibid., p. 31.

30. Ibid., p. 34.

31. Ibid.; all quotes in this paragraph are on p. 36.

32. Ibid., p. 49.

33. Ibid., p. 32.

34. Ibid., p. 30.

35. Ibid., p. 3. Symington suggests that a period be fixed by regulation in which all claims against members of the Backward Classes must be made. These claims would then go before a special court. The court, taking into account government instructions regarding permissible rates of interest, would then make an award of the sum due, and issue an order for payment. The debtor would be represented by government-appointed counsel, and the individual's income, property, and number of dependents would be considered by the court in making its judgment. (p. 95.) Symington acknowledges that "these restrictions will result in the non-satisfaction of many awards of sums due." This is justifiable in his view because of the insolvency of most of the aborigines and because that insolvency has been caused by exploitation at the hands of their creditors: "The sowcar can at present afford to finance them because he can and does keep them on, or slightly below, a starvation level of existence, and because he can and does, by methods of intimidation or violence, force their heirs and relations to take over their debts after death has rescued them from his clutches." (p. 96.)

36. B.G. Kher, then Chief Minister, later said that Symington's report had given him startling facts about the adivasis, and he had determined to do something to ameliorate their grievances. *Bombay Chronicle*, October 24, 1945, p. 2.

37. Government of Maharashtra, *Report of the Committee Appointed by the Government of Maharashtra for Evaluation of Land Reforms* (Bombay, 1974), pp. 8-9.

38. Ibid., p. 9.

39. The Bill was again revised in 1948. See Chapter 9 below for further discussion of the 1948 Act. An attempt to close the loopholes in the Debtors Relief Act of 1939 resulted in the Bombay Agricultural Debtor's Relief Act of 1947 (Bombay Act No. XXVIII of 1947). The 1947 Bill put jurisdiction in the civil courts; under the 1939 Bill, Debt Adjustment Boards of retired sub-judges and Deputy Collectors had been responsible for implementing the law; these had proved unsatisfactory, according to an account in the *Bombay Chronicle*, April 12, 1947, p. 6.

40. Maria Mies, "The Shahada Movement: A Peasant Movement in Maharashtra (India): Its Development and Its Perspectives," *Journal of Peasant Studies*, July, 1976, p. 475.

41. Vijay Kumar Kulkarni, "Shramik Sangathana, Dhule, Maharashtra: A Preliminary Report," *National Labour Institute Bulletin*, November, 1975, p. 13.

42. S.D. Kulkarni, p. 465.

43. Mangesh Rege, "Shahada: January 30 to May 1," *Magowa*, June 1972. Translated from the Marathi in the BUILD Documentation Centre, Bombay.

44. See Francine Frankel, *India's Green Revolution: Economic Gains and Political Costs* (Princeton: Princeton University Press, 1971), passim.

45. Sharad Patil, "Government's War on Adivasis," *Economic and Political Weekly*, October 26, 1974, p. 1808. According to Patil, "About 10,000 families were displaced by the Ukai project alone in the talukas of Nawapur, Nandurbar, Akkalkuwa, Taloda and Shahada in Dhule district."

46. Balmohan Limaye, "Adivasis in Maharashtra and their Movements," *Magowa*, May 1974. Translated from the Marathi by Sandeep Pendse.

47. Some indicators of the extent of the Green Revolution in Shahada include:

1) *Irrigation*: In Maharashtra, the percentage of irrigated land is eight percent. In Shahada, it has increased from seven percent in 1951 to 20 percent in 1971.

2) *Sugarcane*: The area under sugarcane, which brings a tremendous increase in per hectare returns as compared to other crops, increased steadily from 80 hectares in 1951 to 1176 hectares in 1971 to some 3000 hectares in 1973-74.

3) The number of *oil engine pumps* increased from 283 in 1951 to 1008 in 1961 to 2,228 in 1971. These were purchased with government financing.

4) The number of *tractors* increased from 8 in 1951 to over 100 in 1971.

These data compiled from the following:

Chhaya Datar, "The Relationship Between the Women's Liberation Movement and the Class Movement in Shahada—A Case Study," Cyclostyled. 1975. In BUILD Documentation Centre files, p. 4.

Sulabha Brahme and Ashok Upadhyaya, *Study of Economic Conditions of Agricultural Labour in Dhulia District, Maharashtra* (Poona: Shankar Brahme Samajvidnyana Granthalaya, 1975) (unpublished manuscript), pp. 48, 52, 171.

Sulabha Brahme, "Economic Conditions of Agricultural Labour: A Study in Shahada Taluka of Dhulia District," *ICSSR Research Abstracts Quarterly*, January-June 1976, p. 2.

48. Brahme and Upadhyaya, pp. 176-177. Daily wages for male agricultural labor varied from Rs. 2 to Rs. 3 in 1973-74, with the overall average for Shahada taluka being Rs. 2.4. In the 1950s, the wage had been approximately Re. 1. However, using 1961 as the base year, and taking the wage index as 100 in 1963, Brahme and Upadhyaya demonstrate that wages dropped to 90 in 1964-65; 98 in 1966; and from 96 to 99 until 1971. In 1971-72, there was a sharp spurt in prices, but wages lagged behind. Thus the index of real wages was 92 in 1972 and 85 in 1973.

49. Ibid., p. 175; Brahme, p. 6. Increased mechanization has aggravated this problem. In 1974, Shahada had more tractors than any other taluka in Maharashtra. Mies, p. 475.
50. Brahme, pp. 7, 9. Patil, p. 1809.
51. Brahme, p. 9.
52. Ibid., p. 10.
53. Patil, p. 1809; "Organizing the Adivasis," *Economic and Political Weekly*, Annual number, February 1974, p. 174-c.
54. Brahme, p. 10; Brahme and Upadhyaya, pp. 154-55.
55. Brahme, pp. 10-11.
56. Brahme and Upadhyaya, p. 160.
57. As this movement was directed first against the British government and later against the just-elected Congress government in Bombay that was still operating under the British Raj, a thorough discussion of this movement would not add to the theoretical issue being addressed in this essay, namely, the response of a legitimate democratic government to protest. The Congress government in Bombay during the adivasi revolt was not yet in control of the Indian state.
58. This account of the Communist-led revolt has been constructed from several sources, most of which can not be seen as remotely "objective." Godavari Parulekar's book, *Adivasis Revolt* (Calcutta: National Book Agency Private, Ltd., 1975) and the two articles by her husband, S.V. Parulekar, "The Liberation Movement Among the Varlis" and "The Struggle of 1946," both in *Peasant Struggles in India*, ed. A.R. Desai (Bombay: Oxford University Press, 1979) (reprinted from *Revolt of the Varlis* [Bombay: People's Publishing House, 1947]) are written by the two key Communist activists who led the revolt. Articles written in the *Bombay Chronicle* have a distinctly pro-Congress bias. The *Times of India*, traditionally conservative and pro-British, seemed to give the most detailed and balanced reporting. G.V.S. de Silva, et al., whose underlying bias is plainly on the side of the adivasis and activists who work to assist them, have written a useful and scholarly history of radical politics in Thane District in *Bhoomi Sena: A Struggle for People's Power* (Bombay: National Institute of Bank Management, 1978; pre-publication draft).
59. National Archives of India—Home/Political File No. 18/1-18/2, 18 November 1946.
60. *Bombay Chronicle*, December 16, p. 6.
61. Godavari Parulekar, p. 127; and de Silva, et al., p. 20.
62. According to de Silva, et al., p. 24, the purchasers were of three kinds: "1) larger tenants from the non-adivasi producer castes like kunbis who bought cheaply the lands they were renting; 2) former supervisors (often poor relations or sawkars), watchmen...and other underlings of the sawkars...; 3) non-producing petty-traders in the villages and the educated middle class who saw an opportunity for potentially profitable investment. Hardly any land passed into adivasi hands..."
63. Ibid., p. 21.
64. Ibid.

# 8
# THE DEVELOPMENT AND ORGANIZATION OF SHRAMIK SANGHATANA AND BHOOMI SENA

This chapter describes the leadership, ideology and organization of Shramik Sanghatana and Bhoomi Sena. Both are localized, non-party movements that nonviolently demand the passage and implementation of progressive legislation. They hope to politicize the poor and transform them into a powerful political force. While Shramik Sanghatana activists articulate Marxist revolutionary goals and Bhoomi Sena activists do not, the emphasis in both organizations is most strongly on process, or means, rather than a clearly defined end. Although neither group describes itself as anarchist or Gandhian, there are strong elements of these ideologies in their thinking.

The organizational emphasis in the movements is on collective, democratic decision-making and an avoidance of hierarchy. Both stress the importance of instructing the rural poor in their rights and teaching them methods of organizing so that they can build up their own movements. Energy and creativity generated from below are more valued than the advice of outside ideologues or "experts." Activists in Shramik Sanghatana, in particular, are very consciously seeking to avoid the elitist tactics that were in part to blame for the failure of the Naxalites.

The movements refuse to ally themselves permanently to political parties, for they see these as opportunistic; they fear being used by political parties for electoral gain and then being forgotten. They reject political parties, too, because they are hierarchical structures controlled from above. The movements prefer to remain decentralized and organized from the grass roots up.[1]

Gandhian influence is manifested in the energy both Shramik Sanghatana and Bhoomi Sena devote to what Gandhians call "constructive works"; they fight alcoholism and gambling, teach literacy and finances, and organize mutual assistance groups. Women are active participants. All this is part of a strategy of infusing the poor with the sense of personal and political efficacy that is necessary for organization and political action.

Some of the leaders share a Gandhian abhorrence of violence. However, purely tactical considerations, rather than the Gandhian belief in the moral superiority of nonviolence, seem to have had more importance in determining the choice of methods. The Naxalite experience demonstrated the futility of violence in the face of the Indian government's overpowering physical strength and its willingness to use that force against violent revolutionaries.

In contrast to the Naxalite violence, the nonviolent method adopted by Bhoomi Sena and Shramik Sanghatana, while often confrontational and aggressive, is within the parameters of acceptable political activity in India. The government does not approve of these movements but does not feel threatened by or suppress them. Indeed, a democratic government, to retain its legitimacy, should appear responsive to reasonable demands made through legal channels. The movements use this aspect of democratic government to make gradual legal changes, and to build the movements.

Because India is a democracy, public opinion is an important resource for the movement both in inhibiting the physical coercion of activists by the state, and in encouraging the passage of progressive legislation that then opens the door to continuing reform. Although the movements are localized, each has ties to intellectuals and journalists in Bombay and Pune. Consequently, each movement has a wider audience for its actions than just the local officials involved. Bombay, the most commercial and wealthy of Indian cities dominates the economy of Maharashtra. There is more money to support social programs than in many other states in India and there is, generally, a liberal electorate. Indeed, in Maharashtra, as in much of India, a politician must sound like a socialist to be successful. It is good politics to decry the power of the wealthy, to urge development of rural resources and to insist on the uplift of the rural poor. In addition, a number of governmental commissions and the Constitution itself recognize tribals as a particularly exploited and downtrodden segment of India's poor.

Therefore, there is incentive not only for legislators who *are* progressive, but also for those who wish to *appear* progressive, to vote for the kind of legislation the movements support. This is particularly true when the movements are able to focus public attention on a particular issue of tribal exploitation. The passage of legislation, however, certainly does not guarantee that legislation will be quickly, if ever, implemented. At the local level where implementation takes place, vested interests often have considerable power to obstruct government activity that is harmful to them. Even without this pressure, the attempt to implement a law fully may put tremendous strain on government's financial and administrative resources.

## Shramik Sanghatana amd Bhoomi Sena

Thus, once progressive legislation has been passed, the movements turn their attention to its implementation. Because the law exists, the demand that it be implemented is a completely legitimate demand. The demands of the movement thus pose a challenge to government's abilities and, ultimately, to its legitimacy: if government does not respond to a demand that it implement its own laws, it risks losing its legitimacy in the eyes not only of the activists, but of onlookers throughout the state. When government responds positively to movement demands, however, it demonstrates the efficacy of political organization and may therefore aid the movement.

The movements hope through the achievement of such small victories to teach the poor the value of organization and agitation. As they become increasingly educated in the art of politics, their demands may increase, and center on the need for overall system change. Thus, while the changes sought in the short run are progressive, but not revolutionary, the hope of the organizers is that the process of political consciousness raising and confidence building may ultimately yield profound, even revolutionary change.

### *Shramik Sanghatana: Antecedents and Early Development*

The history of Shramik Sanghatana begins in 1956 with the visit of the Sarvodaya leader Vinoba Bhave to Dhule and the subsequent creation of Sarvodaya offices. Bhulabhai Mehta, the first Sarvodaya worker, initiated efforts to restore illegally alienated land to the adivasis, but he was met with violent opposition from the landowners. The Sarvodaya organization, the Gram Swarajya Samiti, thereafter confined itself to "constructive works."[2]

In 1969 a local, high-school educated adivasi who worked with the Sarvodaya organization, Ambarsingh Suratvanti, tried to interest a variety of local officials in the exploitation and beatings the adivasis experienced at the hands of the landowners; the harassment and rape of adivasi women were major concerns. He first approached the Deputy Superintendent of Police with his complaints. The Deputy Superintendent wrote to the Subinspector of Police; but when Ambarsingh met with the latter, he produced a letter signed by a number of adivasis asserting that nothing was wrong. He refused to make an independent inquiry. Ambarsingh then approached the adivasis' MP (a Congressman) and asked him to visit the area. Ambarsingh offered to pay his bus fare, but the MP insisted on traveling by jeep; as this was beyond Ambarsingh's financial capability, the visit did not occur.[3]

Frustrated by these attempts to move government, Ambarsingh began to organize among the adivasis. When a group he had formed decided to build an office for its fledgling organization, the Bhil Adivasi Seva Mandal, sixty-one huts in Ambarsingh's village were burned down.[4]

A further radicalizing event occurred in May 1971. 1971 was a famine year in Maharashtra. In the village of Patilwadi, ten miles from Shahada, a number of poor adivasis went to their landlord and asked for a loan of grain to see them through the lean times. He refused, and they threatened him. Finally, he opened the doors to the granary and allowed each adivasi to take a measure of grain. While they were doing so, he sent word to the police that his granary was being looted. The police, joined by a number of the Gujar landlords, who arrived on their tractors, intercepted the adivasis on their way home. The landlords demanded that the police open fire on the adivasis. The Subinspector in charge refused to do so, whereupon the landlords themselves opened fire on the crowd, killing one adivasi and injuring several more. More than a hundred Bhils were arrested, along with several landlords; charges were brought against the landlords, all of whom were acquitted.[5]

The incident created quite a stir throughout Maharashtra, and the attention of a number of activist groups was drawn to the region. Under the leadership of Ambarsingh, several groups — the Gram Swarajya Samiti, the Bhil Adivasi Seva Mandal, the Lal Nishan Party's Landless Agricultural Labourers and Poor Peasants Union, and the Marathi journal *Manoos* — organized a conference in Manooshahada.[6] Prior to this conference, a Sarvodaya-sponsored survey had found that in the two talukas of Shahada and Taloda, 10,000 acres of adivasi land had been taken over by non-adivasi landlords either by force or through certain legal manoeuvres.[7] The return of adivasi land became a major organizing theme. The conference itself was called the Bhu Mukti, or Liberation of the Land, Conference, and was attended by 5,000 adivasis and a number of non-adivasi activists. Among those attending were several educated young men, high-caste Hindus, who had met while working at Baba Amte's leprosy center in Chandrapur district.[8] These included Vijay Kanhare, who had recently completed his B.Sc. degree, and Kumar Shiralkar, an engineer. These activists, who were soon to form Shramik Sanghatana, elected to stay in Dhule, although they were reluctant to be known as Sarvodaya workers because they were not committed to the path of class cooperation for which Sarvodaya stood. By the end of the conference, however, it was agreed that those working in Dhule would do so under the aegis of the Gram Swarajya Samiti, but with three carefully articulated provisos: 1) The group must have no allegiance to any political party. 2) All decisions on adivasi welfare must be made by the adivasis themselves. 3) The Samithi would initiate no violence.[9]

The Conference developed a program of action and a list of demands. Most important was the intention to immediately occupy and cultivate lands which rightfully belonged to the adivasis. The target of the action here was the landlords, but it was also necessary that the government authorities remain, at the minimum, neutral, and allow the people to implement the laws.

The second call for action was to build organized pressure on the government to implement its Employment Guarantee Scheme, and thus provide jobs.[10] Other demands directed to government were: 1) the cancellation of all adivasi land transfers after August 15, 1947; 2) the cancellation of all adivasi debts to government institutions; and 3) the announcement and implementation of a minimum wage.[11] It is useful to note the differences in the two types of programs put forth. The first two underscore the need for government to fairly and systematically enforce laws already in existence, or, barring that, to allow organized groups to implement the laws themselves. The second group of demands requires the passage of new laws. Thus, from its earliest inception, the adivasi organization in Dhule had a dual strategy of pushing for more progressive legislation and at the same time pressing government to enforce legislation already on the books.

Despite their initial agreement to work in one organization, the educated activists from outside the area soon split off and formed Shramik Sanghatana, the Toilers' Union, which, however, continued to work closely and amicably with the Gram Swarajya Samithi. The groups divided because of their differing political analyses. The Gram Swarajya Samithi saw the issue of exploitation as a local problem; it wanted to concentrate on resistance to atrocities committed by non-tribals and harassment by local government officials. While the Gram Swarajya Samithi saw these atrocities as local anamolies in the broader system, Shramik Sanghatana was more critical of the "entire feudal-cum-capitalist system" and wanted to use local organizing and local issues to eventually challenge the overall economic and governmental structure.[12]

## Organizational Structure of Shramik Sanghatana

Several facts about the organization of Shramik Sanghatana are striking. Although primarily active among tribal landless labor and tribal poor peasants, efforts were also made from the outset to organize the local non-tribal poor as well.[13] Part of the reason for this came from practical imperatives: whenever the tribal laborers threatened to strike, the landlords would try to employ non-tribal laborers.[14] Another reason for the inclusion of the non-tribal poor in Shramik Sanghatana stems from the radical political perspective of the original organizers, who stress the class, rather than the ethnic or caste divisions in society.[15]

Another key aspect of Shramik Sanghatana organization is the emphasis on mass participation and democratic decision-making. The activists who came to Dhule from outside the district strongly believe that building consciousness among India's rural poor is the key to lasting political change.[16] The movement has emphasized the need to develop organizing talent among the adivasis themselves. One young activist has stressed the long-term strategy: to build

## Shramik Sanghatana amd Bhoomi Sena

on principles of socialism and democracy a good movement, a solid organization.[17] Fearing the alienating effects of elite decision-making in hierarchical organization and wary, too, of political opportunism, Shramik Sanghatana has refrained from aligning itself with any existing political party.[18] The emphasis instead is on building a grass roots movement which will ultimately become a political force by building the people up, rather than attempting, like the Naxalites, to create sudden, violent revolution. As S.D. Kulkarni said of both Shramik Sanghatana and Bhoomi Sena, "These are people's organizations. They go directly to the bottom."[19]

The Thane Communist movement of the 1940s relied heavily on the skill of outsiders. The Naxalites, too, were elitist in their organizing. Maria Mies points to the lesson learned by Shramik Sanghatana activists from the terrible failure of the Naxalites:

> The Shahada movement started in 1972, at a time when the repression of the Maoist Naxalite Movement had reached its high-water mark. It is evident that the political line, the strategy and tactics adapted in Shahada, were an indirect criticism of the "annihilation line" of the Naxalites, who believed that the revolution could be sparked off in India by planned terrorism against the individual class enemy. One of the main points of criticism against the Naxalites was their neglect of mass mobilization. In Shahada, therefore, the "mass line" was the guiding principle of action....i.e., the organization of masses through democratic struggle, using all means of non-violent agitation: strike, boycott, satyagraha, *gherao*, processions, *bundhs*.[20]

In order to build what they hoped would become the backbone of a permanent class organization and movement, the early activists established two types of committees: the Tarun Mandals, or youth committees, and the Mazdoor Samitis, or Workers' Associations.[21] The latter groups negotiate with the landlords about wages and working conditions. Each Samiti is responsible for its own negotiations; this principle encourages the development of leadership qualities among the adivasis. The Tarun Mandals are the basic permanent unit of the Shramik Sanghatana. They organize and plan agitational actions, lead struggles against alcoholism and gambling, and help illiterate peasants to maintain proper financial accounts. Night schools for adult literacy and political education have been established.[22] These tasks are seen as crucial to the socio-economic development of the adivasis.

About 40 percent of the membership of the Tarun Mandals have been, from an early date, female. Women are credited with being exceptionally militant in all activities—demonstrations, organizing and negotiating against the landlords, and in the fights against gambling and alcoholism. Shramik Sanghatana has taken special pains to develop the leadership capacities of this group.[23]

On the whole, then, Shramik Sanghatana seeks to include and politicize as many poor people as possible in all levels of participation and decision-making. This, it is hoped, will lead to a strong organization that will outlive the founders; new leaders should emerge from the local population. Additionally, this characteristic should make it more difficult for government to claim that Shramik Sanghatana is an organization of opportunistic outsiders, as was charged of the Communist Party in Thane and the Naxalites in Srikakulam.

## The First Struggles of Shramik Sanghatana:
## Building the Organization

Shramik Sanghatana raised a variety of issues that were keenly felt on the local level, but which often had statewide importance. As the movement matured, the target of protest frequently changed from the local landed population and local officials to state-wide officials and policies. The difference was one of emphasis; at no time were the targets exclusively one or the other.

The activities of Shramik Sanghatana received press coverage from a number of journals and newspapers and this clearly added power to their efforts. The editor of the Marathi weekly *Manoos*, S.G. Majgaonkar, was one of the organizers of the January 30, 1972 Bhu Mukti conference. A daily Marathi newspaper, *Maratha*, also covered events in Dhule, as did a monthly Marathi journal, *Magowa*. The English language press also followed some Shramik Sanghatana actions; the highly regarded *Economic and Political Weekly* ran frequent articles throughout the 1970s, giving the organization a significance beyond the confines of Dhule District.

One of the first major activities undertaken by Shramik Sanghatana was an attempt to implement existing law. This was the effort by Shramik Sanghatana to reclaim adivasi land that had been alienated through fraudulent methods. Later on, the issue of land which had been alienated "legally" but through coercive and usurious methods was also raised, but as this required the creation of new legislation and the ability to influence state level officials, this was a second step.

The primary method used by the Shramik Sanghatana to recover illegally alienated land was the organization of the adivasis to forcibly harvest standing crops on such land. The target in this instance was not so much the government as the landowners themselves. The landowners did call in the police and there were violent incidents.[24] But the combination of the newly organized strength and militancy of the adivasis; the fact that they, and not the wealthy landed individuals who had usurped their property, were on the right side of the law; and the attention given to Dhule by the Bombay and Pune press meant that the landowners and police were careful.[25] In addition to forcibly occupying the land, the adivasis, with the help of the educated activists, also were able to move the courts. They would obtain the transaction documents the illiterate peasants had signed with their thumb prints, and bring these as evidence.[26] Utilizing both of these methods, the adivasis were able, in 1972, to recover several thousand acres of illegally alienated land.[27]

The next action was directed solely against the local landowners, not against government. This struggle was for the payment of higher wages for saldars and day laborers.[28] Saldars' pay ranged from about Rs. 400 to Rs. 800 per annum for days that often included sixteen hours of work, with one day's vacation per year. In addition to agricultural work, they were also frequently called upon to do domestic labor for the landlord, which was deeply resented.[29] Despite these harsh conditions of employment, saldars were considered relatively fortunate, for at least they had assured jobs throughout the year.[30] The Shramik Sanghatana and Gram Swarajya Samiti called for a mass meeting to take place in Shahada on May 1, 1972, in order to organize saldars and casual laborers. A leaflet announcing the conference, signed by Ambarsingh, stated "The government has given us the slogan, work to those who demand it. To get work for us according to that slogan, all are to march and organize."[31] Thus, while the government was not a direct target of this organizing, the goals proclaimed by government were invoked to legitimize the rally. Baba Amte was the main speaker at the conference, which was attended by some 8,000 laborers.[32] The demands put forward by the organizers of the rally, which became the basis for planning the next phase of the movement, included: 1) a 50 percent increase in the yearly pay of saldars; 2) paid leave of thirty days per year plus a weekly holiday for saldars; 3) grain to be sold to saldars at the previous year's prices; 4) fixed hours for work, and no non-agricultural work for saldars; 5) proper accounts to be kept of all money and grains given to the saldar; and 6) payment of Rs. 4 for male agricultural workers and Rs. 3 for female agricultural workers for an eight-hour day.[33]

The landowners refused to concede any of the demands. When the saldars of Raiked village went on strike, they were joined by agricultural laborers and poor peasants. Shramik Sanghatana sent representatives to the village to negotiate with the landlords, who soon conceded most of the demands. Spurred on by this triumph, strike committees formed in some seventy villages throughout Shahada, composed of agricultural laborers and poor peasants, and including women in almost all cases. These committees were coordinated at the taluka level by Shramik Sanghatana. As the strikers held on, the landowners eventually gave in to a number of demands, among them the raising of the minimum contract price for saldars by 50 percent.[34]

Within a week of the May 1 conference, the landowners had met and "decided that it was best to concede some of the saldars' demands rather than invite more trouble by obduracy." One observer hypothesized that this logic of the "doves" among the landowners prevailed over the hard line of the "hawks," who preferred framing the adivasis with false charges, or setting their gundas on them.[35] The "dovish" concessions lasted only long enough, however, for the harvesting season to be completed. A Gram Swarajya Samiti publication states that the new contracts were implemented for only two months; following the busy season, the landlords used their bargaining power to force the laborers to work at lower wages. Only in the villages where the labor committees were strong and vigilant did the new wages continue.[36] Although the triumph was short-lived, the power of organized action had been demonstrated, and a new organization, Shramik Sanghatana, was now more firmly in place throughout the villages of the region. Within a few years, the government would pass a minimum wage law, which would give Shramik Sanghatana more power to press for higher wages.

The next issue raised by Shramik Sanghatana was that of the acquisition of cultivable wasteland. Shramik Sanghatana insisted that much government-owned "forest land" was in fact not forested at all, and demanded that such unused land be turned over to landless adivasis for cultivation. The Minister of Forestry did visit the area and acknowledged that much of the "forest land" was largely devoid of trees;[37] however, no official action was taken on the Shramik Sanghatana demands. Shramik Sanghatana then began direct action: without permission, adivasis started to clear several hundred acres of land for cultivation. The Forest Department deemed this action illegal encroachment, and in July and August 1972, the police arrested over 150 adivasis and activists, who were sentenced to simple imprisonment of one or two weeks after being initially detained for one or two weeks.[38] A large number of those arrested in this first major confrontation with the police were women.[39]

The time in jail was fully utilized by Shramik Sanghatana for continued political education. It has been a consistent Shramik Sanghatana tactic to include one political activist in each group courting arrest, who then holds classes and organizes still further within the jail.[40] On October 2, 1972, an open *dharna* was held on the forest land, and 200 were arrested. The fight for the acquisition of such land was to continue for many years; by the late 1970s legislation favorable to the adivasis' encroachment of forest land would be passed. But in the meantime, the adivasis were being trained in the power of organized action, and this time, the target was the state government.

In 1972-73, a drought scorched much of Maharashtra. Dhule was less affected by the drought than many other districts, but was nonetheless the site of a number of government drought relief works. The organized strength of

## Shramik Sanghatana amd Bhoomi Sena

Shramik Sanghatana can be credited with this achievement.[41] "The Shramik Sanghathna (sic) organized mass rallies, demonstrations, seminars on the Famine Legislation, *gheraos* of government officials. On an average, some sort of agitation took place every week."[42]

Shramik Sanghatana's success in obtaining government works and in insuring rightful wage payments can be seen by contrasting the situation in Shahada with that in Sakri Taluka, also in Dhule. In mid-1973 the staff of the Arts and Commerce College at Sakri conducted a sample survey of the taluka to assess the impact of the famine.[43] While the report, "The Nature, Range and Intensity of the Famine in Sakri Taluka (1972-73)," indicated that a large number of unemployed agricultural laborers did find jobs with the scarcity relief works, payment of wages was "irregular and fraudulent." The daily wages were supposed to be Rs. 3, but the workers were in actuality receiving only Re. 1 to Rs. 1.50.[44]

In a 1975 study of Shahada, Brahme and Upadhyaya[45] found that *all* of the families in their sample reported having worked on relief projects during the 1972-73 drought. In contrast to the systematic underpayment in Sakri taluka, "Generally, they received wages between Rs. 2 to Rs. 3 mainly because the Shramik Sanghatana organizers were vigilant about the payment and also organized the workers properly and efficiently so that they can put enough work [sic] to reach the maximum volume of work in a day and get the ceiling rate..." Also because of Shramik Sanghatana efforts, Brahme and Upadhyaya reported, some government works were continued beyond the drought and "provided supplementary employment to a large number of workers in some of the villages."[46]

In Shahada, Shramik Sanghatana organized workers around demands for more relief projects and the continuation of these projects after the drought, higher wages, equal wages for men and women, more and cheaper foodgrains, the opening of more ration shops, and better working conditions.[47] In addition to making these demands on government, Shramik Sanghatana also took direct action against hoarders; in March and April of 1973 there were organized morchas against grain shops on the Gujarat border during which marchers confiscated hoarded grains.[48] Looting of grain in trucks and carts was also stopped.[49]

On May 16, 1973, an all-Maharashtra Bandh took place around the issues of relief works, wages, grain supplies, and working conditions. In Shahada, there was a total strike of the relief workers on that day. Shramik Sanghatana had built up to this strike with a study camp of women activists, a series of small and large meetings informing people of their rights under the drought regulations, the consolidation of the Tarun Mandals, and a 5,000 strong morcha in April against police repression.[50] According to an account in *Economic and Political Weekly* of the May 16 action in Shahada,[51] 6,000 people marched to the Tehsildar's office. A deputation of thirty, including two full-time Shramik Sanghatana activists, presented the Tehsildar with their demands, most of which centered on charges of frequent breaches of government regulations and assurances. The Tehsildar assured the marchers that he was sympathetic and would convey their demands to the Collector and other higher authorities. The marchers, unsatisfied, continued to occupy his office. After three hours, the Collector and the Pranth Officer (above the Collector in the local hierarchy) arrived in town, and the marchers shifted locale to confront them, bringing the Tehsildar with them. The Pranth Officer assured the crowd of his concern, but they wanted more concrete promises, and remained. By this time, the *dharna* had become a *gherao*; the Tehsildar, Collector and Pranth Officer were inside a building surrounded by angry people who refused to release them. The special police from Dhule were called, and the crowd grew increasingly restive.

> At last...the Pranth Officer came out again and gave various assurances: commencement of construction of percolation tanks from May 17, more relief works to follow within a week to create employment for 5,000 to 10,000 persons, adequate food rations, and tools which were not till then given to relief workers to be supplied within two days.
>
> That seemed concrete enough for many but not for all. As the crowd became more restive, the Pranth Officer announced that five more road projects would start on May 18.

The success of this eight hours of *dharna* and *gherao* would not have been achieved without the organizational efforts of over a year. The account given above describes a crowd that was angry but tightly disciplined and organized. Shramik Sanghatana had shown itself capable of bringing prolonged and repeated pressure to bear on local officials both to uphold the law and to use their discretionary powers on behalf of the welfare of the landless.

The increasing strength of Shramik Sanghatana can also be measured by the violence of the local landholders, who came to see it as a threat necessitating serious reaction. As Shramik Sanghatana's members generally acted within the law, or in nonviolent, traditionally acceptable ways to push for implementation of the law, the local authorities were not moving against them. To protect their own interests, local powers went outside the law.

Early in the 1970s, the landlords began organizing "crop protection societies" which were accused by local activists of such illegal acts as detaining adivasis, collecting fines of up to Rs. 100 for petty and often false charges, burning villages, poisoning wells, and beatings.[52] But as Shramik Sanghatana grew in strength and the adivasis became increasingly organized and active, a wealthy landholder, "a rich Gujar and Congressman of Shahada," P.K. Patil, sought to organize a sophisticated private army, complete with hierarchical military organization, jeeps, motorcycles, horses and rifles, to protect "the property interests of a well-to-do section of society."[53] Patil sought to finance this "army," which would have four ranks ranging from "watchman" to "major," with an annual levy on the land, which would be paid by the landlords. The annual total levy that was anticipated and suggested in a letter in fall 1973 to the local landlords came to Rs. 2,035,000.[54] Patil was an influential man who had reason to believe he would be able to obtain the official government sanction he needed to make the improved Crop Protection Society "a registered body with arms and ammunition licensed by the District Magistrate."[55] Patil was at the time Chairman of the Dhule District Central Cooperative Bank, Chairman of the Shree Satpura Tapi Area Cooperative Sugar Mills, Ltd. in Shahada (on whose stationery the letter went out), Vice-Chairman of the Maharashtra Central Cooperative Bank, and Chairman of the Shahada Taluka Panchayat Samiti.[56]

However, the Shramik Sanghatana obtained a copy of the letter and gave it widespread publicity.[57] Questions were raised both in Parliament and in the Maharashtra State Assembly by Opposition parties. Not only did the Maharashtra daily paper *Maratha* and the weekly *Manoos* pick up the story, but so did the English language press.[58] Under the pressure of this national publicity and political opposition, the Maharashtra Home Minister announced that government would not permit the Crop Protection Society without further enquiry.[59] Government's own authority, its monopoly on the legitimate use of force, was here being challenged, and government moved to reclaim it. P.K. Patil then withdrew the scheme from consideration. One year later, a faint effort was again made to launch the scheme, following a Shramik Sanghatana sponsored satyagraha to protest government inaction on land transfers, but the effort did not succeed.[60] Shramik Sanghatana, nonviolent and seeking redress of legal grievances, was the object of liberal minded support and sympathy. With publicity bringing the movement to the attention of government at the state and national levels, local authorities were pushed towards an impartiality which favored Shramik Sanghatana at the expense of the landowners, whose actions were themselves threats to the legitimacy of government authority.

In these first several years of its existence, Shramik Sanghatana, through local organizing and wide publicity, had moved government in incremental ways. To government, Shramik Sanghatana was certainly no more than a gadfly rather than a threat. Their actions were not illegal, or were agitational within an acceptable range of nonviolent direct action. Consequently, there was no obvious need to suppress them. But a process had begun in which government, by acceding to legal and concrete demands that would lead to improved lives for poor and landless adivasis, spurred the growth of continued demands. In a sense, government allowed itself to be pushed; but given the publicity afforded the movement in a broader sphere of public opinion, the government could do little else and still maintain its claim to legality and authority.

## *The Development of Bhoomi Sena: Origins and Early Struggles*

Bhoomi Sena is an adivasi-based movement in Palghar Taluka of Thane District. It has branches in over eighty of the 100 villages in Palghar,[61] where 85,000 of the total population of 250,000 are adivasis. The adivasis are generally extremely poor; while they constitute 65 percent of the population, they own less than 20 percent of the land. In most villages landless laborers far outnumber landowning adivasis, and even the latter are mainly small farmers who seldom own more than five acres of land.[62] The resulting land hunger was a prime force in the founding of Bhoomi Sena.

Bhoomi Sena's origins date to the 1970 "Land Grab" movement organized throughout much of India by a wide coalition of left opposition political parties; its goal was to put pressure on national and state governments to implement land reforms. Although the Land Grab movement had national implications, it was organized around local issues. In Palghar, the movement was organized locally by the Praja Socialist Party, which was strong in the taluka. The tactic was a satyagraha on two thousand acres of land belonging to the Anjuman Trust. This Trust is a religious organization which took advantage of a loophole in the Maharashtra Agricultural Lands (Ceiling on Holdings) Act, 1961 that allows religious trusts to hold property in excess of that allowed to private owners. The satyagrahis claimed that the better part of the income from the land owned by the Anjuman Trust did not in fact go for religious purposes, but was appropriated by an individual to whom the Trust had given tenancy rights. The satyagrahis therefore demanded that the ceiling law should be made applicable to this land.[63] About 150 people participated in the satyagraha; all were arrested and sentenced to fifteen days in jail.[64]

A number of adivasis were among those who had been organized by the Praja Socialist Party to participate in the satyagraha. One of them, Kaluram Dhodhade, was a young man who had been working as a full time organizer with the P.S.P. In jail during those two weeks, Kaluram and other adivasis had the opportunity to discuss their recent activities and came to the conclusion that the political parties, including the P.S.P., were more interested in

## Shramik Sanghatana amd Bhoomi Sena

broad symbolic actions than in concretely helping the adivasis to regain land that, they felt, had been improperly alienated. Disillusioned with the parties, this group of adivasi activists headed by Kaluram decided to form their own organization, Bhoomi Sena, or Land Army, whose first goal would be the reclamation of lost adivasi lands.[65]

From the outset, the battles waged have most often been for the implementation of already existing legislation. Bhoomi Sena has consistently pressed not for structural change, but for the dramatic change that would occur if laws were actually obeyed. Their demands have consistently been made nonviolently and legally.[66] Pressure has been brought to bear less on those who make the laws than on the local officials who implement the laws, or who can step aside and allow the adivasis to implement the laws themselves. Bhoomi Sena is less revolutionary in its strategic thinking than Shramik Sanghatana,[67] but its tactics bear a close resemblance.

The first action taken by Bhoomi Sena was a dramatic example of direct action aimed at moving local government to implement laws that were in the best interest of the poor adivasis and not of the landlords. The laws in question were a series of Tenancy Acts that were designed, and refined over the years, to establish "protected tenants"—tenants with fixity of tenure;[68] they later gave rights of *ownership* to tenants cultivating the land.[69]

Bhoomi Sena's first activity was to organize an investigation of land ownership in ten villages.

> The investigation...revealed that there were innumerable cases where the sawkars were actually occupying the land which the revenue records showed as belonging to the adivasis; or the sawkars had managed to transfer the title of adivasis' land to themselves.[70]

The initial tactic used by Bhoomi Sena was to forcibly harvest the crops on adivasi land that had been—illegally—cultivated by the sowcars. In the first action, some 600 adivasis bearing sickles harvested the crops on one sowcar's land.[71] Initially, there was no resistance from the surprised landowners. But as the harvesting continued, they called in the police. The police threatened the adivasis with arrest, but they stood their ground, explaining to the police that they were acting legally by taking the crops from lands that rightfully belonged to them; they told the police it was they who were acting illegally by defending the sowcars.[72]

While these confrontations were occurring locally, they were publicized at the state level by the MLA for Palghar, Navinit Shah. Shah was a member of the Praja Socialist Party and had been an important influence on Kaluram's political development; he was wholly in sympathy with Bhoomi Sena's actions.

Shah argued in the Maharashtra Assembly that the government should give protection to the adivasis, who were only demanding that the law be enforced. As a result of these dual pressures, the District Sub-Divisional Officer agreed to come to Palghar, and to decide cases of disputed land ownership on the spot. To the surprise of Bhoomi Sena, and of Shah, the Sub-Divisional Officer not only brought his court to the villages, he ruled in favor of the adivasi complainant in 799 of the 800 cases he heard; the adivasis won back several thousand acres of land.[73] Navinit Shah firmly believes that it was the power of the organized adivasis that had produced the most impact; in previous years, when he as MLA had tried to get the land laws implemented, he had not been successful. As MLA he could be useful to the movement by adding pressure and bringing its case to the attention of state officials; but bureaucrats, he found, would not listen to an MLA unless he had an organized movement behind him.[74]

Following this victory, the Bhoomi Sena came to the attention of a number of outside, urban-based political activists. Control over the development of the movement was soon yielded by the local adivasis to a voluntary organization for adivasi uplift, the Bhumi Putra Pratisthan, which was intent on improving the production methods used by the adivasis. New agricultural methods, it was hoped, would lead to general social and economic uplift. In 1972, the Shetkari Mandal (Farmers Association) was established in Palghar to administer loans provided by the Bank of Maharashtra, which agreed to cooperate with the program on the urging of the Bhumi Putra Pratisthan.[75] Over the next three years, the Shetkari Mandal undertook a number of economic schemes they hoped would bring increased prosperity to the adivasis: in addition to administering the bank loans, it entered the grass trade, serving as middleman between the adivasis and the grass traders in a failed effort to secure higher prices, and dug costly wells, a number of which proved to be dry.[76] The major failing of the Shetkari Mandal, however, was its mismanagement of the bank loan program. Although an audit by the bank showed that there had been no misappropriation of funds, the funds had been diverted for unauthorized and uneconomic projects.[77] Kaluram, the adivasi leader, had lent his support to this venture, and in 1975 he publicly admitted his part in its failure. In 1976, the Bhumi Putra Pratisthan workers left the area, and Kaluram and others worked once again to establish Bhoomi Sena under local control.[78]

Now in its third incarnation, Bhoomi Sena has worked to become a grass roots political organization with sufficient power to have an impact on local officials and landlords and to insure the application of the law. In addition to taking on specific issues—notably the struggle against illegal land alienation and bonded labor, and for the implementation of the minimum wage law— Bhoomi Sena has worked for "conscientization,"[79] or what westerners might call "consciousness raising," among the adivasis. The effort is to educate and politicize, both to eliminate wasteful social evils, such as alcoholism and gambling, and in order to create a pressure group capable, like the vested interests, of being heeded. The effort is entirely within the legal structures of society, and is gradualist; but it is potentially threatening to the dominant class in the countryside whose support has been important to state and union governments. To the extent that such pressure can motivate local officials to vigorously enforce the law, and can push on the state level for more progressive legislation which then in turn serves as a rallying point for more organization, such movements can have a gradual but potentially profound effect. Government cannot legitimately move against groups acting entirely within the law and, indeed, embarrassing the government into enforcing the law. The attention paid to the rural efforts by urban intellectuals and journalists is thus absolutely crucial to widening the impact that can be made at the local level, for government must be pushed to act vigorously by a wide audience.

### *Organizational Structure of Bhoomi Sena*

Following the failure of elite control in the Shetkari Mandal debacle, Bhoomi Sena has fostered more grass roots organization and the selection of issues for struggle through the spontaneous development or articulation of a grievance. There is a central group of eight or nine activists who maintain an office and serve both as facilitators of village-level organizing and as coordinators of actions spanning more than one village.[80] But at the heart of Bhoomi Sena are the Tarun Mandals (youth leagues); these are organized at the village level by villagers who have usually attended a Bhoomi Sena-organized discussion group, and who thereafter operate autonomously. There are no office holders, no elected or appointed officials; the emphasis is on collective decision making:

> The role of Tarun Mandal is to provide a systematic forum for deliberation about collective tasks and to organize such tasks, and to review experience.

> The Tarun Mandals hold meetings once every week. Their activities include negotiating with and confronting the sawkars in the village as the need arises on issues of bondage, minimum wage, other conditions of work; to managing collective savings funds and to advancing khauti [consumption loans] to the more distressed among the adivasis; undertaking activities like mutual aid in production and joint farming; obtaining and managing bank loans for cultivation purposes;

and more recently setting up people's courts and people's schools.[81]

From time to time Bhoomi Sena holds a *shibir*, or "camp for collective reflection."[82] At these meetings, after hearing a brief history of Bhoomi Sena, its accomplishments and problems, approximately twenty-five to fifty adivasis discuss the problems faced by their villages, their objectives, and possible strategies for obtaining them. Thus inspired and energized, the activists often attempt to organize Tarun Mandals in their own villages. Once created, a Tarun Mandal

> is interlinked with other Tarun Mandals through participation in the movement and in the Shibirs, and through direct exchanges. It learns from its own experience, from other Tarun Mandals, and from the center. But it is not a local branch of Bhoomi Sena; it is fully autonomous and free to move on its own.[83]

The commitment to generating issues and solutions "from below" rather than from an elite does seem to inhibit the development of a strategy that would be system threatening. Unlike Shramik Sanghatana, Bhoomi Sena does not have a long range strategy or a long range desire for revolutionary structural change. Until recently, the emphasis has been on local issues and local solutions.

But as will be described in Chapter Nine, in the late 1970s Bhoomi Sena did join in a temporary alliance with several other organizations, including Shramik Sanghatana, to create a state-wide pressure group to agitate for tribal access to forest lands. The willingness of small localized movements to form coalitions in pursuit of common goals may give them considerably more power to pursue legislative changes at the state level. This, in turn, gives the movements tools for organizing locally.

De Silva, et al., point out that "All the activities hitherto undertaken by Bhoomi Sena—the present struggle for land...minimum wages, employment, abolition of bonded labour, etc.—are not in any way incompatible with, but rather within the framework of, capitalist relations of production."[84] But at the same time, the movement is threatening to the power of the sowcars whose position is often maintained by breaking or ignoring the law. That the landed are able to do so indicates the frequent failure of local government officials to implement laws that work against the interests of the local elites. When the movement attempts to force government to implement such laws, it is attempting to make the local government move against its traditional supporters. While this problem is manageable in one locality, if modest movements like Bhoomi Sena multiplied in number, local demands for implementation of various land laws, minimum wage laws, and employment guarantees could pose serious problems of capacity and political will for government.

## Shramik Sanghatana amd Bhoomi Sena

### NOTES

1. Godavari Parulekar, who organized the 1940s revolt in Thane, is still very active in Dahanu and Talasari talukas. She is now a member of the CPI(M). Because of her nearly forty-year commitment to Thane's adivasis, she has gained the respect of many Maharashtra government officials, and exerts considerable power locally. While CPI(M)'s activities under her direction have thus been very important in generating change, this political party's workings will not be detailed below. As part of a national political party, the local CPI(M) differs substantially in organization and strategy from the non-party movements with which this study is concerned.
2. Vijay Kumar Kulkarni, "Shramik Sangathana, Dhule, Maharashtra: A Preliminary Report," *National Labour Institute Bulletin*, November 1975, p. 14. "The Bhil Movement in Dhulia," *Economic and Political Weekly*, Annual number February 1972, p. 207, reports that Sarvodaya activities in Shahada were "limited to organizing free kindergartens, ashram schools, health centres, fair price shops, campaign against alcoholism, etc."
3. Mies, p. 476.
4. Ibid.
5. The essentials of this incident were reported in Mies, p. 476; "The Bhil Movement in Dhule," p. 205; "Agricultural Workers in Action: The Story of the Shramik Sangathan," *How*, June 1978, p. 29; and in an interview with Chhaya Datar, an activist and writer whose involvement with Shramik Sanghatana dates to 1972, January 29, 1980. "The Bhil Movement in Dhule" reported that the Subinspector who refused to open fire was suspended from his job soon afterward.
6. Reports of the conference appear in "The Bhil Movement in Dhule," pp. 205, 207; Mies, pp. 476-477; "Agricultural Workers in Action," p. 29; Vijay Kumar Kulkarni, p. 14; *The Times of India*, February 6, 1979; and interview with Chhaya Datar, January 29, 1980.
7. *The Times of India*, February 6, 1979; and Mangesh Rege, "Shahada: January 30 to May 1," *Magowa*, June 1972, translated from the Marathi in BUILD Documentation Centre.
8. Baba Amte is a respected, apolitical social worker whose work among the poor in Chandrapur is in the Indian "saintly" tradition. He has striven to inspire youth to become involved with the problems of the poor. His early support for Shramik Sanghatana was a source of positive publicity for the organization. Interview with Chhaya Datar, January 29, 1980.
9. *The Times of India*, February 6, 1979; "Agricultural Workers in Action," p. 29.
10. The EGS is examined fully in Chapter 10 below.
11. Mies, p. 477; "The Bhil Movement in Dhule," p. 207.
12. S.D. Kulkarni, "Class and Caste in a Tribal Movement," *EPW*, Annual Number, February 1979, p. 467. In a 1980 interview, one Shramik Sanghatana activist (J) said that the short and medium range goals of the organization are to work on the passage and implementation of good legislation, but that the activists do see their goal, ultimately, as revolution. Chhaya Datar cited the distinction between "constructive" and "agitational" work and the increasing radicalism of the Shramik Sanghatana activists as the reasons for the split. January 29, 1980.
13. See S.D. Kulkarni, pp. 466-467; "Organizing the Adivasis," p. 176-B.
14. S.D. Kulkarni, p. 467.
15. Datar, p. 10, states, "The activists had a perspective of the radical transformation of the society through proletarian revolution." In a February 13, 1980 interview, S.D. Kulkarni described the current Shramik Sanghatana as "completely Marxist."
16. Interview with Chhaya Datar, January 29, 1980; interview with Vahru

Sonawani, full-time worker with Shramik Sanghatana and an adivasi, January 29, 1980. This point is further emphasized in Vijay Kanhare, "A Meeting at Night," *How*, December 1979, p. 28. Kanhare is one of the founders of Shramik Sanghatana.

17. Interview, "H", January 17, 1980.

18. This insight gained from a number of sources, including interviews with Sudheer Bedekar, editor of *Magowa*, January 31, 1980; S.D. Kulkarni, February 13, 1980; and H, January 17, 1980.

19. Interview, February 13, 1980.

20. Mies, p. 480.

21. Mies, pp. 477-478, and Datar, pp. 10-11, both describe these groups.

22. Vijay Kumar Kulkarni, p. 16.

23. Mies, p. 478; Vijay Kumar Kulkarni, pp. 15-16; Datar, p. 1.

24. "The Bhil Movement in Dhule," p. 207; P.B., "Organizing the Landless," *Economic and Political Weekly*, March 10, 1973, p. 502.

25. Datar, p. 9; Mies, p. 477.

26. Mies, p. 477.

27. "Rise to Support Our Friends in Shahada," *Magowa*, October-November, 1973, translated from the Marathi in the BUILD Documentation Centre, reported that 3,000 acres were recovered at this time. *The Times of India*, February 6, 1979, claimed 3,500 acres had been recovered. Datar, p. 9, Mies, p. 477, and P.B., "Organizing the Landless," p. 502, all cited 4,000 acres.

28. Saldars are laborers who are hired under a yearly contract.

29. See P.B., "Organizing the Landless," pp. 502-503; Mangesh Rege, "Shahada: January 30 to May 1," *Magowa*, June 1972, translated from the Marathi in the BUILD Documentation Centre.

Government of Maharashtra, *Report of the Study Committee on Employment Conditions of Agricultural Labor in Maharashtra State (With reference to Minimum Wages)* (Bombay: Central Government Press, July 1973), p. 58, described the job of the saldars in these terms:

> "The worker is required to attend a variety of duties from early morning till about 11 p.m....He is a person for all unskilled jobs. The hours of work range from 10 to 16 hours a few rest intervals of half an hour, interspersed with. (sic)
> 
> The question of granting weekly off, annual leave, etc. does not arise as the nature of work is such that either the worker must provide a substitute from his family members or attend without any interruptions."

The report also found "certain unfair practices": "A monthly worker works for thirty-two days and gets one month's salary. A yearly worker works for thirteen months, and gets yearly wages....Loans given for marriages and other purposes are adjusted by making the worker work as saldar for years together on meagre pay." (p. 75)

30. Brahme and Upadhyaya, p. 175, reported that the number of work days per year available for male agricultural workers in Shahada averaged 170 days; women could expect to be employed only 125 days per year. Mangesh Rege reported that the average male wage for a 12-hour day was Rs. 2; a woman received 75 paise for an 8-hour day.

31. The leaflet is described in Rege.

32. Rege; P.B., "Organizing the Landless," p. 503; Vijay Kumar Kulkarni, p. 15.

33. Rege.

34. This account of the strike draws on Vijay Kumar Kulkarni, p. 15; Rege; P.B., "Organizing the Landless," pp. 502-503; and *The Times of India*, February 6, 1979.

35. P.B., "Organizing the Landless," p. 503.

36. The publication, *Shahada Chalwal* (Bombay: Gram Swarajya Samithi [Shahada] Publication, 1974), is translated in a cyclostyled manuscript kindly made available by Arvind Das.

Despite the limited success, in 1973 the *Report of the Study Committee on Employment Conditions of Agricultural Labour in Maharashtra State* praised the work of Gram Swarajya Samiti and Shramik Sanghatana (although not by name), stating: "Recently, in October 1972 on account of the sustained and peaceful struggle by social workers the wages of Saldars have been raised by agreement in Shahade-Talode area of Dhule District." (p. 100)

37. See Mies, p. 477.

38. P.B., "Organizing the Landless," p. 503.

39. Datar, p. 10.

40. P.B., "Organizing the Landless," p. 503; *The Times of India*, February 6, 1979.

41. "Where the Bandhs Lead Further," *Economic and Political Weekly*, June 2, 1973, p. 970; Mies, p. 478.

42. Mies, p. 478. "Where the Bandhs Lead Further," p. 970, also reported that "On an average there was one morcha every week, several meetings, distribution of leaflets, and study and propaganda meetings."

43. The Report, "The Nature, Range and Intensity of the Famine in Sakri Taluka (1972-73)" was issued in Marathi, and was subsequently summarized in English in the following two articles, which are nearly identical: Sharad Patil, "Famine Conditions in Maharashtra: A Survey of Sakri Taluka," *Economic and Political Weekly*, July 28, 1973, pp. 1316-1317; and Sharad Patil, "On a Survey of Famine Conditions in Sakri Taluka of Maharashtra," *Social Scientist*, August 1973, pp. 69-73.

44. Patil, "Famine Conditions...," p. 1317; Patil, "On a Survey...," p. 72.

45. Brahme and Upadhyaya, p. 134.

46. Ibid.

47. "Where Bandhs Lead Further," pp. 970-971.

48. Ibid.

49. "Agricultural Workers in Action: The Story of the Shramik Sangathan," *How*, June 1978, p. 30.

50. Ibid.

51. "Where the Bandhs Lead Further," p. 971.

52. Datar, p. 6; *Shahada Chalwal*.

53. *Indian Express*, November 12, 1973.

54. *Indian Express*, November 12, 1973; and an Untitled Pamphlet, cyclostyled, 6 pages, issued in 1974, evidently by Shramik Sanghatana or its sympathizers, regarding the possibility of a private army being raised by Dhule landlords; in BUILD Documentation Centre. Much of the letter is reprinted in this pamphlet.

55. Quote from Patil, *Indian Express*, November 12, 1973.

56. *Indian Express*, November 12, 1973; and Untitled Pamphlet.

57. It is interesting to note that the *Indian Express* article, November 12, 1973, is in substance completely in agreement with the Untitled Pamphlet, which appears to have been issued either by Shramik Sanghatana itself, or by activists close to it.

58. Interview, Shramik Sanghatana activist "J," January 26, 1980; "Offensive Against Poor Resumed," *Economic and Political Weekly*, March 18, 1978, p. 516.

59. Untitled Pamphlet.

60. Ibid.

61. Harsh Sethi, "Rural Development: Alternative Strategies," in Arvind Das and V. Nilikant, eds., *Agrarian Relations in India* (New Delhi: Manohar, 1979), p. 106.

62. G.V.S. de Silva, et al., *Bhoomi Sena: A Struggle for People's Power*, p. 4.

63. Interview with Navinit Shah, former MLA from Palghar, February 18, 1980.
64. de Silva, et al., p. 31.
65. Interview with Navinit Shah, February 18, 1980; de Silva, et al., p. 32; and de Silva, Mehta, Rahman, and Wignaraja, "Bhoomi Sena: From the Village to the Global Order," *National Labour Institute Bulletin*, January-February 1979, p. 16.
66. Amit Bhaduri, G.V.S. de Silva, Niranjan Mehta, Anisur Rehman, Datta Sevale, Ponna Wignaraja, "The Emergence of People's Power in Palghar and Some Reflections Growing Out of It," ("A note prepared August 1977," cyclostyled), in BUILD Documentation Centre. This paper notes that "these legal demands represent some of their immediately pressing problems."
67. Interview with S.D. Kulkarni. Kulkarni suggested that Shramik Sanghatana is more radical because its constituency is almost entirely landless, while there are more small farmers among Bhoomi Sena's constituency. Another reason for Shramik Sanghatana's relative radicalism may be that the landlords in Shahada are much wealthier than in Palghar; the gap between rich and poor is greater.
68. Bombay Tenancy Act of 1939 and Bombay Tenancy and Agricultural Lands Act of 1948.
69. The Bombay Tenancy Act as amended in 1955. According to this law, landlords were allowed to resume land for their "personal cultivation" within the limits of the ceiling law. Lands not so resumed by the landlord were to become the property of the tenant. Government of Maharashtra, *Report of the Committee Appointed by the Government of Maharashtra for Evaluation of Land Reforms* (Bombay: 1974), p. 16, explains: "After the time set for landlords to file their claims for resumption of leased land expired on 31st of March, 1957, the tenants holding land on lease, not so claimed by the landlords, were to be deemed to have become owners of the land from the 1st of April 1957. Therefore this day was designated as the Tillers' Day in the Act."
70. de Silva, et al., *Bhoomi Sena: A Struggle...*, p. 33.
71. Ibid.
72. Ibid., p. 34; interview with Navinit Shah.
73. de Silva, et al., *Bhoomi Sena: A Struggle...*, p. 34; interview with Navinit Shah; and Nitish R. De, "India's Agrarian Situation: Some Aspects of Changing the Context," in Arvind Das and V. Nilikant, eds., *Agrarian Relations in India* (New Delhi: Manohar, 1979), pp. 251-252.
74. Interview, Navinit Shah.
75. Interview, Navinit Shah; de Silva, et al., *Bhoomi Sena: A Struggle...*, p. 37.
76. de Silva, et al., *Bhoomi Sena: A Struggle...*, pp. 40-41.
77. Ibid., p. 42; De, p. 252. Navinit Shah stated in an interview his view that the intentions of the Shetkari Mandal leaders were honest, but that the experiment was extended beyond their capability to manage it.
78. De, p. 252; de Silva, et al., *Bhoomi Sena: A Struggle...*, p. 42.
79. This word is used by a number of the intellectuals writing about Bhoomi Sena and other tribal movements in Maharashtra. de Silva, et al., *Bhoomi Sena: A Struggle...*, which perhaps introduced the phrase in this context, ascribe it to Paulo Friere: "As defined by Paulo Friere [*Cultural Action for Freedom*, Penguin, 1972], conscientization is a process 'in which men, not as recipients, but as knowing subjects, achieve a deepening awareness both of the sociological reality which shapes their lives and of their capacity to transform that reality.' As opposed to spontaneous (unconscious) action of the masses mobilized by a conscious Vanguard, conscientization is a process that generates consciousness in the masses themselves." p. 95.
80. de Silva, et al., *Bhoomi Sena: A Struggle...*, pp. 100-101; interview, Navinit Shah.
81. de Silva, et al., *Bhoomi Sena: A Struggle...*, p. 101.
82. Ibid., p. 49 and Annexure 2, which gives a detailed description of one shibir; see also De, p. 252.
83. de Silva, et al., *Bhoomi Sena: A Struggle...*, p. 102.
84. Ibid., p. 108.

# 9
# STATE AND MOVEMENT INTERACTIONS: ISSUES OF TRIBAL LANDLESSNESS

In the 1970s, the Maharashtra government initiated a number of projects and passed many laws designed to improve the socio-economic condition of the poor, and of Scheduled Tribes and Castes in particular. This chapter and the following chapter will juxtapose the evolution of government policy making and implementation with the activities and demands of organized adivasi-based movements throughout the state, particularly Shramik Sanghatana in Dhule, Bhoomi Sena in Palghar Taluka of Thane, and the CPI(M) Kisan Sabha movement in Dahanu and Talasari Talukas of Thane. This chapter focuses on issues of tribal landlessness, and Chapter 10 will discuss issues of work and wages.

One of the issues that proved to be among the most galvanizing in the early struggles of both Shramik Sanghatana and Bhoomi Sena was the insistence on the restoration of agricultural lands that had been lost by the adivasis either through illegal means or because of debt obligations. As was shown in Chapter 8, both movements had some early success in regaining lands that had been illegally usurped. Because the adivasi activists were on the side of the law, and because their cause was publicized in the press and supported by some sympathetic elected officials, local government cooperated with the demand that the laws be enforced. The existence of laws that upheld adivasi rights made the process possible; the movements were making no radical demands, but merely pressuring government to act legally by implementing laws it had often failed to enforce.

As will be seen in this chapter, the legislation that existed when the movements were formed in the early 1970s was flawed; there were numerous loopholes that could be used to protect those who had illegally or through usurious methods acquired land from the tribals. The adivasi movements were one influence in the 1970s that led the Maharashtra government to write improved legislation. Once that legislation was in place, the movements could

*Tribal Landlessness*

push locally for its implementation.

However, this chapter will show, current legislation does not provide the movements with the tools they need to push government much further. Although laws with regard to *illegally* alienated land have been tightened, the law regarding the return of land alienated to non-tribals legally is written in such a way as to have little practical use for the tribals. Similarly, the 1972 law imposing a ceiling on land holdings is little improvement over its flawed 1961 predecessor.

Movements based on the rule of law need, in effect, the cooperation of the government in passing progressive legislation. Democratically elected governments in India at state and union levels often provide such legislation. At these levels, legislators have an electoral incentive to pass progressive laws. On the local level, however, where implementation occurs, and where the influence of vested interests is greater, the picture is far less sanguine. Nonetheless, as the state government passes increasingly progressive legislation, the movements, in turn, are then able to push for its implementation. In passing the legislation, the government gives the movements a tool for organizing and bringing legitimate pressure to bear on government.

Despite the pressure coming from the movements, and to some extent from the union government, Maharashtra has thus far been unwilling to pass legislation that severely threatens the land holdings of the vested interests in the countryside. This is a step that legislators are politically unwilling to take. The movements themselves seem to have accepted the political and practical difficulties of regaining land that has been legally in the private possession of others for years; they have turned their attention away from the demand that *privately*-held lands be returned to the demand that *government*-owned lands be distributed.

The decision to pursue this tactic seems a politically realistic one. In order to grow, the movements must win battles, and they will do better to take on struggles at which they can succeed. The movements do not yet have the strength to force the return of lands that have been legally, if, perhaps, unethically, taken from them. If they are lacking the political clout to create such legislation, they do better to pursue legislation that is politically possible. This chapter concludes with a discussion of the movements' struggle to gain legislation that would provide government-owned land for the landless.

### *Land Alienation*

Major pieces of legislation designed to protect tenancies and give ownership of land to the tiller were passed in 1939, 1948, and 1955. However, each of these laws has proved seriously deficient because of gaping loopholes that have allowed the expressed intent of the legislation to be easily circumvented.

## Tribal Landlessness

In June 1968, the Government of Maharashtra created a Committee for Evaluation of Land Reforms that was empowered "to study the working of various land reform measures such as Tenancy Laws, Abolition of Intermediaries, Land Ceiling Acts, etc., with a view to pin-pointing the defects, if any, in the implementation programme." It was further empowered

> To assess how far the implementation programme has been successful particularly with reference to its impact on the two main objects, namely—
> i) increasing agricultural production, and
> ii) enlargement of social justice.[1]

The report issued by the Committee gives a detailed analysis of why the laws had not provided social justice. While ownership had been given to cultivators in the Bombay Land Revenue Code of 1879, "tenancies in land in the raiyatwari region of Western Maharashtra [in which both Thane and Dhule lie] remained practically unregulated by law till 1939. In effect, a tenant was a pure tenant at will."[2] Land should have been inalienable under the provisions of the 1879 Bombay Land Revenue Code, in which formal ownership of land was given by the state to the actual cultivator of the land at the time of the original surveys and settlement operations of the 19th century.[3] However, the combination of difficult agricultural conditions, the required revenues due the British, and the entry of non-adivasi traders and moneylenders into adivasi regions led to the loss of adivasi ownership and the transformation of adivasis into unprotected tenants or agricultural laborers.

> The number of famines, droughts, and general uncertainty of outturn of crops rendered the peasant incapable of paying a revenue fixed over time and in cash, without the aid of the money-lender... The effects...were the disposition of the peasantry and their transformation into tenants or share-croppers or agricultural labourers. For the landless labourers, the debt obligation was even more degrading since it involved the mortgage of one's labour to the creditor.[4]

In 1939, with the first Congress government in place in the Bombay Presidency, the Bombay Tenancy Act of 1939 was enacted "to provide for the first time some measure of protection to tenants."[5]

> The Land Revenue Code, 1879 had defined a class of permanent tenants. The rest were all tenants-at-will. The 1939 Act defined

> and created a class of protected tenants, gave them fixity of tenure and protection against eviction except under some specified circumstances, laid down a procedure for the determination of "reasonable rent" payable by these tenants, fixed the duration of lease of ordinary tenants and prohibited the levy by landlords of any cess, rate, tax or service of any kind.[6]

This law did not come into force until 1941, and then only in Thane and Dhule districts. In 1946, with the return of Congress officials to government, the Act was significantly amended and applied to the entire Province. Under the new law, protected tenants were deemed to be those who had held land continuously for six years immediately preceding either January 1, 1938 or January 1, 1945. "The Act required every tenant on a specified date to be recorded as a protected tenant

> unless the landlord had made an application during the year preceding and acting on such application a competent authority had declared the tenant not to be a protected tenant. *The Act thus put the burden of proof squarely on the landlord.*[7]

However, a major loophole in this Act allowed the landlord to resume the leased land "after due notice, in case he wanted the land for personal cultivation or for any non-agricultural use."[8] There was no ceiling limit to the amount of land that could be so resumed by the landlord; this provision negated the tenant's protection, and rendered the 1946 amendment as ineffectual as the 1939 Act.

Unprotected, or ordinary, tenants were, however, given some security of tenure by the same amendment. New leases had to be of at least ten years' duration, and could be terminated only for nonpayment of rent or other failure of the tenant to abide by the standard lease arrangements,[9] not because of the landlord's desire to use the land for personal cultivation. The amendment allowed the maximum rent payable by a tenant to be no more than one-fourth of the crop on irrigated land, and no more than one-third of the crop on unirrigated land.[10]

In 1948 a new Act, the Bombay Tenancy and Agricultural Lands Act, was passed in order to correct defects that had been noted in the 1939 Act and its 1946 amendment. Again, in the 1948 Act, the protected tenants were recognized, and again, the landlord had rights of resumption of land for his personal use. But, in the 1948 Act, there was a change: the landlord was permitted to resume land only until he had reached a limit of fifty acres under his personal cultivation. While this qualification might have been important, it was in fact negated by another provision of the Act, through which a tenant could at any time "voluntarily" surrender his land to the landlord, who "could retain to himself the lands so surrendered without any ceiling restrictions whatsoever."[11] This meant that tenants could easily be coerced into "surrendering" their land "voluntarily." As Dandekar and Khudanpur succinctly note, "this single loop-hole made all provisions for protection ineffective in practice."[12] Indeed, Dandekar and Khudanpur's overall assessment of the 1948 Act, cited in the Government report on land reforms,[13] was entirely bleak, noting severe deficiencies both in the legislation and in its implementation.

> The main facts brought out by this investigation are, firstly, the extensive resumption and changes of tenants that took place even after the enforcing of the Act showing that *the protection given to tenants could not be effective in practice*; secondly, a more or less normal market in land showing that the *provisions for promoting the transfer of lands into the hands of the tillers were not quite effective*; and thirdly, an almost *complete absence of any signs of lowering the share and cash rents* or of any changes in the tenancy practices....The first two of these failures are attributable to certain *inherent weaknesses of the original Act of 1948*....The third failure, namely the failure to regulate rent, is however the most distressing for it is *entirely a failure of implementation*....there have been more cases of raising than of lowering the rents. The surprising element of the situation is that even the landlords reported to us the true rents they received and that they found no reason to conceal the facts....*For all practical purposes the Act did not exist.*

The Maharashtra government recognized the utter "failure of the 1948 Act to secure the tenure of tenancies, regulate rent and promote ownership of leased land by tenants," and so prepared "a comprehensive amendment of this Act, not so much with a view to regulating tenancy relation as to abolishing it altogether."[14] The result was an amending Act (Act 13 of 1956) passed in 1955 and brought into force in 1956. The amendment was designed to eliminate tenancies "by enabling the landlords to resume, within specified limits, their leased land for self-cultivation if they so wished and by making the tenants the owners of the remaining leased land."[15] Lands not resumed by landlords converted to tenant ownership on April 1, 1957, known in the legislation as Tiller's Day.

Nonetheless, in the 1970s a wide range of reports indicated that large numbers of adivasis, once in possession of land, had lost it. *Economic and*

*Tribal Landlessness*

*Political Weekly* declared

> ...large scale alienation of lands belonging to the scheduled tribes into the hands of non-scheduled tribe persons has taken place in the post-independence period. Adivasis all over India have been victims of this process....A non-official committee headed by S.M. Joshi toured the adivasi areas in Shahada taluka in Dhulia district and expressed the view that about 10,000 acres had passed into the hands of non-adivasis in Shahada taluka alone.[16]

A number of state documents also cite "land alienation" as one of the primary aspects of the "exploitation" of tribals.[17]

In 1974, the Maharashtra government issued an Ordinance (number 13 of 1974) designed to prevent further land alienation and to restore already alienated lands. The Ordinance acknowledged that "in a number of cases, particularly from Dhulia, Thana, and certain other districts, lands previously held by persons belonging to the scheduled tribes have gone into the hands of non-tribals." How did this situation come to be?

The 1956 Amendment was, like its predecessors, a flawed piece of legislation. The Act allowed for the transfer of land held by adivasis to non-adivasis. Based on their research in Dhule, Brahme and Upadhyaya describe how a large number of adivasi landholders were indebted, prior to the passage of the 1956 Amendment, to non-adivasi moneylenders; the latter were prohibited from purchasing adivasi land under the provisions of the Land Revenue Code. But with the passage of the new Amendment, such purchase was allowed. The non-adivasis were already utilizing the adivasis' lands; because of their indebtedness, the adivasis were working on their own lands as saldars in the employment of the moneylenders. Since the moneylenders were technically "tenants" on the land owned by the adivasis, they had only to apply as "tenants" under the Amendment in order to be named legal owners. Thus, quite within the law, the adivasi land was transferred to non-adivasi hands.[18]

In the early 1970s this issue of the alienation of adivasi lands, and the failure of legislation to have prevented it, became targets of organized direct action by the adivasi-based organizations.[19] Within a few years, their struggle was aided by the promulgation of an Ordinance (Number 13 of 1974) and the subsequent passage of two new pieces of legislation, all designed to return land to adivasis and to help them keep that which they already had. From the time of the passage of these two Acts—the Maharashtra Land Revenue Code and Tenancy Laws (Amendment) Act 1974 (Act No. 35 of 1974), which came into force on July 6, 1974; and the Maharashtra Restoration of Land to Scheduled Tribes Act 1974 (Act No. 14 of 1975), which came into force on November

1, 1975 – the movements worked to obtain their implementation.

S.D. Kulkarni attributes much of the impetus behind the issuance of the Ordinance as well as the passage of the Acts to the struggles of the adivasis over land alienation, particularly those led by Shramik Sanghatana in Dhule:

> Since 1972, the adivasis of Dhulia have carried on a struggle against these alienations. In 1973 the Government of Maharashtra appointed three special tahsildars to inquire into the legality of the alienations...they have reported that these alienations were more or less in accordance with the provisions of the law. This naturally did not satisfy the adivasis or their leaders. In February 1974 the adivasis in Dhulia district launched a satyagraha to regain these lands. The government has now come up with an Ordinance (No. 13 of 1974) supposedly to meet the adivasis' demands...[20]

However, while the adivasi actions may have added important pressure, the Maharashtra government seems to have become interested in the problem of adivasi land alienations prior to 1972. In March 1971, a committee under the Chairmanship of the Minister for Revenues had been appointed to examine the transfer of land from adivasis to non-adivasis in evident contravention of the Maharashtra Land Revenue Code of 1966, which had put certain restrictions on such transfers.[21] Government sources suggest that it was the report of this committee, received in April 1972, that was the impetus to the creation of the two pieces of legislation designed to restore and protect adivasi lands.[22]

The Maharashtra Land Revenue Code and Tenancy Laws (Amendment) Act 1974 (Act 25 of 1974) provides to the original adivasi landholders restoration of "all their lands which have gone into the hands of non-adivasis prior to July 6, 1974, as a result of illegal transactions, i.e., transactions effected in contravention of any law for the time being in force." Under this law, adivasis could bring cases to the attention of the Collector. More importantly, the Revenue Officers were empowered to start inquiry on their behalf. The Maharashtra Restoration of Land to Scheduled Tribes Act 1974 (Act 14 of 1975) is more far reaching in that it provides for restoration to the original tribal owners lands which were *legally* transferred to non-adivasis, either through purchase or exchange, any time *between April 1957 and July 6, 1974.*[23]

How effective have these acts been? A study analyzing their impact was published in 1979 by the Tribal Research and Training Institute, a research organization "under the direct control of the Secretary and Tribal Commissioner of the State."[24] Entitled *Land Alienation and the Restoration of Land*

## Tribal Landlessness

*to Scheduled Tribes People in Maharashtra*,[25] the study was conducted in Dhule, Thane, Nashik and Chandrapur districts because of the large number of tribals there, and because "these districts have experienced growing incidence of agitation by the tribal people on the issue of land problem (sic)."[26]

According to the report, "no actual assessment of the alienation of the tribal land could be made and it is therefore not possible to report the number of cases and area involved in such alienations."[27] Although the report does not, therefore, judge the full dimensions of the problem, it does examine 1) the registration of cases brought under Act 25 of 1974; 2) the government's initial scrutiny of the cases; 3) the issue of orders for restoration of land; and 4) the actual possession of registered land taken by the tribals. The study determined the following:

1) 14,770 cases were registered with the proper officials.
2) 14,201 cases (96 percent) were judged after preliminary investigation to be fit cases to order restoration of land to scheduled tribes.
3) After detailed scrutiny:
    a) in 6,267 cases (44 percent) land was ordered restored. The amount of land was 13,076 hectares to 7,545 adivasis.
    b) in 7,934 cases (56 percent) it was judged that transfer had taken place from one tribal to another, and the cases were therefore dropped.
4) Of the 6,267 cases in which land was ordered restored, *actual possession* had been taken in 4,895 cases (78 percent). In 9 percent of the cases in which land had been ordered restored, stays had been issued at various levels (Collector, Revenue Tribunal, Courts); and in 12 percent of the cases, possession was still to be handed over.

The author of the study deemed this progress of the disposal of cases to be "satisfactory."[28]

The same questions were asked of the Maharashtra Act 14 of 1975, regarding *legal* transfers. The findings were:

1) 31,404 cases were reported.
2) As of February 2, 1979, 23,724 cases had been decided (76 percent), with 24 percent of the cases still pending.
3) Of the 23,724 cases, land was ordered restored in 9,347 cases (39 percent). In 14,377 cases (61 percent), the land was not ordered restored.

4) Out of the 9,347 cases ordered restored, *actual possession* had taken place in 6,404 cases, or 68 percent of those ordered.

The conclusion reached by the author of the study is that "at the State level, the progress of the implementation of this Act, due to stay and other reasons, does *not* seem satisfactory."[29]

A number of explanations have been advanced for the unsatisfactory implementation of the Act. The author of the report concluded that three factors inhibited the impact of the protective legislation: "1) lacuna in the laws; 2) ignorance of the tribal people; and 3) complicated legal procedures involved in land restoration."[30]

The major lacuna in the law, which is not directly addressed by the report, is in its clause requiring the tribal receiving the land to pay a large sum:

> an amount equal to 48 times the assessment of the land or the amount of consideration paid by the non-tribal transferee for the acquisition of the land whichever is less *plus* the value of the improvements, if any, made by the non-Tribal transferee...[31]

On the face of it, this provision is absurd. To be sure, the government has an interest in protecting the rights of those non-tribals who in the past legally acquired land, and the law does accomplish that. But as a tool of land *restoration* to impoverished tribals, it cannot help but fail because of this clause. Only the wealthiest tribals would be able to raise the funds required by this law; it is hardly an aid to the poor. In contrast, there is no payment required under the provisions of the Maharashtra Land Revenue Code and Tenancy Laws (Amendment) Act, which relates to transfers that occurred illegally; this fact alone may account for the relative success of this Act compared to Act 14 of 1975.[32]

Another problem with the Act is that it provides for the return of lands only if they were originally transferred after April 1957. Many applications for land restoration have been rejected because they have asked for land that was sold prior to April 1957.[33] One state official formerly involved at a high level with tribal problems, while pointing to this dilemma, did not think the government could do much to correct it:

> This law really did not undo all that the tribals had been deprived of for 100 years before British rule ended. It undid only so much — just touched the fringe of the problem. The better land, the more fertile land, had been alienated over a hundred years ago, and government couldn't touch it. There's nothing that can be done under the constitution.[34]

These problems, along with the difficult legal procedures and the

## Tribal Landlessness

delays brought about by legal actions of the non-tribal landholders, may be more pertinent than the tribal ignorance of the law cited in the report.

In a breakdown of the state data into districts, the Tribal Research and Training Institute study found that the implementation was weaker in some areas than others; Thane and Dhule Districts were among those where implementation was less successful. In Thane, out of 326 cases in which land had been ordered restored, actual possession had taken place in 164, or 50 percent of the cases. In Dhule, out of 870 cases in which land had been ordered restored, possession had taken place in only 167, or 19 percent of the cases, a figure far lower than the state-wide average of 68 percent implementation.[35] Yet, these are districts that have organized movements.

Interviews with Shramik Sanghatana activists seemed to indicate that Shramik Sanghatana has, since the early 1970s, concentrated its attentions elsewhere. One Shramik Sanghatana activist explained,

> The landless...are not interested in land restoration. In their memories, they never had land; so they don't have any to "reclaim." So the whole issue of "reclaiming land" applies only to middle and upper sections of the adivasi population.[36]

Thus, the activists in Dhule seem to have recognized the limited utility of the Act. First, its applicability only to post-1957 transfers, while understandable, addresses the problems of only a few. Second, the law's insistence on financial payment of forty-eight times the land tax, plus improvements, severely limits its practical application. The law is simply not useful to the impoverished individual who cannot raise a large sum of money. Nor is it in the power of these political movements to raise cash. Because implementation of the law requires a cash outlay by those it seeks to benefit, it is no wonder that implementation is slow. Thus, while there has been greater success in returning illegally alienated lands, the movements' demand for the restoration of legally alienated lands seems to have been at least temporarily halted by these limitations in the law.

### *Land Ceilings*

Nor have the movements had greater success with state laws imposing ceilings on land holdings. Here, the political power of the vested interests has been stronger than the power of the movements. As in the case of laws regarding legally alienated land, the laws creating land ceilings have not provided the movements with good weapons for organizing demands. The 1971 amendment to the plainly defective 1961 Ceiling Act was introduced only after a delay lengthy enough to provide those with too much land the opportunity to circumvent the law. By the time the law came into effect, in 1975, there were few teeth left in it, and thus little a movement could legally demand. A movement whose tactics consist largely of demanding the rule of law must have a progressive law with which to work; in the case of land ceiling laws, as in the case of land alienation laws, the state government has so far not provided these.

Throughout India, the number of landless agricultural laborers has increased during the independence period.[37] As Brahme and Upadhyaya note,

> The increase in landlessness has led to considerable agrarian tensions and the Government has passed various Land Ceiling Acts attempting to curb the size of ownership and effect some kind of redistribution of land. For instance, the Maharashtra Government enacted in 1961 "The Maharashtra Government Agricultural Lands (Ceiling on the Holdings) Act" to effect redistribution of land.[38]

Even the Government of Maharashtra acknowledged that its implementation of this law was "rather slow," at least until 1966. As of 1966, according to a Government publication, of the 37,795 hectares of land declared surplus that were held by individual owners, only 533 hectares had been distributed.[39] *The Patriot* editorialized in 1971 that the 1961 law had been "totally ineffective...The total surplus land made available for distribution to the landless is so small an area that it has made no difference to the structure of land ownership."[40]

1971 was a national election year, and Mrs. Gandhi put pressure on state Congress governments to impose stricter land ceiling measures. The *Hindustan Times* of October 29, 1971 reported:

> Giving up its strong resistance to the lowering of land ceilings in Maharashtra, the Naik cabinet decided to fall in line with what he described as the national policy on the subject and issue an ordinance to further restrict the ceiling on cultivated and uncultivated land.

The same news article also noted the strong resistance to this new policy by the Naik cabinet:

> Though the Government was not unanimous on this matter, it came to the conclusion after long deliberation that it was now not possible to keep the present ceiling law which gives each individual in a family the right to have up to 155 acres of dry land.

> The Cabinet also decided, despite the misgivings of most of its members, to declare a family as the unit, in place of an individual, for fixation of the ceiling...
>
> The decision to issue an ordinance and not to call a special session of the legislature to pass the Bill on the subject would save the Government from the criticism that might come not from the Opposition, but from members of the Assembly Congress Party, *a majority of whom are themselves owning more land than might be prescribed.* (emphasis added)

Despite these misgivings, and the fear reportedly felt by Chief Minister Naik that food production would be adversely affected, plans to issue the Ordinance were made because "Prime Minister I. Gandhi...conveyed to Mr. Naik and other Congress Chief Ministers that they would find it difficult to go to the polls in February unless such a step...was taken."[41]

Although it felt pressured by the Union government to implement ceiling reform, the Naik government did so in such a way as to allow considerable evasive action; by announcing in advance the new regulations that were to be imposed, the Naik government provided ample opportunity for holders of large tracts of land to circumvent the law. *The Times of India* editorialized on November 29, 1971:

> Already the rich farmers in the State have taken full advantage of the Chief Minister's notice that legislation will soon be enacted to usher in the reform and make the family, instead of the individual, the basis for new ceilings. Thousands of acres of agricultural lands are said to have changed hands in the past week or two...the sleepy district officials, who normally take months to register such transfers, have suddenly turned into fiends for work and are actively helping the rich farmers....If the Maharashtra Government meant business, the least it could have done was to keep its own counsel before actually issuing the ordinance. Its failure to take this elementary precaution can hardly be ascribed to oversight.

Mr. Mohan Dharia, Union Minister of State for Planning, in a similar spirit criticized the Maharashtra cabinet's advance notice of its proposed ordinance, saying it had given rich farmers in the State a chance to "revolt" against the proposed lowering of the land ceiling.[42]

The delaying tactics continued; in January 1972, the Maharashtra Pradesh Congress Committee expressed the view that the State Government should not promulgate such an ordinance, but should await the results of the Assembly election and then introduce a bill.[43] The MPCC did state, however, that it would uphold the national policy on agricultural land ceilings that was part of Congress' 15 point *garibi hatao* (abolish poverty) program.[44] In 1972, the Maharashtra Assembly did indeed pass the Maharashtra Agricultural Lands (Lowering of Ceilings on Holdings) and (Amendment) Act 1972, which was not, however, brought into effect until September 19, *1975*,[45] thus prolonging the period in which the rich could find ways to evade the law.

The new amendment was expected to make available one and one half lakh (150,000) hectares for distribution. The 1961 Act had made available approximately one and one quarter lakh (125,000) hectares.[46] Of this land, the government decided to reserve half for distribution among scheduled castes and tribes, nomadic castes and tribes, and other backward landless;[47] in other words, about 1.38 lakh (138,000) hectares would go to the weakest sections. The 1971 census counted 29.54 lakh (2,954,000) scheduled tribes in Maharashtra.[48] Given these numbers, one can see how *The Times of India* concluded that "there is not much hope of giving land to the landless," and urged instead an emphasis on increased employment and better working conditions to improve their lives.[49] Even with perfect implementation, the land ceiling laws would make only a small dent in the problems of the landless. And, the problem of the limited amount of land available for distribution was compounded by the fact that "nearly all the land that has been distributed has been dry and barren. Only 250 of the 125,000 hectares that...the Maharshtra government acquired after implementing its ceiling law in 1962 was irrigated land."[50]

Thus the land ceiling laws did not provide the adivasi movements with good tools for organizing demands that government implement its own laws. The laws were, from the movements' perspective, barely worth implementing. The organized adivasis have pressed for more land by instead demanding the regularization of encroachments on government-owned forest lands.

## *Forest Encroachment Regularization*

The loss of adivasi land that began in the nineteenth century was paralleled by decreasing rights to the forests. In 1894 the British government imposed severe restrictions: customary tribal control over the forests and their resources was lost. The restrictions were further tightened in 1952, leaving the tribals with no legal rights except for the right of way and the right to water courses.[51]

With the loss of livelihood that had derived from cultivation, and the further loss of subsidiary income from the collection of forest products, many adivasis who had lost their lands moved into interior areas and began to cultivate

## Tribal Landlessness

the forest lands. Their economic predicament left them little alternative.[52]

> However, these occupancies were treated as encroachments, and occasionally the cultivators were forcibly made to discontinue cultivation. Sometimes, fines were levied and cultivation was allowed for the season. Sometimes, however, the cultivators were imprisoned and their crops destroyed.[53]

Numerous adivasi demonstrations throughout the 1970s have demanded the regularization, or legalization, of these encroachments. The struggle in this instance was initially not for the implementation of existing legislation, but for the passage of new legislation. Recognizing that this is a state-wide issue, a number of localized movements formed a temporary coalition, the Joint Action Committee, to put pressure on state government; the coalition in turn became allied to several opposition political parties, particularly CPI(M) and Janata. This alliance put sufficient pressure on the Congress-Congress I government of Maharashtra to win a significant concession. A change in government followed soon after the announced concession, and the new coalition included the CPI(M) and Janata. As will be seen below, once in power these parties introduced legislation that provided a partial victory for the movements. The movements, seeking further change, have continued their agitational activities against the political parties, now incumbents, which had formerly fought on their side.

In the 1960s, the Government of Maharashtra legalized some forest encroachments, but also issued orders to have some encroachers forcibly removed.[54] In 1969, the government announced that it planned to distribute more than 17,000 hectares of forest lands among the adivasis in Thane. *The Times of India* editorialized that the government, in so doing, "has merely yielded to local political pressures....It is also an admission of its failure to deal with the adivasi agitation led by extremists of the Left and the local Congress leaders who entered the fray in the hope of containing the Leftist challenge."[55] Two years later, during a satyagraha held in Thane to protest government eviction of some adivasis from encroached land, Godavari Parulekar charged that the government's claim to have distributed this forest land was "bogus," for the distribution had been "only on paper." Even that land which had been given to the adivasis, she maintained, was too rocky to be cultivable without further help from the government.[56]

Indeed, the difference between the government's pronouncements and government's actions regarding regularization appear to be great. Mrs. Mrinal Gore, a Socialist MLA from northern Bombay in 1972-77, and in 1977-79 a Janata MP, relates a series of events that occurred in Chandrapur District, in which she charges the government's apparent efforts to give forest land to be adivasis were insincere:

> The Manikghad area of Chandrapur had been entirely a forest area. In the late 1950s and early 1960s, government gave leases to contractors to cut the trees. After the land was cleared, adivasis settled and started cultivating it. Then, in 1972, the government issued a resolution throwing them off because the land was forest land. The harvest that was ready was burned down by the government, as were some of the adivasis' huts.
>
> Some progressive MLAs argued that [the adivasis] had worked the land and should be allowed to stay. In 1973, the Socialist Party organized a satyagraha. Thousands of adivasis participated, and occupied the land. Government brought in a large number of police, and over a thousand were arrested. Agitations continued for the next two years, and in 1974, government issued a resolution allowing the encroachers to stay.
>
> But, instead of correctly implementing this resolution, government instead put the lands in the name of adivasis who were not actually occupying it. So the people who, according to government records, now had legal possession could not cultivate the land because others were already doing so. Those who were actually cultivating the land did not have ownership rights to it. This government-created situation served to divide the adivasis.
>
> The whole thing was just a showpiece for the Assembly — just an effort to fool the Assembly. Those who made the decisions weren't really connected with the problem, and they wouldn't accept the advice of those people who actually worked in and understood the area. The decision-makers never took a real interest in the problem; they just wanted to show they'd done something. There was no real sincerity there.[57]

In 1972, government issued a resolution regularizing certain encroachments made up to August 15, 1972.

> The order was, however, limited to government fallow land, village grazing lands and forest lands in control of the Revenue Department. Encroachments on forest lands in control of the Forest Department

were excluded from the operation of the order. Most of the above orders were not implemented properly and a considerable number of encroachments were not regularised.

As a result, there were continuing agitations "in almost all the districts where adivasis have considerable population."[58]

In 1974, there were major demonstrations in Dhule District around the issue of forest encroachments, and the government responded with considerable police power. On June 5, 1974, following the Shramik Sanghatana-organized strikes that took place in Dhule around wage issues, the Maharashtra Minister of Home Affairs began a tour of the adivasi areas in Shahada and Taloda Talukas, promising to see to the implementation of the Minimum Wages Act. At the same time, 400 to 500 Special Reserve Police were sent into Nawapur Taluka to forcibly remove 4,000 adivasi families from 20,000 acres of forest lands they had been cultivating for a number of years.[59] While essential to these adivasis' livelihood, these encroachments were not legal. Mies reports that the government decided that this land should be reserved for the planting of teak trees; the police cleared the land for this purpose by asking the people to leave their huts, burning the huts to the ground, and then transporting the adivasis by truck far away from their original villages.[60] Patil and the opposition party leaders alleged a worse "reign of terror," including beatings of men and women, raping, and looting, as the encroachers were driven from the land.[61]

The adivasis in Nawapur had been organized into Kisan Sabhas by the CPI(M). These groups and others, including Shramik Sanghatana, joined together in a march to the Collector's Office, where they presented him with demands that included the withdrawal of the Special Reserve Police and the regularization of the encroachments. A week later, on July 1, the Collector held a press conference in which he alleged that the CPI(M) had established a parallel government in Nawapur and Sakri Talukas, and in which he further declared government's determination to remove the encroachers.[62] The charge of parallel government seems to indicate that the government was seriously alarmed by the level of organization shown by the adivasi encroachers. More Special Reserve Police were brought into the area following the press conference.[63] More violence between police and adivasis occurred throughout July and August,[64] and nearly 1,000 adivasis were arrested in satyagrahas led by the CPI(M) and Shramik Sanghatana.[65]

Although the District Collector had stated in his July 1 press conference that there was no problem of encroachments in the Shahada and Taloda Talukas, the number of SRP units in those areas was also increased.[66] On August 2, Chief Minister Sharad Pawar announced in the Legislative Assembly that the government had decided to raise two new units of SRP in order to post them to the districts of Dhule, Nasik and Jalgaon. On August 25, he stated that the SRP had been stationed in Shahada for the purpose of defending the adivasis from oppression by the landlords.[67] However, some observers saw the dramatic increase of police in the area as evidence of an effort to intimidate and suppress the adivasis, and to limit the influence of the groups organizing them:

> When the landlords saw that the peasants did not stop at certain symbolic actions, but wanted land, and their organisation [Shramik Sanghatana] was taking on a more clearly Marxist character, they did not bother about the non-violent character of the movement, but took to their traditional means of violent repression and terror. At this point it also became evident that the government, which to a certain extent had encouraged the mass mobilisation and the non-violent struggle because it wanted to co-opt the movement, put in all its machinery of armed law and order forces to control the movement.[68]
>
> The real reason for the state government's campaign to evict the landless, mainly adivasis, from forest waste-land in Dhulia district...may be the Congress Party's fear of losing its influence over the whole of the adivasi belt due to the rapidly increasing following of the CPI(M) and the Shramik Sanghatana. Local Congressmen have been persistently urging the Forest Minister, who is also in charge of Dhulia District, to crush the adivasi and other "encroachers" on forest land together with their organisations. The brutality with which the operation has been carried out and the degree of force used suggest political motives on the part of the government.[69]

On June 13, 1974 a committee was appointed by the Government of Maharashtra to prepare an Adivisai Sub-Plan, designed to speed up the socio-economic development of the tribals. Given the amount of agitation that had taken place among adivasis throughout the state, especially in Thane and Dhule, the establishment of the Sub-Plan appeared to be a repetition of the same carrot-and-stick strategy seen on a more dramatic scale in Srikakulam: the repression of the movement with police power, followed by the attempt to co-opt the demands of the nascent movements in order to weaken their appeal to the impoverished.

The encroachers in these events were legally in the wrong, which allowed the government, with some legitimacy, to remove them from the forests. But the intense poverty of the adivasis and their widely recognized exploita-

## Tribal Landlessness

tion gave them some moral standing. Thus the government had to defend its use of police power, and the movements were then able to press forward to achieve more favorable legislation.

During the Emergency, the government "took harsh steps to vacate encroachments on forest lands."[70] With the Emergency's end, and the re-emergence of competitive electoral politics, agitations designed to obtain the legalization of encroachments picked up steam. In January 1978 a two-day Maharashtra Adivasi conference was held in Thane district, attended by 2,000 delegates from around the state and a large number of non-delegate adivasis belonging to several different political parties.[71] The conference was organized by opposition parties—Janata, CPI(M), the Peasants and Workers Party, and the Republican Party—and was presided over by Godavari Parulekar. Speakers at the conference included the secretary of the All-India Janata Party, Surendra Mohan; the president and secretary of the Maharashtra unit of Janata, S.M. Joshi and Pannalal Surana; and the CPI(M) MP from Dahanu, L.S. Kom.[72]

The Janata Party's interest in the adivasis' plight seemed tied to its electoral ambition for state control following the Emergency. Its involvement at the grass roots level generated publicity for the party as the defender of the downtrodden. Among the pledges made in its election manifesto published before the Maharashtra Assembly elections in February was one to regularize encroachments that had occurred up until a certain date. When the elections were held, no party received an absolute majority. Congress and Congress (I) together formed a ruling coalition and on March 7, 1978, Vasantrao Patil was sworn in as Chief Minister. Janata, still in the opposition, continued its agitations.

In early May, the state Janata Party announced plans to organize a satyagraha in conjunction with the CPI(M), Bhoomi Sena, and Gram Swarajya Samiti (a group combining "constructive work" and political organization, based in Jawhar taluka of Thane District)[73] to demand regularization of land encroached upon by adivasis. The Janata leaders of the satyagraha cited a "recent incident at Agari in Dhule district where about 14 adivasis were evicted from the land occupied by them and fined Rs. 500 and sentenced to undergo a month's simple imprisonment" as a reason for organizing the satyagraha.[74] The satyagraha, demanding "pattas" (documents) to legalize the encroachments, was held in front of the tehsildars' offices in Thane and Dhule Districts.

At the same time that he announced this satyagraha, state Janata Party Secretary Pannalal Surana also told reporters that the party would soon be organizing morchas to demand that elections to the Bombay Municipal Corporation and 23 zilla parishads be held soon after the monsoon. Other demands of the morchas would include debt cancellation for small and medium farmers; the filling of vacancies in government and cooperatives reserved for scheduled castes, scheduled tribes and neo-Buddhists; as well as the "reduction of penal charges in respect of slum dwellers." Surana also announced an upcoming state-level political conference, to include 500 Dalits, the "main purpose" of which would be "to mobilize public opinion against the present coalition Government which had showed its inability to run the administration and curb goondaism."[75] Clearly, the plight of the "weaker sections" had become an important political tool for Janata. At the same time, the agitations and publicity kept the adivasis' cause in the public eye.

On June 28, 1978, *The Indian Express* reported that Janata intended to launch another satyagraha in the first week of August to highlight the problems of adivasis and landless labourers. Pannalal Surana said that morchas would go to Collectors' offices, and there would be cultivation of lands encroached on by the adivasis; they would demand that encroachment land belonging to the Forest and Revenue Departments be regularized.

These agitational activities did succeed in moving the government. On July 11, the Deputy Chief Minister for Forests, N.K. Tirpude, announced in the Maharashtra Assembly that the Forest Department had prepared a scheme to regularize encroachments on the Department's land, if the encroachments had occurred prior to March 31, 1978.

> Mr. Tirpude pointed out that there had been encroachment on 1,42,000 hectares of the Forest Department's land. Under the scheme, either the encroached land would be retained with the adivasis or an alternate land would be provided to him (sic) so that he would not be deprived of his economic activities. The adivasis...had encroached upon the forest land as they had no other means of livelihood, he pointed out.[76]

With this announcement, the Congress-Congress I government acceded to partial, but significant, demands of the adivasi movements, and also duplicated the Janata call for regularization. The adivasi claim, pressed by major as well as minor opposition parties, had become a cause to be politically embraced.

The success of achieving positive legislation strengthened the adivasi movement's ability to press for more, and to organize forces to demand implementation. It has been around this issue of forest encroachment that the unity of disparate adivasi-based movements and political parties has most successfully coalesced.

Although the Patil government had announced its intention to regularize encroachments, the Congress-Congress I coalition resigned on July 17, and was replaced with a non-Congress ministry, the Progressive Democratic Front, composed of several parties including Janata, CPI(M), and the Peasants and

## Tribal Landlessness

Workers Party, and headed by Sharad Pawar. The new government made good on Janata's election manifesto, and on December 27, 1978, issued a Resolution to regularize encroachments on government fallow lands, grazing lands, and forest lands "as existing on March 31, 1978."[77] The resolution provided that encroachments would be regularized if the encroacher belonged to a scheduled caste or scheduled tribe and/or if the person's annual family income did not exceed Rs. 3,600.

There were, however, several conditions which met with protest from the organized adivasis, now pressuring the political parties who had argued against the Congress government on their behalf. The order applied only to those encroachments in existence on March 31, 1978. But during the Emergency, the government had taken "harsh steps to vacate encroachments on forest lands" and "some people had been prevented from cultivating the land after the Emergency"; those earlier encroachments were not eligible for regularization under the new law.[78] Adivasi-based groups therefore organized and demonstrated to demand that all encroachments *which had existed* between 1960 and 1978, not just those existing *on* March 31, 1978, be regularized.[79]

The issue at this time was one of legislating, not implementing, and a number of adivasi-based groups, initially from Thane, but soon from around the state's adivasi belts, formed a coalition in a unified attempt to influence state legislative policy.[80] The CPI(M) was initially active in this struggle, but it demanded regularization only for encroachments that had occurred between 1972 and 1978. In a 1980 interview, Godavari Parulekar said about this demand, "We should not make demands which are so extreme that they may be absurd."[81] Of course, the fact that CPI(M) was a partner in the new ruling coalition also no doubt contributed to the "moderation" of CPI(M)'s demands.

In late June 1979, the coalition organized a satyagraha; between June 28 and July 4, 1058 people courted arrest, and 55 were sentenced to 15 days' imprisonment.[82] On July 4 an adivasi delegation, including the MLA from Palghar, met with the Chief Minister, who promised a reconsideration of the matter and a Cabinet decision by July 12. At his request, the satyagraha was suspended. To maintain the pressure and the publicity, the CPI(M) organized a dharna in front of the Assembly on July 9; MLAs of both the Janata and CPI(M) parties addressed the rally, promising to join it if the Cabinet did not meet the adviasis' demands.[83]

On July 13, the Revenue Minister announced in the Assembly the results of the July 12 Cabinet meeting which, while favorable to the adivasis, did not go as far as most of the groups wanted. The new decision was to regularize all encroachments which had existed between April 1, 1972 and March 30, 1978, provided the land was not presently being used by the Forest or other government Departments and was not scheduled for such use. All other encroachments were to be summarily evicted.[84]

The adivasis have responded by continuing their demands for the regularization of encroachments from 1960 to 1978. On July 20, over 1,200 adivasis from Thane, Dhule, Chandrapur and Yeotmal Districts demonstrated before the state legislature. A satyagraha campaign was begun on August 20.[85]

Despite the continuing agitations, the adivasis have been unable to make any further legislative changes. There has thus been a partial victory. According to Shramik Sanghatana activists in Dhule, the law has reduced the amount of government interference with the encroachers. "The threat of fines for working forest land has diminished," said one, "but nothing has been done to implement the decision of the government. So far, there has not even been an enquiry commission set up to determine who is going to be given title to the land."[86]

The impact of the struggle has been mixed; a government resolution more favorable to the adivasi position was ordered, but the resolution was not as sweeping as the adivasis wanted and therefore eliminated from regularization a large number of encroachments. The implementation has not been prompt,[87] but the existence of the order has limited government interference with the encroachers.

The struggle also saw a state-wide coalition emerge capable of effecting legislative change. Such coalition-building would seem to be essential if localized groups are to have an impact on the formulation of state legislation. The ability of the groups to come together, even temporarily, in pursuit of common goals at the state level would seem to portend a stronger future for them.

But there is a deep ambivalence among the movements about coalition-building. The leaders of Shramik Sanghatana in particular are wary of permanent coalitions, especially coalitions with political parties. They do not want the movements to be used by opportunistic politicians, and they suspect most, if not all, political parties of opportunism. They want decision-making to emerge more and more from below, not from a coalition of elites. Consequently, they enter into coalitions gingerly and as a temporary measure.

As will be seen in the next chapter, the state government has already passed useful legislation regarding key areas of concern to Shramik Sanghatana and Bhoomi Sena. The movements' immediate growth may therefore rest less on the passage of new legislation than on their success in gaining the implementation of legislation that already exists. And implementation remains a more localized problem, requiring local pressures. The movements' ability to grow will continue to rely heavily on the local, immediate changes they are able to make for individuals through implementation of the law.

## NOTES

1. Government of Maharashtra, *Report of the Committee Appointed by the Government of Maharashtra for Evaluation of Land Reforms* (Bombay, 1974), p. 1. The Committee relied heavily in the sections relating to the 1937 and 1948 laws on a study done in 1957 by the Gokhale Institute of Politics and Economics on behalf of the Research Programmes Committee of the Planning Commission: V.M. Dandekar and G.J. Khudanpur, *Workings of Bombay Tenancy Act, 1948: Report of Investigation* (Pune: Gokhale Institute of Politics and Economics, 1957).
2. *Report of the Committee...for Evaluation of Land Reforms*, p. 8.
3. Ibid., p. 7.
4. Brahme and Upadhyaya, pp. 39-40. See also "Organizing the Adivasis," p. 173; and the Symington Report.
5. *Report of the Committee...for Evaluation of Land Reforms*, p. 8.
6. Ibid.
7. Ibid., p. 9. Emphasis added.
8. Ibid., p. 9.
9. E.g., the performance of any act injurious to the land, the failure to cultivate it personally, or the use of the land for nonagricultural purposes. Ibid., p. 9.
10. Ibid., pp. 9-10.
11. Dandekar and Khudanpur, p. 5.
12. Ibid.
13. Ibid., p. 187; *Report of the Committee...for Evaluation of Land Reforms*, p. 11. Emphasis added by present author.
14. *Report of the Committee...for Evaluation of Land Reforms*, p. 12.
15. Ibid.
16. S.D. Kulkarni, "Alienation of Adivasis' Lands: Government Not Serious," *Economic and Political Weekly*, August 31, 1974, p. 1469.
17. See, for example, Government of Maharashtra, *Draft Sixth Five-Year Tribal Sub-Plan, 1978-83*, p. 8.
18. Brahme and Upadhyaya, pp. 43-44. Brahme and Upadhyaya drew in part from a pamphlet by S.D. Kulkarni, published in Marathi, and cited as *Alienation of Adivasi Land—A New Act* (Gramayan, Poona, 1974).
19. See Chapter Eight above for descriptions of some early agitations.
20. Kulkarni, "Alienation of Adivasis' Lands...," p. 1469.
21. Government of Maharashtra, Directorate-General of Information and Public Relations, *Decade of Progress: Land Reforms* (Bombay, January 1976), p. 10. P.R. Sirsalkar, *Land Alienation and Restoration of Land to Scheduled Tribes People in Maharashtra* (A report of the Tribal Research and Training Institute, Pune, 1979), p. 3. (This report is also summarized in the *Tribal Research Bulletin*, September 1979.)
22. Ibid.
23. *Decade of Progress*, p. 12.
24. Government of Maharashtra, Department of Social Welfare, Cultural Affairs, Sports and Tourism, *Draft Annual Tribal Sub-Plan (1980-81)*, p. 14.
25. P.R. Sirsalkar, *Land Alienation and Restoration of Land to Scheduled Tribes People in Maharashtra* (Pune, 1979).
26. Sirsalkar, in *Tribal Research Bulletin*, p. 3.
27. Sirsalkar, *Land Alienation...*, p. 11.
28. Ibid., pp. 11-12. S.D. Kulkarni also writes that this law "has been more or less satisfactorily implemented." "Problems of Tribal Development in Maharashtra," *Economic and Political Weekly*, September 20, 1980, p. 1599.
29. Sirsalkar, *Land Alienation...*, p. 14. Emphasis added.
30. Sirsalkar, in *Tribal Research Bulletin*, p. 5.

31. Act No. XIV of 1975, subsection 4, clause b. Emphasis in original.
32. This point is made in Gautam S.G. Vohra, "Return of Land to Adivasis: Slow Pace of Progress," *The Times of India*, May 18, 1976. The Sirsalkar report does stress the poverty of the tribals—"the main reason of land alienation is poor economic conditions of the Scheduled Tribes"—but does not point to the economic demand the law places on the tribals which is clearly out of the reach of most of them. Quote from *Tribal Research Bulletin*, p. 5.
33. Vohra.
34. Interview with "B," February 28, 1980.
35. Sirsalkar, *Land Alienation...*, p. 15.
36. Interview with "J," January 26, 1980.
37. The percentage of landless agricultural labour households among all agricultural labour households increased from 50.07 percent in 1950-51 to 61.17 percent in 1963-64. Ranjit Sau, "Indian Economic Growth—Constraints and Prospects," *Economic and Political Weekly*, Annual Number, January 1970; cited in Brahme and Upadhyaya, p. 4.
38. Brahme and Upadhyaya, p. 6.
39. *Decade of Progress...*, p. 2.
40. *Patriot*, November 23, 1971.
41. *Hindustan Times*, October 29, 1971.
42. *The Hindu*, November 23, 1971; see also *The Times of India*, November 29, 1971.
43. *The Times of India*, January 2, 1972.
44. *The Times of India*, January 3, 1972.
45. *Decade of Progress*, p. 3.
46. Ibid., pp. 2-4; *Times of India*, October 20, 1974.
47. *Decade of Progress*, p. 4; *The Times of India*, October 20, 1975.
48. Cited in *Draft Annual Tribal Sub-Plan (1980-81)*, p. 1.
49. *The Times of India*, October 20, 1975.
50. Gautan S.G. Vohra, "Land Reforms a Failure in Maharashtra," *The Times of India*, February 23, 1979.
51. "Organizing the Adivasis," p. 174-A.
52. The government has an ecological interest in preserving forest land. As was noted in the Srikakulam discussion, in 1952 the Government of India decided to try to restore 33.3 percent of India's land to forest. The response of Maharashtra's adivasis to the ecological argument is that the lands they have taken over for cultivation have been wastelands, de-forested for years, and that regularization of encroachments on such lands would not affect the present forests. See Kulkarni, "Encroachments on Forest Lands: The Experience of Maharashtra," *Economic and Political Weekly*, November 10, 1979, pp. 1847-1848.
53. Ibid., p. 1846.
54. In 1960, certain encroachments in Nasik were regularized, and in 1961, some in Thane were regularized. In 1968, however, a Resolution was issued to take possession of encroached lands without waiting for the cutting of standing crops by the encroachers. Ibid., p. 1846.
55. *The Times of India*, August 18, 1969. See also Sharad Patil, "Forest Development or Adivasi Oppression in Maharashtra?" *Social Scientist*, October 1974, p. 53.
56. *People's Democracy* [Organ of the Communist Party of India (Marxist)], August 15, 1971, p. 12.
57. Interview with Mrinal Gore, February 15, 1980.
58. Kulkarni, "Encroachments on Forest Lands...," p. 1846.
59. The following account is drawn from Mies, pp. 479-480, and two articles by Sharad Patil: "Forest Development or Adivasi Oppression in Maharashtra?" *Social Scien-*

## Tribal Landlessness

tist, October 1974, pp. 54-55, and "Government's War...," p. 1809; the figure of 500 and the number of adivasis involved were given at a press conference held by four opposition party leaders demanding the withdrawal of the police from the area. The four opposition leaders were Pannalal Surana, General Secretary of the State Socialist Party; Datta Deshmukh, Lal Nishan Party; N.D. Patil, Peasants and Workers Party, and S.Y. Kolhatkar, CPI(M). *The Indian Express*, July 23, 1974.

60. Mies, p. 479.
61. "Forest Development...," p. 54; "Government's War...," p. 1809; report of press conference in *The Indian Express*, July 23, 1974.
62. "Government's War...," p. 1809.
63. Mies, p. 480.
64. "Government's War...," p. 1810; press conference, *The Indian Express*, July 23, 1974.
65. "Government's War...," p. 1810; "Forest Development...," p. 55.
66. Mies, p. 480; "Government's War...," p. 1810.
67. "Government's War...," p. 1810.
68. Mies, p. 481.
69. "Government's War...," p. 1809.
70. "Encroachments...," p. 1847.
71. *The Times of India*, January 11, 1978.
72. *The Times of India*, January 10, 1978; January 11, 1978; and January 9, 1978.
73. S.D. Kulkarni, "Problems of Tribal Development in Maharashtra," *Economic and Political Weekly*, September 20, 1980, p. 1600.
74. *The Indian Express*, May 4, 1978.
75. *The Indian Express*, May 26, 1978.
76. *The Indian Express*, July 12, 1978.
77. Cited in Kulkarni, "Encroachments...," p. 1847.
78. Ibid.
79. Joint Action Committee, *Forests We Will Not Destroy; Our Lands We Will Not Quit: An Open Call/Challenge*. 2-page cyclostyled leaflet, August 14, 1979.
80. A number of press releases describing demonstrations and explaining demands were issued by the "Joint Action Committee." Two press releases issued in July listed the following organizations under the title Joint Action Committee: Bhoomi Sena, Palghar; Kashtakari Sanghatna, Dahanu-Talasari; Kranti-Sena, Talasari; Plot Dharak Sanghatna, Wada; and Gram Swarajya Samithi, Jawahar; all these are in Thane District. In a press release of August 12, 1979, Shramik Sanghatana, Dhule; the Yeotmal District Adivasi Andolan Action Committee; Bhoomi Sangharsha Samithi of Chandrapur District; and the Tribal Conscientization Centre, Pune, were also listed. Plot Dharak Sanghatna was no longer listed.
81. Kannan Srinivasan, "Organizing Tribals in Thane," *Economic and Political Weekly*, October 4, 1980, p. 1647.
82. *Regarding Regularisation of Encroachments on Government Waste/Gairan/Forest Land in Maharashtra in reference to the Government Resolution (GR) of 27th December 1978 and amendments to the GR announced in the assembly on 13th July 1979*. Press release issued July 18, 1979 by the Joint Action Committee.
83. Ibid.; *Forests We Will Not Destroy...*; "Encroachments...," p. 1849; and interview with Godavari Parulekar, February 26, 1980.
84. In addition, encroachments in the middle of the forest or on land above 10 percent gradient would not be regularized. "Encroachments...," p. 1847.
85. Joint Action Committee, *Forests We Will Not Destroy...*"; Encroachments...," p. 1849.
86. Interview with "K," January 29, 1980. This information was confirmed in a

separate interview with "I," February 5, 1980.

87. The implementation of the government order published on December 27, 1978, was to be completed by May 31, 1979. S.D. Kulkarni reported in November 1979 that the initial listings of encroachments had not yet been prepared "in a number of villages." "Encroachments...," pp. 1847-48. In February 1980 a forest official in Thane stated that regularizations there had begun. Interview with "D," February 16, 1980.

# 10
# STATE AND MOVEMENT INTERACTIONS: WORK AND WAGES

In Maharashtra, and throughout India, there is frequently a gap between government's intentions, as articulated in legislation, and government's capability, as measured by the *implementation* of law. For a variety of reasons ranging from scarce resources and administrative limitations to the power of local vested interests to influence officials, implementation at the local level does not keep pace with progressive legislation.

This chapter demonstrates the effectiveness with which organized agitations by Shramik Sanghatana and Bhoomi Sena have been able to achieve local implementation of two existing laws: the Employment Guarantee Scheme and the Minimum Wages Act. As will be seen below, many government officials openly acknowledge that government does not have the capacity to fully implement either of these laws. The movements have discovered that government is more likely to direct its resources to implementation in a locality where organized groups make vigorous demands. When such demands are localized, and few in number, the government has the capacity to respond.

However, when the government responds more positively in localities that have organized movements than in those that do not, it helps to legitimize and strengthen the notion of grass roots organization. Although government resents the legal, but aggressive, pressure from below, its positive response to that pressure demonstrates its utility. The government may thus become a collaborator in the growth of such movements. In the short run, government must respond to demands that the laws be implemented. But by so doing, government may be helping to create a broader movement whose increased demands it would be incapable of meeting; this is certainly the hope of the movements.

### *Employment Guarantee Scheme*

The Employment Guarantee Scheme (EGS) is an excellent example of a government program that works best with pressure from below. The law is filled with loopholes that undermine the stated intent of the program, for if every citizen who was eligible demanded his or her rights under the scheme it could not function. In reality, the state does not have the capacity to fully implement the law.

The existence of the EGS, however, enables elected and bureaucratic officials to claim that the state is generous and just to its poor. When the organized rural poor set out to plug the loopholes, they are frequently regarded as trouble makers. Yet it is clear that implementation of the law occurs more fully when there is organized pressure from the people whom the law was designed to benefit.

### *History of the Employment Guarantee Scheme*

Maharashtra is chronically deficient in the production of foodgrains;[1] its agricultural production has stagnated in the years since independence.[2] It is a state with two faces: one, the prosperous industrialized Bombay region, and the other, an underemployed impoverished countryside.[3] The introduction of the EGS may be seen as government's acknowledgment of the severe problems of rural unemployment and underemployment; it is an effort to minimize crises in the countryside that would threaten the position of landlords and also, via emigration of workers in search of jobs, the stability and relative prosperity of the cities.[4]

Forerunners of the EGS date back to the mid-1960s.[5] In 1964-65 a pilot scheme for integrated area development sponsored by V.S. Page, then head of the Legislative Council, was initiated in one block. Its aim was to provide productive employment for the rural poor, specifically agricultural laborers, rural artisans, and small and marginal farmers. The program provided loans and subsidies for wells, the purchase of animals and other developmental projects. In 1968-69 the program was expanded, and for the first time offered an employment guarantee. The lessons learned from these early efforts were applied to the initiation on a state wide basis of the Employment Guarantee Scheme, introduced in April 1972.[6] The scheme was designed, according to Chief Minister V.P. Naik, to guarantee employment to able-bodied adults in the rural areas who could not obtain any work in agriculture or departmental works.[7] The EGS first was mentioned as an election promise made by the ruling state Congress Party during the period of the drought in 1970-71, and was then one of the items in the 15-point program adopted by the state legislature in September 1971.[8] Mrinal Gore, former Socialist Party MLA from Northern Bombay, contends that Congress responded primarily to agitational activities:

During the famine, there were many agitations for the right to work. The EGS is to the credit of government; but it came into being because of pressure from the opposition.[9]

The scheme was barely initiated when, in 1972, it was postponed in order to undertake relief works that were necessitated by the increasingly widespread and harmful drought affecting most parts of the state. The postponement temporarily put off the criticism that opposition parties had already introduced concerning the wages to be paid under the EGS. The wages were to be fixed in such a way that workers would not receive more than the prevailing minimum agricultural wage during the non-harvest season "so that the scheme did not have any adverse effects on agricultural operations."[10] This feature of the scheme was intended to prevent agricultural workers from being attracted away from private to state employment. In effect, this wage policy spoke to the interests of the landowners of Maharashtra for cheap labor; it also meant that the laborers on EGS would be working for wages that were less than those necessary to sustain life.

State officials readily acknowledge that it is virtually impossible for government to ensure that private agricultural workers are paid the legal minimum wage. One former official in Thane District explained that with so much unemployment, the landowner can always find someone who is willing to work for less than minimum wage. Workers will actually sign documents stating that they have received more wages than they actually have, because this is the only way to get employment at all. That is why, the official explained, it is impossible for government to monitor wages and why EGS wages have been designed to be slightly less than minimum so as not to take people away from private jobs.[11]

On the other hand, the 1973 Page report on agricultural employment suggested that EGS wages should be equal to the legal minimum wage in order to encourage landowners to obey the minimum wage law.[12] Members of the opposition in the state legislature also insisted that government pay minimum wage for those employed under the scheme.[13] Organized labor in the state echoed this demand; in May 1972 the Maharashtra state conference of the AITUC stated in a resolution

> When nothing is being done to raise and implement minimum wages for agricultural labourers in the state, which happen to be one of the lowest in the entire country (sic), the wage policy pursued through this scheme will only serve to depress the wages of agricultural labourers and actually inhibit any trend or movement toward getting them raised.

## Work And Wages

During the most serious drought year, 1972-73, four million workers were employed in scarcity projects in addition to the four hundred thousand who were employed at normal departmental works throughout the state. These workers constituted about 45 percent of the labor force in the drought affected areas. However, not only were many of the works unproductive in terms of staving off future famines,[15] but the wages paid to workers on these projects were so low that, in one estimate, "people are unable to meet even half their foodgrain requirements with these earnings."[16]

As with the famine relief works, the ambitious aims proclaimed by government for the EGS, which began again in 1974-75, have not been reached. The existence of the scheme allows government officials to take credit for being progressive and caring for the needs of the poor, while at the same time loopholes in the scheme ensure that while some of the rural poor will indeed be helped, no significant change in the status quo will result. Such legislation can be approved by legislators in the full knowledge that while their vote makes them appear progressive, and may indeed have some positive consequences for the poor, the limited implementation of the legislation will largely safeguard the interests of the rural powers.

The law does, however, provide political activists with a legitimate channel for making demands on government. Having a law on the books which promises employment enables activists to organize for precisely that. Given the existence of progressive legislation, demonstrators ask for nothing radical, but merely the rule of law. The demand that government implement existing legislation cannot be repressed by the coercive machinery of the state without a loss of state legitimacy.

### *Characteristics of the Employment Guarantee Scheme*

A document of the Government of Maharashtra Planning Department proclaims that the objective of the Employment Guarantee Scheme "is to provide gainful and productive employment gainful to the individual and productive to the economy on approved works to all unskilled persons in their rural areas...who need work and are prepared to do manual labour but cannot find it on their own."[17] Among the salient features cited are:

1) A guarantee of unskilled employment is provided to all adult persons residing in the rural areas.

2) The persons demanding work have no choice of work. The guarantee is to provide work *anywhere in the district*, though operationally work is normally provided within the Panchayat Samiti area. (emphasis added)

3) Work is to be provided to any person demanding employment within 15 days of such demand. The work should normally last for at least 30 days.

4) Only productive works are permitted under the scheme. The major types

of works which have been initiated under the scheme are labor intensive components of major and medium irrigation projects, minor irrigation, percolation and storage tanks, soil conservation, etc. Where such productive works are not available, road works are undertaken.

5) Only works in which the cost of the unskilled component is more than 60 percent of the total cost are permitted under the scheme.

6) Wages are linked to the "quality and quantity" of the output; the wages are so designed "that an average person working diligently for 7 hours should earn a total wage equal to the minimum wage for agricultural labor in the lowest zone of the State. This will ensure that the operation of the scheme does not affect agricultural operations and at the same time the agricultural labor is assured of the minimum wage."

7) The works are executed departmentally, and not by subcontractors; "therefore there is no intermediary between the Government and the labour."

8) Blueprints of works which may be undertaken through the scheme are kept ready for each Panchayat Samiti "so that there is practically no time lag between the registration of the actual demand for work and the starting of the work."

In August 1977 the Maharashtra Legislature enacted the Maharashtra Employment Guarantee Act 1977 (Maharashtra Act No. XX of 1978). This Act was hailed by the opposition as a radical measure[18] because the legislation had greater legal force than the scheme and, more importantly, because of an additional provision that the scheme had lacked. The Act states that if the government is unable to provide employment within fifteen days of a properly executed request for it, "the person shall be entitled to receive from the Employment Guarantee Fund an unemployment allowance at such rate as may be fixed by the State Government from time to time, but not less than Re. 1 per day."

Because of this provision the Act met with strong opposition from the Center. Prime Minister Morarji Desai and other Union officials regarded the unemployment allowance as an unacceptable "dole,"[19] even while others criticized the unemployment allowance as inadequate "to keep body and soul together."[20] In June 1978, Desai stated that the Act would not secure the President's assent,[21] but on October 1, 1978, the Act was finally signed. The Center's dismay at the precedent of promising a dole was probably matched by an unwillingness to cooperate with the governing Congress-Congress I coalition in Maharashtra. In July 1978, this coalition was replaced by the Progressive Democratic Front. A September 18, 1978 editorial in *The Times of India* noted that "within two months of another group of parties, of which the state Janata is a prominent member, taking office, the bill has been cleared."

The unemployment allowance and the entire EGS have been important organizing tools. One Shramik Sanghatana activist[22] has said that the EGS has been valuable because it is a lever for pressuring government to start projects for which money has been allocated, but which have not yet been initiated. The fact of the EGS allows an organization to build pressure. However, to date, giving the organizers of rural labor an organizing tool has been the only cost to government of the unemployment allowance provision. One high level official concerned with social welfare acknowledged that the dole has never been paid.[23] He stated further, "there is no penalty to government if we don't give a dole." The law was passed, he said, to show the *intention* of government; the purpose of such a bill is to set the policy and prevent its alteration by the whims of bureaucrats or successive governments.

The Act was written with a large enough loophole to rescue the government from unwanted expenditure. A registered person requesting employment "shall be provided with employment as far as possible on any work within the area of the Panchayat Samiti where he resides, but in any case *not outside the district*."[24] If a person declines a job offered *anywhere* within the *district*, which is a large geographic region, he or she is then ineligible for unemployment allowance for the following three months. A Shramik Sanghatana activist contends that it is common for government to offer jobs that are too distant for people to realistically take;[25] poor peoples' refusal of these jobs prevents them from receiving the dole. An official of the Planning Department, pressed on this issue, corroborated this view, stating, "The problem of unemployment allowance doesn't really come up. That's because EGS works on a district level. The law says that a person must be offered a job within the district. So, if you can't get them a job locally, you can always offer them a job *somewhere* in the district."[26]

In defense of this provision, the Planning Department official went on to say that government provides all transportation, housing facilities, water and other needs on projects distant from the worker's home. A former Assistant Collector of Thane asserted that if the work is further than 5 kilometers away, the government must provide camps for the workers.[27] Other officials, however, contradicted these assertions. A high level official of the Social Welfare Department, asked if labor camps were provided, replied that this was the case only if the work was a very large one, such as a canal building, that would involve as many as 1,000 people for at least a month. But, he said, most of the works are small, and in these cases only minimum amenities such as drinking water are provided.[28]

A Thane official[29] knowledgeable about the workings of the EGS there provided details of EGS planning that also contradicted the assertion that government provides "amenities" at job sites beyond five kilometers. Although the Employment Guarantee Act denotes a distance of five kilometers as the preferred limit, this official explained that because a saturation point has been reached in parts of the district—there are no more projects to be done—the standard distance used in planning has become *eight to ten* kilometers from the worker's home. If the work offered is *beyond eight to ten kilometers*, but *within the same taluka*, only work is provided; no transportation, drinking water, food or child care are offered. Thus, a daily walk of over 20 kilometers is seen as a reasonable condition of employment. Failure to accept a job that might be more than 10 kilometers away results in disqualification from the unemployment allowance.

If work is outside the taluka, the official said, government will provide transportation and housing. The experience in Thane has been, however, that despite the offer of these facilities, laborers are reluctant to travel beyond their own taluka. In fact, transportation and housing have *never* been provided, because workers have refused to go so far from home.[30] Thus, the Act's provision that employment can be offered anywhere within the district and the doubling of the standard five kilometer distance suggested in the Act, combined with the laborers' unwillingness to travel long distances on a daily basis and to leave their homes, make the promise of an unemployment allowance an empty one.

However, as one state official[31] pointed out, the existence of a law guaranteeing the allowance has the potential to put government on the defensive. For example, if questioned in the Assembly, a Minister will have to explain why the dole has not been paid. Thus, the passage of the law gives people a weapon. It gives movements like Bhoomi Sena and Shramik Sanghatana an additional tool for organizing the laborers to make demands of government.

Requests for employment seem to far outstrip the number of jobs available. Mrinal Gore reported after a February 1980 visit to Palghar Taluka in Thane that there were seven to eight thousand people registered for EGS, but that there was employment for less than one thousand.[32] A Thane official, interviewed in March 1980[33] said that there were 36,277 people at work in the district on EGS projects on that particular day. During the peak period for EGS employment in April and May, some forty-five to fifty thousand are employed. Later, during the same conversation, this official noted that at that moment, in March, there were 50,000 people in the two talukas of Jowhar and Mohkada who wanted EGS jobs, but that the government was hard pressed to provide work for them. The EGS schemes had "reached a saturation point" in those areas; that is, there were no more works to be done that met the legal criteria. If there were 50,000 people clamoring for jobs in only two talukas of the district, in the off season, then the number of those in the district as a whole during the peak season for EGS must be many times more. (There are 13 talukas in Thane.) Amidst all this demand, those who make themselves heard, by being organized, are most likely to be served.

The decisions as to where EGS schemes shall be located and what they shall be belong, finally, to the District Collector, subject to budgetary considerations (although, thus far, funding has not been a problem.)[34] There are committees at both the taluka and the district level, consisting of all the bureaucratic officers (i.e., forest, irrigation, and engineering officials) and elected officials. At the taluka level, the MLA chairs the committee. The taluka committee makes recommendations to the district committee. Both committees have only advisory powers, with the actual judgment resting with the Collector.[35] Although two-year blueprints of probable projects are issued, the committees sit every month, or even more frequently in peak season, and revise the schemes on the basis of need, productivity, and practicality.

Sometimes, the determination of "need" is based on local demands; organized pressure or a calm word from a spokesman for a pressure group can result in the creation of new EGS schemes. Two weeks after the interview with Mrinal Gore, in which she asserted there was a pressing need for jobs in Palghar, a Thane official involved with the implementation of EGS there was questioned about Mrs. Gore's statement. He said that the week before, he had been approached by a leader of Bhoomi Sena who impressed upon him the need for more EGS projects. After the discussion, this official expedited three additional projects in Palghar.[36]

It has not always been so easy for Bhoomi Sena to receive a positive response to its requests; in April 1977, de Silva et al. report, Bhoomi Sena undertook an independent survey to discover the number of people requiring work and suggested possible projects that could be begun under the EGS. A delegation presented this information to local officials, but received no response. Bhoomi Sena then organized a morcha to back up its demands. Following the morcha, another delegation spoke with officials, who at this time agreed to start a number of projects.[37] Another local official, of the forestry department, described how in 1978 in parts of Thane there were a number of people clamoring for jobs. "We were under a lot of pressure." Because of that pressure, representatives of the forest department met with the Collector in order to devise some new schemes.[38] A former Assistant Collector of Thane stated in an interview that, with regard to the EGS, "leaders of movements cause a lot of problems for government." The official cited the strength of Godavari Parulekar's CPI(M) organization in Dahanu-Talasari as especially significant. In making policy for that area, the official asserted, decision makers must always keep Parulekar in mind.[39] Thus, according to a number of officials who have administered the EGS, local movements' demands for EGS projects have been able to move government.

The effect of organization can also be seen in the allocation given to the

EGS in Thane in the Tribal Sub-Plan, a subdivision of the state annual and five year plans designed to focus specifically on heavily tribal regions. Tentative figures for the 1980-81 Annual Tribal Sub-Plan project an outlay of Rs. 332.71 lakhs for EGS for the entire sub-plan area; of this amount, Rs. 150 lakhs, or 45 percent of the total outlay, were designated for Thane,[40] although only 19.62 percent of the state's tribals live in Thane.[41] An official involved at a high level with the Tribal Sub-Plan, asked why the allocation was so disproportionate for Thane, cited several reasons.[42] One was the need for jobs there; with little irrigation, agriculture can support workers for only a few months a year. But other reasons were more political. The Thane administration is better organized than most, he said, and successful programs create a demand for yet more programs. Also, he pointed out, in Thane tribals are not geographically cut off from non-tribal areas as they are in most other districts; government, both local and state, is more *accessible*. In other words, the ability to make demands on government makes a difference. While stating that the most pressing determinant of where jobs are allocated is simply need, the official did acknowledge that pressure from local organizations and parties is important. Before EGS, he said, tribals had to beg; now they can *demand*.

In summary, the state Employment Guarantee Scheme and the subsequent Act were written with a number of loopholes that make it easy for local government to evade complete implementation. As was seen in the discussion of Jowhar and Mohkada Talukas, government officials, even when well-intentioned, find it difficult to create enough employment to meet the need. When land and agriculture, the mainstays of the rural economy, are privately owned, there are only so many public works projects that can be initiated. Implementation of the Employment Guarantee Act is made more likely when organized groups demand it. The law provides very real and important benefits to those it serves, and thus encourages organization and the imposition of pressure on government to live up to its stated policy.

## *Wages*

A 1974 article in *Economic and Political Weekly*[43] claimed that "the history of adivasi movements and struggles in Maharashtra shows conclusively that the government acts to improve the lot of the adivasis only under pressure." The article cited as evidence of this proposition the statutory fixing of minimum wages in 1953 by the Government of Bombay in Umbergaon, Dahanu and Mokhada Talukas of Thane District, the area where the Communist movement led by Godavari Parulekar in 1945-1947 had challenged government. The minimum wage was not instituted elsewhere by Bombay until after the Page report was issued in 1973.[44] Since the early 1970s, the demand for a decent minimum wage law, and later, the demand that the law be

*Work And Wages*

implemented, have been tools of organizing for Bhoomi Sena and the CPI(M) in Thane and Shramik Sanghatana in Dhule. Again, we have an example of the use of demands that are legitimate in the eyes of the state and the general public to mobilize movements that have more radical strategic goals.

In November 1971, the Maharashtra Government appointed a committee to examine the question of issuing notifications under the 1948 Minimum Wages Act for agricultural minimum wages. The introduction to the Report that was released in July 1973 — *Report of the Study Committee on Employment Conditions of Agricultural Labour in Maharashtra State (With Reference to Minimum Wages)* — implicitly states that agitational activity and the government's desire to prevent rural unrest prompted the study:

> ...organized public bodies like political parties and trade unions [have] agitated for coverage of all agricultural labour in the state under statutory minimum wage.
> The need for "social justice" to farm labour is felt greater now than before. For the winds of economic change, which have set in particularly during last decade in the rural economy as a result of planning have kindled the aspirations of "rural poor" for better deal (sic).[45]

The Report recommended the implementation of a minimum wage to vary between Rs. 3.50 and Rs. 2.50 depending on the region; for Dhule and Thane the suggested minimum was Rs. 3.00, with men and women to receive the same wage.[46] The suggestion was also made that saldars (yearly workers) be paid Rs. 1200 for a twelve-month year (not the thirteen-month "year" generally figured by the employer) and mahinedars (monthly workers) be paid Rs. 100 per calendar month (not the 32-day "month" that was customary).[47]

On March 14, 1974 a series of notifications fixed the minimum wage for unskilled employees in non-municipal areas at Rs. 3.00.[48] Several of the Report's other recommendations were also adopted: wages of Rs. 1200 for saldars; Rs. 100 per month for mahinedars, and a work day of seven hours work and one hour's rest.[49]

Struggles around wages had been a primary focus of organizing activities by the Shramik Sanghatana since 1971. By early 1974 *Economic and Political Weekly* reported that through a series of Shramik Sanghatana-sponsored strikes and agitations begun in 1971, wage levels for both casual laborers and saldars in Shahada had been brought to levels just below those recommended by the Page Committee.[50] But April 1974 brought dramatic confrontations in two areas of Dhule as local landlords moved violently to protect their interests against increasing wage demands.

In Shahada on April 17, 1974, Shramik Sanghatana held a large conference in the village of Prakashe. Some ten to fifteen thousand peasants, not all of them tribals, attended; the effort was being made to expand the constituency and power of the organization by mobilizing saldars and day laborers whether or not they were tribals.[51] Demands were made at the conference for the implementation of the Minimum Wages Act with regard to saldars; for the cancellation of debts; and for day wages of Rs. 3.50 or the equivalent in grain.[52] The conference was followed by ten days of strikes designed to gain these demands. On April 28,[53] the landlords of the area organized their own conference, at which speeches were made condemning Shramik Sanghatana and declaring that the landlords would crush the movement.[54] The day following this meeting, landlords physically attacked a leader of Shramik Sanghatana, and a fight resulted in which both Gujars and laborers were injured. One hundred thirty-eight adivasis were arrested, while only two Gujars were taken into custody.[55] The landlords lodged a complaint with the police, naming 395 persons as culprits.

> The names included SS leaders and almost all the Bhil persons whose names the complainants could remember. The list also included Neo-Buddhist, Maratha and koli labourers. The case had to be withdrawn as it was noticed that the list included persons who were dead and also those who had left Prakashe years before.[56]

When they did not succeed in prosecuting the laborers, the landlords sent a delegation to the Chief Minister of Maharashtra demanding that Shramik Sanghatana be banned on the grounds that it inhibited production. This request was not granted, but the police forces in Shahada and Taloda were doubled. With this protection, the Gujars broke the strike of the laborers by importing labor from outside the area.[57]

The strike had created a law and order problem in that it evoked violence from the landlords; the adivasis had not initiated the violence. However, the government evidently did not want to punish landlords who were supporters of the ruling Congress Party.[58] They went unpunished, and by treating the problem mainly as a law and order issue, by doubling the police force, the government restored the status quo ante. But of course the restoration of "order" favored the landlords, who continued to pay less than the legal minimum wage. Government attempted to appear even-handed; it restored order, punished no one on either side, and that summer the Home Minister of Maharashtra toured the adivasi areas of Dhule, promising to see to the implementation of the Minimum Wages Act. At the same time, units of armed Special Reserve Police were sent to evict adivasis from forest lands in Dhule they had been cultivating, illegally, for years.[59]

## Work And Wages

Just prior to these events, a similar struggle was evolving in Dhule's Nandurbar Taluka. Following the notification of the minimum wage by the Maharashtra government, an agreement was reached between representatives of the landlords and the laborers of Karajkupa village in which the daily wages were to be raised from Rs. 2 for men and Re. 1 for women to Rs. 3 for both men and women. The wages for saldars and monthly workers were also renegotiated. These agreements, however, were never implemented. On April 8, a CPI activist in the area organized a meeting in Karajkupa to demand the implementation of the wage agreement. Clashes broke out between the landlords and the laborers, with a number of adivasis injured. The police judged the landlords to have been the instigators of the violence, and arrested 19 landlords. The issue of wages, however, remained unresolved; the landlords were not forced to pay the minimum wage.[60]

Other parts of Maharashtra were also witnessing increased demands for wages. In Talasari in Thane District, the Maharashtra unit of the CPI(M)-led All-India Kisan Sabha organized an adivasi conference. This rally, attended by 25,000 adivasis, called for a minimum daily wage of Rs. 5 for at least 300 days a year. Godavari Parulekar, the leader of the 1945-47 movement in the same area was, according to the *Economic and Political Weekly* account, "very much in command" of the conference.[61]

While this goal was for a wage higher than the minimum prescribed by law, the demands made in Dhule were simply for the implementation of existing legislation. Yet this demand was enough, in two instances, to provoke violence by the landlords. And while the landlords did not succeed in punishing the activists through legal means, they certainly were not obliged themselves to act in a legal manner and pay the wage required by law. The government appeared willing to provide armed force to maintain the peace and the status quo, but not willing to enforce the minimum wage which would mean a change to the detriment of the landlords. However, by endeavoring to put a stop to the violent excesses of the landlords, the government attempted to appear on the side of the law.

Despite the failure of early attempts to procure implementation of the existing minimum wage law in their area, the activists persisted. Eventually, some of these efforts bore fruit. The change from a Congress-Congress I government to the non-Congress Progressive Democratic Front government that occurred in July 1978 also seems to have brought a more sympathetic state government; if not itself active in prosecuting landowners who paid less than the minimum wage, the PDF appeared more willing to step aside and let organized workers demand the wage through strikes.[62] The most important component continues to be the organized strength of the workers: government responds to this; it does not itself initiate action.

## Work And Wages

On July 20, 1977, *The Times of India* reported that thousands of adivasi agricultural laborers under the leadership of the Kisan Sabha had been on strike in Dahanu and Talasari since late June, demanding wages of Rs. 5 a day. By late July, an agreement had been reached at a meeting of "farmers, adivasi farm labourers and social workers" that the laborers would receive Rs. 4 a day, one rupee more than the minimum wage. The meeting had been addressed by the Minister for Agriculture, who had appealed to the farmers to "be realistic" and pay more to the adivasis.[63] Government in this instance plainly supported the workers' legally made demands.

In April through June of 1976, Bhoomi Sena had organized a struggle for the payment of minimum wages in Palghar that was largely unsuccessful. They had, in addition to striking against the sawkars, surveyed seventy villages and issued a detailed report documenting over one thousand cases of violation of the minimum wage.[64] However, no action was taken by the officials concerned at that time.[65] Bhoomi Sena continued their organizing efforts and in July 1978 there was a total strike against the paddy growers. This time, an official of the Labor Department toured the area, accompanied by Bhoomi Sena members, and announced to the sawkars that if they did not pay the minimum wage he would prosecute them. Government stood with the workers in demanding the rule of law. Government had not initiated action against those guilty of paying less than the minimum wage, but it did follow the lead given by Bhoomi Sena. The sawkars gave in under this pressure and paid the legal wage; in some areas where the strikers were especially strong, they paid more than the minimum.[66]

There have been a number of wage strikes in Dhule organized by Shramik Sanghatana. Here, as in Thane, the ultimate target of the strikes has been the landlords, but it has also been necessary to gain the cooperation of government officials whose responsibility it is to implement the law. In Dhule, this has been accomplished by forcibly pressing home to the officials their legal responsibility. In September 1977

> About 2,000 men and women led a morcha to the office of the Tehsildar at Taloda, the taluka headquarters, 8 miles from Moyde [a village in which a wage action was in progress. The workers there were refusing to accept wages less than Rs. 3 per day.] Poor peasants from other villages also participated in the morcha and agricultural labourers of the neighborhood joined in the march. Officers of Revenue, Block Development and Police Departments were called before the morcha. The workers enquired from the officers if they knew of the Minimum Wages Act promulgated by the Government of Maharashtra on 24 March 1974....The demonstrators

insisted that officials should explain publicly the provisions of the Act and also tell the labourers what had been done to implement it. The agricultural workers knew the details of the Act but they wanted to impress on the local officials how they had been negligent in the performance of their duty....The workers...forced the officials to give a specific assurance: they would conduct an enquiry into the whole affair and if the maldars had not paid the legal dues, they would be compelled to respect the Act.[67]

The agricultural workers soon raised their demands to include payment of arrears for the entire season, during which the landlords had never paid the minimum wage. The Block Development Officer at first took the side of the landlords in this, asking for proof that the laborers had been underpaid. The laborers turned this around, asking the officials to show them the records maintained by the maldars; according to the Minimum Wages Act, *employers* must keep detailed records of wage payments, which are to be co-signed by the employee. The Block Development Officer, Tehsildar and District Magistrate are responsible for seeing to the implementation of this procedure, but this is rarely done. In Moyde, the agricultural laborers, pressing this demand, made clear that they were acting within the law. Having gained the neutrality of the local officials, who would now not intervene to protect the maldars, the laborers were able to win their strike.[68]

From interviews conducted with a number of activists and government officials, and from the evidence seen in these individual cases, it seems evident that the minimum wage law is almost never actively enforced and that on those rare occasions when the wage is paid, its payment is directly attributable to pressure brought to bear by an organized movement. This is certainly the position taken by the activists and their sympathizers, but it is not a view that is contradicted by government officials.

Vijay Kanhare, one of the founders of Shramik Sanghatana, explained in a 1980 interview[69] that the main road open to laborers seeking to obtain the minimum wage legally due them is to agitate locally against the landlords. The government, in the form of the Block Development Officer and other local officials, has power that extends only to telling the landlords that they must pay the minimum wage. Aside from so informing them, the only power the BDO has is to take them to court with the accusation that they have not kept accurate *records* of the wages paid; the BDO is not authorized to take the landlords to court for not *paying* the minimum wage. This accusation can legally be brought only by the workers themselves. But, Kanhare explained, the legal process ordinarily takes from three to four years and consequently is of little use to the laborer. Rather than addressing these legal channels, then, the organized laborers turn to direct action in the form of local agitations against recalcitrant landlords. The BDO will sometimes serve as a negotiator between the two sides, but aside from his powers of moral persuasion and his ability to charge the landlord with inadequate record keeping, a crime for which the penalty is very small, he has little real power. If the BDO is sympathetic to the laborers, it is helpful to them; if he is not sympathetic, he can help the landlords skirt the law. But, as the government's local administrative representative, he is almost powerless.

Consequently the laborers, once organized, become the instruments through which the law of the state is implemented. While government ordinarily does not actively implement the law itself, the refusal of government to intervene on behalf of landlords who are in violation of the law allows the organized laborers' strikes to have effect. In other words, the laborers do the work of the government. This means that only in those cases in which the laborers are sufficiently organized to have an impact on the landlords is the minimum wage operative. The fact that the law is on the books gives the laborers moral standing, but, more importantly, it can sometimes provide for the benign neglect of the repressive machinery of government. While government will not take the initiative to force landlords to pay minimum wage, neither, often, will the government come to the defense of landlords facing a peaceful strike demanding that the law be obeyed. The passage of a minimum wage law allows the government to straddle the fence between the laborers and the landlords; it does not implement its own law, but it will allow those who are sufficiently organized to implement it themselves. Since very few of Maharashtra's agricultural laborers are so organized, for the most part the government's actions in passing such laws have little effect, but give the appearance of protecting the workers' rights.

One official concerned with Tribal affairs[70] expressed his suspicion of the motives of those who organize agricultural workers; he believes they are primarily concerned with seeking power for themselves. "The political parties make use of them," he said, "but are not useful to them." The same official nonetheless acknowledged that the main redress for those not receiving their rightful wage is not legal, but *political*. He admitted that individual cases are not frequently resolved because of the time necessary for a case to be brought through the court system and the complications that process entails for the workers. When specifically questioned, he conceded that in Dhule "the landlords have become scared of Shramik Sanghatana—and that is good." But while he would acknowledge that agitation is most likely to bring the agricultural laborers the minimum wage due them under the law, he remained, it seemed, deeply resentful and suspicious of the activists who undertake the necessary organization.

*Work And Wages*

Thus, a peculiar relationship is created between government and movements demanding, in the first instance, the rule of law. The movements put pressure on the government, and while it is admitted by government officials that such pressure is effective, it is also resented; it makes the work of officials that much more trying. As many officials cited above have stated, it is difficult if not impossible to insure the payment of minimum wage in an agricultural economy of such scarcity. The laborers themselves, acting under fear of future unemployment, may not be reliable witnesses. The Block Development Officers are granted very limited powers under the law. Similarly, creating Employment Guarantee Scheme projects that fit within the limitations set by the law is a difficult task: how many roads can be built in one taluka?

And yet, when an organized movement initiates strikes which might in turn lead to violence, government has an interest in preserving order. When it is the *movement* that is on the side of law in demanding minimum wages, not the landlords, and when these movements are furthermore receiving the attention of those outside the immediate locality, the government has incentive to maintain order by implementing the law. The movements succeed not because they *break* the law, but because they demand the *implementation* of the law. Government then has a choice of acting legally or illegally; given the government's wish to maintain its own legitimacy, it is likely to act legally, and support the movements that have initiated action. Thus, paradoxically, the government's desire to project its own legitimacy furthers the aims of the movements and may lead to their growth in size and in number.

## NOTES

1. Sulabha Brahme, "Drought in Maharashtra," *Social Scientist*, July 1973, p. 49.
2. Norman Reynolds and Pushpa Sundar, "Maharashtra's Employment Guarantee Scheme: A Programme to Emulate?" *Economic and Political Weekly*, July 16, 1977, p. 1151, report that Maharashtra has emphasized large development works, partly in hopes of capturing additional financial resources from the Centre. Politically, this has allowed the State to maintain control of development works, while enabling it to assuage local political interests. Developmentally, however, there has been little benefit: "Maharashtra's irrigation potential is amongst the lowest in Indian and its exploitation remains tardy. Large schemes, inter-state water disputes and the relative neglect of small schemes explain the state's poor performance." Another cause of the poor agricultural accomplishments since independence, according to Reynolds and Sundar, rests with the effects of India's war efforts under the Raj. "During both World Wars 'grow more food' campaigns and programmes to save coal and oil fuel as energy sources together depleted many forest lands....As forest and pasture lands disappeared, the uplands were denuded, leaving Maharashtra's agricultural land vulnerable to erosion. The degradation of agricultural land over at least half the state plus the spread of civilization onto more marginal land are important causes of the state's agricultural stagnation as well as the instability of rural incomes....The overall agricultural stagnation has aggravated the employment problems in the countryside. Recurring drought years...have forced the poorest in the countryside to move to towns, both as seasonal migrants as well as permanent settlers."
3. Two thirds of the population of 51 million are engaged in agriculture. Eighty-six percent of the 18 million classified as workers live in the countryside in 36,000 villages. Reynolds and Sundar, p. 1151.
4. In Brahme's estimation, government undertakes relief works only to the extent necessary to maintain the status quo. Brahme, "Drought in Maharashtra," p. 50.
5. The principle was first articulated in Article 41 of the Indian Constitution, which guarantees the right of all citizens to work. But this article is in the "Directive Principles" section of the constitution, which outlines aspirations but not responsibilities for which government can be held legally accountable.
6. This history is drawn from Reynolds and Sundar, p. 1149; Sudam Deshmukh, "Employment Guarantee Scheme: Introduction and Review," *How*, October 1979, p. 19; and a cyclostyled paper obtained from the Government of Maharashtra Planning Department, entitled *Employment Guarantee Scheme in Maharashtra*, 12 pps., no date.
7. Speech to Legislative Assembly on March 29, 1972. *The Times of India*, March 30, 1972.
8. Reynolds and Sundar, p. 1149; and *The Times of India*, March 30, 1972.
9. Interview, February 15, 1980.
10. *The Times of India*, March 30, 1972.
11. Interview with "E," February 8, 1980.
12. Government of Maharashtra, *Report of the Study Committee on Employment Conditions of Agricultural Labour in Maharashtra State (With Reference to Minimum Wages)* (Bombay: Central Government Press, July 1973), pp. 104, 107. The committee was chaired by Sri V.S. Page. The Report also stated, p. 110, "All witnesses without exception have deposed before the Committee that the provisions of the Minimum Wages Act, so far as the agricultural labourers are concerned, have remained on paper not only in Maharashtra but even elsewhere and the only hope for honest implementation is the Employment Guarantee Scheme. Hence we have recommended the application of the minimum wage to that Scheme."
13. *The Times of India*, April 7, 1972.
14. Quoted in *New Age* (Central Organ of the Communist Party of India), June

# Work And Wages

18, 1972, p. 3. AITUC is the labor union federation controlled by the CPI.

15. Brahme, "Drought in Maharashtra," p. 51, states "Scarcity conditions and relief works are recognized facts of life in Maharashtra. Yet no effort has been made to draw up and keep in readiness adequate number of projects of productive works which could employ the drought-affected population meaningfully and help minimize the hardships imposed by failure of rains. Metal breaking [breaking stone into small pieces for use in road-building] is one of the important relief works undertaken. This reflects the poverty of planning....the metal broken as relief operation twenty years ago during the 1952-53 famine is still lying around in many of the drought affected areas..." Brahme calculates that only six percent of the land that potentially could be irrigated has been irrigated. p. 53.

16. Brahme, "Drought in Maharashtra," p. 51.
17. *Employment Guarantee Scheme in Maharashtra.*
18. *The Times of India*, November 23, 1977.
19. Ibid.; *The Indian Express*, June 20, 1978.
20. *The Hindustan Times*, August 10, 1977, editorial.
21. *The Indian Express*, June 20, 1978.
22. Interview with "I," February 5, 1980.
23. Interview with "A," February 22, 1980.
24. Maharashtra Act No. XX of 1978, section 8(3), emphasis added.
25. Interview with "I," February 5, 1980.
26. Interview with "C," February 28, 1980. This statement was echoed by an official in Thane District who said, "There hasn't been occasion to pay the cash dole, because the jurisdiction area is the *district*." Interview with "F," March 1, 1980.
27. Interview with "E," February 8, 1980.
28. Interview with "A," February 19, 1980.
29. Interview with "F," March 1, 1980.
30. This reluctance of workers to leave their own areas was also noted by Mrinal Gore, interview, February 15, 1980.
31. Interview with "A," February 22, 1980.
32. Interview with Mrinal Gore, February 15, 1980.
33. Interview with "F," March 1, 1980.
34. Interview with "A," February 19, 1980, who said there is plenty of EGS money to go around; there is more money in the fund than there is demand.

Statistics from the Government of Maharashtra Planning Department cited in Reynolds and Sundar, p. 1154, show that the budget expenditure for EGS has always been considerably lower than the budget allocation:

| Year | Budget Allocation (Rs. million) | Budget Expenditure (Rs. million) |
|---|---|---|
| 1972-73 | 24 | 18.8 |
| 1973-74 | 44 | 18.8 |
| 1974-75 | 150 | 137.2 |
| 1975-76 | 500 | 344.3 |
| 1976-77 (up to October 31, 1976) | 500 | 233.0 |

It does appear to be true that the availability of funding is not the problem standing in the way of more jobs.

35. Interview with "F," March 1, 1980.
36. Ibid.
37. de Silva, et. al., *Bhoomi Sena: A Struggle*, p. 56.

## Work And Wages

38. Interview with "D," February 16, 1980.
39. Interview with "E," February 8, 1980.
40. Government of Maharashtra, Department of Social Welfare, Cultural Affairs, Sports and Tourism. *Draft Annual Tribal Sub-Plan (1980-81)*.
41. S.D.Kulkarni, "Problems of Tribal Development in Maharashtra," *Economic and Political Weekly*, September 20, 1980, p. 1598. Dhule was projected to receive Rs. 65 lakhs, with Nasik scheduled for Rs. 45 lakhs, and Chandrapur, Rs. 33.75 lakhs. All other districts were to receive less than 10 lakhs. *Draft Annual Tribal Sub-Plan (1980-81)*.
42. Interview with "A," February 27, 1980.
43. "Organizing the Adivasis," *Economic and Political Weekly*, Annual Number, February 1974, p. 175-A.
44. Government of Maharashtra, *Report of the Study Committee on Employment Conditions of Agricultural Labour in Maharashtra State (with reference to Minimum Wages)* (Bombay: Central Government Press, July 1973). A minimum wage was instituted in 1954 in three districts of present day Maharashtra State—Parbhani, Amraoti, and Yeotmal—by the governments of Hyderabad State and Madhya Pradesh, which then had jurisdiction. *Report of the Study Committee...*, p. 1.
45. Ibid., p. 1.
46. Brahme and Upadhyaya, p. 177, writing in 1975 noted that if the Page recommendations were to be adopted at that time, the Rs. 3 would bring the real wages in Dhule up to only 91, using 1961 as the base year and taking the wage index as 100 in 1963. In 1973-74, wage rates for men in Dhule varied between Rs. 2 and Rs. 3; in Shahada Taluka, the average was 2.40. Thus, in real terms, wages were below the 1961 level by 15 to 20 points. Wages for women, in 1973-74, were about 70 percent those of men.
47. *Report of the Study Committee...*, pp. 75, 111. It was suggested that the saldar be guaranteed twenty-four holidays with pay per year, and that the mahinedar be guaranteed two holidays per month. A work day of eight hours, to consist of seven hours actual work and one hour rest was suggested for all types of employees. pp. 112-113.
48. Government of Maharashtra, *Notifications Fixing/Revising Minimum Wage Rates of Wages Under Minimum Wages Act, 1948 for Various Scheduled Employments in Maharashtra State, 1976*. (Bombay: Commissioner of Labour and Director of Employments, Government of Maharashtra, 1976), pp. 243, 246.
49. Ibid., pp. 243, 248. While saldars and mahinedars were given the number of holidays suggested by the Page Report, no notification was made concerning the number of hours they could work per day.
50. "Organizing the Adivasis," p. 176-A.
51. S.D. Kulkarni, "Class and Caste in a Tribal Movement," *Economic and Political Weekly*, Annual number, February 1979, p. 468; Maria Mies, "The Shahada Movement: A Peasant Movement in Maharashtra (India): Its Development and Its Perspectives," *Journal of Peasant Studies*, July 1976, p. 478.
52. Mies, p. 479.
53. The date is according to Kulkarni, "Class and Caste...," p. 468; Mies, p. 479, puts the date at April 27.
54. Kulkarni, "Class and Caste...," p. 468; Mies, p. 479.
55. Mies, p. 479.
56. Kulkarni, "Class and Caste...," p. 468.
57. Mies, p. 479.
58. Ibid.
59. Ibid.
60. The above paragraph is derived from Brahme and Upadhyaya, p. 15; "The Long

Haul," *Economic and Political Weekly*, April 20, 1974, p. 615; and *Patriot*, August 28, 1975.

61. "Organizing the Adivasis," pp. 175-A - 175-B.

62. The research for this study examines the period of the 1970s; thus, the impact of the return of Congress to office in 1980 is not discussed.

63. *The Times of India*, July 29, 1977.

64. The events outlined here are detailed in de Silva, et al., *Bhoomi Sena: A Struggle...*, pp. 51-55. The study done by Bhoomi Sena was summarized in a number of articles, including: Husain Dalwai, "Bonded Labour Continues," *Economic and Political Weekly*, May 28, 1977, pp. 868-869, and is cited in a later government report, also chaired by V.S. Page: Government of Maharashtra, *Report of the Committee on Problems of Illicit Money Lending and Bonded Labour (October 1977)*, p. 46.

65. de Silva, et al., *Bhoomi Sena: A Struggle...*, p. 55.

66. Ibid., p. 62.

67. "Agricultural Workers in Action: The Story of the Shramik Sanghathan," *How*, June 1978, p. 25.

68. The details of this incident are related in Ibid., pp. 26-27.

69. Interview, February 5, 1980.

70. Interview with "A," February 22, 1980.

# CONCLUSION TO PART 2

Through the introduction of new values, Shramik Sanghatana and Bhoomi Sena may ultimately threaten the equilibrium of India's political system. They are teaching the poor that they have the right to demand improved social and economic conditions, and that in organization they can find the power to realize their demands: the poverty in which they live is neither justifiable nor inevitable. Will government be able to re-establish harmony between the environment of the movements' constituents—an environment of grim poverty brought on by centuries of exploitation and governmental neglect—and the new values of autonomy, self-worth, and empowerment taught by the movements?

At present, these movements are too few in number and small in size to pose a threat to the overall equilibrium of the Indian polity. The demands for environmental alteration that they make of the government can often be met because government does have the capacity to respond on a limited basis. Shramik Sanghatana and Bhoomi Sena alone cannot disequilibrate the system. But many movements like them, working in a similar mode, might be able to do so; and the number of such groups has already grown into the thousands.[1]

These groups represent a new, decentralized form of political organization. It has been seen that neither Shramik Sanghatana nor Bhoomi Sena want to be associated with any political party. They want to insure that decision making remains on the local level, not with a hierarchical party elite. They view political parties with suspicion, afraid of being used by them for opportunistic reasons.[2]

In a 1980 interview, Godavari Parulekar, a member of CPI(M)'s Central Committee and President of the Maharashtra Kisan Sabha of CPI(M), expressed a generally positive opinion of Shramik Sanghatana, which works in a district other than her own; claimed that Bhoomi Sena "is very minor—but they are at present working with us"—a statement which exaggerates the limited cooperation; and leveled charges that a recently formed organization operating in Dahanu and Talasari, the Kashtakari Sanghatana, was funded by American

## Conclusion to Part 2

agents.[3] The suspicions of the non-party-based groups about the political parties appear to be borne out by the divisiveness of these attitudes. S.D. Kulkarni responded to Parulekar's attack on Kashtakari Sanghatana:

> Godvari Parulekar's attack on Kashtakari Sanghatana is a part of CPI(M)'s policy and several groups have taken a note of this attack. These groups may support the CPI(M)'s national policies but they will have to oppose it in any election in their area. If CPI(M) wins the first target of attack will be the group in their area.[4]

Disillusionment with political parties appears to be growing. In a 1982 article in *The New York Times*, a number of Indian scholars, including Rajni Kothari, Mohan Ram and George Verghese, commented on the burgeoning throughout India of non-party organizations representing the hopes of the downtrodden. The author of the article commented:

> It is a decentralized movement in a basically decentralized society, but according to some of India's most respected political scientists and commentators, the aggregate effect of their work is becoming a significant factor. The social activism, the commentators say, is moving into a vacuum left by the decay of older political institutions.[5]

George Verghese, editor of *The Indian Express* and a former official of the Gandhi Peace Foundation, stated in the article that "the greatest innovative energy results when local people identify problems in their lives and seek their own remedies."[6] These ideas are echoed by S.D. Kulkarni:

> The number of groups working among the poor and not affiliated to any political party is increasing day by day. These groups can take up local issues and have some advantages over political parties which, caught in the muddle of elections, cannot take up certain issues. They are building up people's power and are bound to pose a threat to political parties as they are organized today.[7]

Thus, the grass roots, decentralized character of the movements may ultimately prove to be a strength. Both Shramik Sanghatana and Bhoomi Sena have begun to include the non-tribal poor among their members.[8] A multitude of small grassroots movements, based among the poor, may prove to be the most effective way to fight the vested interests at the local level, the level of implementation; Shramik Sanghatana and Bhoomi Sena have both won significant con-

*Conclusion to Part 2*

stituencies at this level. Political parties engaged in electoral politics can be effective in introducing and passing legislation; but as implementation occurs locally, local groups may be a more powerful source of pressure.[9] And, the aggregate effect of a number of local movements pushing for similar changes seems, in Maharashtra, to have had a real impact on the legislative process as well. The next, and concluding, chapter asks how likely it is that these movements will eventually be able to force systemic changes. Do the decentralized grassroots movements pose a greater challenge to governmental power and legitimacy than did the Naxalites?

*Conclusion to Part 2*

## NOTES

1. Michael T. Kaufman, "Social Activism Sprouts as India's Politics Decay," *The New York Times*, June 15, 1982, p. A2, writes that "there are at least several thousand" non-party organizations working among the poor, "though attempts to count them have been incomplete."

2. These insights were presented by a number of interviewees, including "H," January 17, 1980; Sudheer Bedekar, January 31, 1980; Navinit Shah, February 18, 1980; and Sulabha Brahme, January 30, 1980.

3. Interview, Parulekar, February 23, 1980. The charges against Kashtakari Sanghatana are expanded in an interview in *Economic and Political Weekly*, October 4, 1980, pp. 1647-1649.

4. S.D. Kulkarni, "Letters to Editor: Organizing Tribals in Thane," *Economic and Political Weekly*, November 1, 1980, p. 1873. Kulkarni is the Director of the Centre for Tribal Conscientization, an organization that helps to coordinate activities among several adivasi-based movements in Maharashtra.

5. Kaufman, p. A2.

6. Ibid.

7. Kulkarni, "Letters...," p. 1873.

8. S.D. Kulkarni, "Class and Caste in a Tribal Movement," *Economic and Political Weekly*, Annual Number, February 1979, p. 468.

9. George Verghese claims that even the increasing numbers of caste conflicts in India are a hopeful sign of the power of local groups: "It is of course tragic that people are being killed...but the assaults by vested interests show that they are growing fearful of the increasing assertiveness and self-assurance of the dispossessed." In Kaufman.

# 11
# CONCLUSION: PROTEST'S CHALLENGE

Chapter 1 of this study took note of the hopes held by many of India's elites at independence that the politicization of India's poorest citizens would take place gradually under the tutelage of a local leadership loyal to the institutions of party politics and democratic government. These institutions, however, have failed to provide economic growth and political power for many of India's poor. As a result, increasing numbers are finding their political voice through movements that operate outside the channels of government and parties, and that constitute a challenge to this institutional framework.

Chapters 2, 3 and 7 above have shown how the actions of government elites contributed to the development of disequilibriums that provided fertile soil for the growth of these movements. In all three districts studied, the rights of poor tribals were trampled upon by more sophisticated people from plains areas, initially in some instances with the help of laws that facilitated land transfers and tribal indebtedness or, in more recent times, with the collusion of local officials who took no steps to protect the tribals against illegal abuses.

A disequilibrium, however, does not ensure a revolutionary response, and certainly not a successful one; it merely provides an opportunity to aspiring revolutionary leaders. Whether a challenge is successful depends on the resources of the revolutionary movement relative to those of the governmental system it opposes. The government's strength lies ultimately in its access to instruments of coercion; but its most important resource for avoiding crisis altogether or, failing that, for having the ability to use coercion during a time of crisis is the public's belief in the government's legitimacy. A movement's strength, its ability to mobilize the public to support and participate in its actions, rests in substantial part on the quality of its leaders, their ability to create an effective organization, and their promotion of an ideology that both generates enthusiastic followers and outlines a viable plan of action.

The movements studied in this book have had dramatically different

## Protest's Challenge

ideologies and approaches to leadership and organization. The Naxalite vision of the overthrow of the state was far removed from the everyday life of those it sought to mobilize. Naxalite ideology was not understood by the mass participants, who were used by the leadership for ends they did not share. The Naxalites claimed to be Maoists, and they did indeed look to an agrarian-based revolution to establish a communist regime. However, unlike Mao, the leaders of the Naxalite revolution largely directed operations from afar; local leadership became subordinated to a centralized elite with little grassroots experience and no ties, either ideological or personal, to the local participants, most of whom had so little understanding of the leaders' ideology that they thought they were engaged in upholding the law rather than in overthrowing the state. The leaders scorned mass organization and education in favor of spontaneity. As a result, they received support only in regions where painstaking political organization had preceded them. They fomented violence, but offered their followers no protection from the state's retaliation. They trusted that the annihilation of landlords would result in an outburst of mass rage that would destroy the forces of government. Instead, the brutality of their violence left them isolated and provided the government with the political support it needed to crush the Naxalites with impunity.

For although local government may indeed have lost its legitimacy for many in Srikakulam, the system of government had not lost its legitimacy generally throughout India. Thus, when the Naxalites engaged in violence, government was able to move against them with full force, even with force that may have been in excess of the law, and pay no political price for doing so. Indeed, had the government done any *less* to protect the lives of those the Naxalites attacked, and to assert its own authority, government's legitimacy would have been sorely compromised. When the Naxalites used violence, the government had no rational choice but to respond with the full violence necessary to stop them.

Government's rehabilitative efforts in the aftermath of Naxalite violence may be seen as an attempt to insure that the Naxalites remained isolated. The socioeconomic programs that were introduced were directed as much, if not more, at the broad public as at those tribals immediately involved with the violence. The government needed to demonstrate its commitment to the welfare of the impoverished tribals, a group recognized as entitled to special attention, and to reestablish its own legitimacy in the face of its obvious failings.

The government introduced economic aid into the troubled area in order to show the tribals that their best interest lay in cooperation with the government rather than with the Naxalites. This reduced the need to use force; it also demonstrated to the broader public the government's commitment to the protection of the innocent—of whatever class—and to social justice. Had the government wanted only to destroy the Naxalites, force would have been sufficient. The fact that in addition government officials took ameliorative economic steps reveals their understanding that they should evince concern for the welfare of those affected. The government needed to restore public faith in its abilities and in its commitment to socioeconomic progress; the government needed to safeguard its legitimacy.

Shramik Sanghatana and Bhoomi Sena pose a less dramatic but ultimately, perhaps, a more sustained and deeper challenge to government authority. Unlike the Naxalites, the leaders of Shramik Sanghatana and Bhoomi Sena share an ideology that stresses means over any specific ends; their central concern is to build mass participation and political sophistication and to generate new leaders. Shramik Sanghatana's leaders hope that a strong grassroots movement will ultimately press for class-based revolutionary change. But while their preferred outcome is a socialist revolution, their means are the antithesis of the Leninist vanguard party. Fearing that hierarchical organization and centralized leadership will lead to the opportunistic use of the poor rather than to their liberation, the leaders of both Shramik Sanghatana and the less ideological Bhoomi Sena instead are trying to generate self-sustaining, decentralized, non-hierarchical organizations that they hope will generate enough power to be able to pressure and perhaps, ultimately, to challenge the system itself.

Bhoomi Sena and Shramik Sanghatana have utilized tactics that echo a legitimate Indian political tradition: nonviolent direct action against intransigent government. The movements are indigenous. Their use of constructive works to improve the lives of the poor while simultaneously politicizing them rings familiar. Their demand that government live up to its moral commitments and that it obey the rule of law also has roots in the nationalist tradition.[1]

Because these movements offer the possibility of radical transformation through traditional modes of action, they have found support among urban intellectuals and others who seek dramatic social change but who have been either repelled by the Naxalites or discouraged by their failure. Their friends have helped to give these small movements a stronger voice and have provided a protective shield against arbitrary or unlawful response; press attention has lifted them from the isolation that so limited the first attempts to organize the girijans in Srikakulam.

The movements have a legitimacy that the Naxalites lacked; government therefore cannot suppress them without considerable political cost. By proceeding in an agitational, but legal, style of action, the movements have succeeded in making the government an unwilling collaborator in their growth. A democratic government, to retain its legitimacy with a wide constituency, must respond positively to legal demands, legally made. Similarly, appeals

## Protest's Challenge

that, in effect, request government to live up to its *moral* commitments often meet with positive response from politicians and governments who may share that concern and who, in any case, seek to maintain their own popularity. When the government responds to these appeals through the passage of improved legislation, it gives the movements tools with which to press government still further. When government responds positively to agitational activity, it demonstrates the efficacy of agitation; it encourages continued political organization.

Can these movements continue to grow? And do they pose a threat to government's legitimacy? Or have these movements developed a grassroots form of political education and development that may be integrated into the political system? The answers depend very much on the flexibility of government and its ability to honor growing demands for social and economic change while they are still being made through legitimate channels.

The Naxalite experience demonstrated government's culpability for allowing exploitation and violence to develop to a point at which the seeds of revolution planted by outside leaders could land on fertile soil. Furthermore, the peaceful movement that preceded the Naxalites was not merely rebuffed; some of its members were murdered by landlords while representatives of government looked away. Laws designed to help the poor regain land, obtain living wages and escape from the virtual slavery caused by indebtedness were not enforced. The poor tribals of Srikakulam had good reason to view a government that protected violent and exploiting landlords and moneylenders as illegitimate.

As seen in Chapter 6 above, the government of Andhra Pradesh's development efforts in the wake of Naxalite violence have had only limited success; the fundamental conditions of poverty and exploitation that fostered Naxalite violence remain. They exist, too, in other parts of India. The impoverishment of tribals in Thane and Dhule Districts in Maharashtra bore striking resemblance to the process that took place in Srikakulam; more sophisticated outsiders were able to obtain the tribals' land, enslave them through indebtedness and exploit their labor for painfully low wages.

It is important, though, to recall that impoverishment, unemployment and indebtedness are not confined to India's tribals. Nor are the emerging grassroots movements limiting their organizing efforts to any one tribe or caste; their appeal is to the vast pool of landless rural labor. Thus far, the Maharashtra movements representing these rural poor have been able to gain incremental improvements from a government that, it would seem, has also learned some lessons from the example of the Naxalite revolt and is aware of the potential for rural unrest.

Can government transform the energies generated by these movements

## Protest's Challenge

into support for the system? Can government coopt these movements? It has been outside the scope of this study to evaluate the capacity of the present system of government to meet the challenge of economic development. The movement leaders believe government does not in fact have the resources to meet the demands of the poor in the absence of a radical transformation of the economy. Their skepticism is shared by many scholars. Francine Frankel, for one, has concluded that "adequate progress toward the multiple economic, social and political goals of development cannot be accomplished in the absence of radical agrarian reform....[It] is essential to alter patterns of economic concentration in the rural sector."[2] Yet, the reliance of Indian state and central governments on the support of dominant landholding elites is well known.[3] Increasingly, the struggle for continuing governmental legitimacy will be cast as a battle between the conservative landed elite that has upheld the system and the newly emerging movements of the rural poor and their urban supporters that challenge it.

Obviously, if movements such as Shramik Sanghatana and Bhoomi Sena remain few in number, government is not troubled by them. The potential of such movements lies in their ability to generate imitative movements. In the absence of the rapid economic development that may not be possible under the present structure of concentrated landholding and wealth, widespread decentralized demands may outstrip the system's capacity to respond as law and political culture dictate it must. As the legitimacy and power of the movements grow, those of the government will decrease.

This strategy is painfully slow for those who would like to see rapid change. But barring the unlikely event of a swift destruction of state power from some outside source such as war,[4] there will be no rapid revolution in India. The transmission to the poor of a sense of their own power, so that they may attack the legitimacy of a government that does not live up to its legal and moral commitments, is a strategy that has appeal despite its moderate pace. It is precisely because the tactics are gradualist and legitimate that the government cannot move against the activists, and that the strategy therefore poses a significant challenge.

## NOTES

1. One is reminded, for instance, of the successful Bardoli Satyagraha of 1928, in which the sole demand was that the British implement their own laws.

2. Francine Frankel, *India's Political Economy 1947-1977* (Princeton: Princeton University Press, 1978), p. 548.

3. See, for example, Frankel, p. 547; Barrington Moore, Jr., *Social Origins of Dictatorship and Democracy* (Boston: Beacon Press, 1966), p. 391; and Robert L. Hardgrave, Jr., *India: Government and Politics in a Developing Nation* (New York: Harcourt Brace Jovanovich, Inc., 1980), pp. 127-8.

4. Theda Skocpol, *States and Social Revolutions* (New York: Cambridge University Press, 1979), p. 23, discusses the international arena as a factor influencing the emergence of revolutions.

# Appendix A
# IDENTIFICATION OF MAHARASHTRA INTERVIEWEES

A number of people interviewed about Shramik Sanghatana, Bhoomi Sena, and Government of Maharashtra policies requested anonymity. These people have been coded by letter so that it is possible, through the footnotes, to maintain their separate identities.

The following is a brief description of each of the interviewees. The affiliations of government officials are given as specifically as possible without endangering their anonymity; the dates during which they held these posts cannot be given.

*State Officials*
"A": Department of Social Welfare, Cultural Affairs, Sports and Tourism.
"B": Department of Social Welfare, Cultural Affairs, Sports and Tourism.
"C": Planning Department.

*Local Officials*
"D": Forest Department, Thane.
"E": Deputy Collector, Thane.
"F": Deputy Collector, Thane.
"G": Collector, Thane.

*Activists*
"H": Joint interview with two social workers, activists among tribals in several Maharashtra districts.
"I": A non-adivasi founder of Shramik Sanghatana.
"J": A non-adivasi activist with Shramik Sanghatana.
"K": An adivasi activist with Shramik Sanghatana; interview conducted in Marathi, and translated by Chhaya Datar.

# GLOSSARY

adivasi(s): scheduled tribes; so-called because they are part of a list or "schedule" of tribes denoted by the union government for constitutional purposes

bandh (or bundh): strike

banjar land: waste land

benami: in name only; land held illegally

Bhil: a tribe living in Dhule District

Bhoomi Sena: Land Army

coolie or cooly: laborer

coupe: an area of forest rented for the purpose of gathering minor forest produce and timber

CPI: Communist Party of India

CPI(M): Communist Party of India (Marxist)

dacoity: armed gang robbery

dalam: organized guerrilla band

dharna: demonstration

gherao: a sit-in demonstration that detains an official

girijan: hill people or "children of the hills"; a name used to describe the tribal people of Srikakulam District

gunda: thug, goon

hectare: a measure of land equal to 2.47 acres

jotedar: landowner

lakh: one hundred thousand

maldar: large landowner

Marathi: language spoken in the state of Maharashtra

MLA: Member of Legislative Assembly (state level)

MP: Member of Parliament

morcha: demonstration, march

paise: one-hundreth of a rupee

panchayat: village government

panchayati raj: system of local government with three ascending tiers: panchayat, panchayat samithi, and zilla parishad

patta rights: legal rights

podu: slash and burn cultivation; shifting cultivation

Re.: abbreviation for one rupee; a rupee is approximately one-eighth of a U.S. dollar

Rs.: abbreviation for rupees

ryot: cultivator

saldar: a laborer hired on a yearly contract

samithi: association

sangham (or sangh): association

satyagraha: non-violent civil disobedience

satyagrahi: one who performs satyagraha

shandies: markets

Shramik Sanghatana: Toiler's Union

sowcar (or sahukar, or sawkar): moneylender

taluka (or taluk): a subdivision of a district

Tarun Mandal: Youth League of Bhoomi Sena

Tehsildar (or Tahsildar): title of a local official

zamindar: owner of large amounts of land; the rights to this land were conferred by the British, and removed by the new government soon after independence

# BIBLIOGRAPHY

The bibliography is arranged in the following manner:

I. Introduction: General Works
II. The Srikakulam Naxalite Movement
   A. Books and Articles
   B. Government Documents
      1. Government of Andhra Pradesh
      2. Government of India
   C. Unpublished Works: Typescripts and Ph.D. Dissertations
   D. Interviews
III. The Maharashtra Movements: Shramik Sanghatana and Bhoomi Sena
   A. Books and Articles
   B. Government Documents
      1. Government of Bombay
      2. Government of Maharashtra
      3. Government of India
   C. Unpublished Typescripts
   D. Interviews
IV. Newspapers

## I. Introduction: General Works

Arora, Satish K. "Political Participation: Deprivation and Protest." *Economic and Political Weekly* [hereafter referred to as *EPW*], January 1971, pp. 341-50.

Bayley, David H. *The Police and Political Development In India*. Princeton, N.J.: Princeton University Press, 1969.

Frankel, Francine. *India's Political Economy 1947-1977*. Princeton, N.J.: Princeton University Press, 1978.

Gurr, Ted Robert. "The Revolution—Social Change Nexus." *Comparative Politics*, April 1973, pp. 359-392.
―――――. *Why Men Rebel*. Princeton, N.J.: Princeton University Press, 1970.
Hardgrave, Robert L., Jr. *India: Government and Politics in a Developing Nation*. New York: Harcourt Brace Jovanovich, Inc., 1980.
Huntington, Samuel. *Political Order in Changing Societies*. New Haven: Yale University Press.
Johnson, Chalmers. *Revolutionary Change*. Boston: Little, Brown and Co., 1966.
Kothari, Rajni. "More Opposition." *Seminar*, January 1971, pp. 22-27.
Linz, Juan. *The Breakdown of Democratic Regimes: Crisis, Breakdown and Reequilibration*. Baltimore: The Johns Hopkins University Press, 1978.
Lowi, Theodore J. *The Politics of Disorder*. New York: Basic Books, Inc., 1971.
Maxwell, Neville. *India'a China War*. New York: Anchor Books, 1972.
Moore, Barrington, Jr. *Social Origins of Dictatorship and Democracy*. Boston: Beacon Press, 1966.
Skocpol, Theda. *States and Social Revolutions*. New York: Cambridge University Press, 1979.
Tilly, Charles. *From Mobilization to Revolution*. Reading, Mass.: Addison-Wesley Publishing Co., 1978.
Weber, Max. "Politics as a Vocation." *From Max Weber*. Ed. H.H. Gerth and C. Wright Mills. New York: Oxford University Press, 1946.
―――――. *The Theory of Social and Economic Organization*. Ed. Talcott Parsons. New York: Free Press, 1947.

## II. The Srikakulam Naxalite Movement

*A. Books and Articles*
"A Report on the Girijan Struggle." *Liberation*, December 1968, pp. 33-41.
"The Bhargava Commission." *EPW*, 23 July 1977, p. 1169.
Dasgupta, Biplab. "Naxalite Armed Struggles and the Annihilation Campaign in Rural Areas." *EPW*, February 1973, pp. 173-188.
―――――. *The Naxalite Movement*. Bombay: Allied Publishers, 1974.
―――――. "The Naxalite Movement—An Epilogue." *Social Scientist*, July 1978, pp. 3-24.
District Communist Committee, Srikakulam. "Report on Srikakulam." *Liberation*, May 1969, pp. 58-79.
" 'Encounters' Are Murders." *EPW*, 21 May 1977, pp. 827-29.
Ghosh, Sankar. *The Naxalite Movement: A Maoist Experiment*. Calcutta: Mukhopadhyay, 1974.

Haubold, Erhard. "Srikakulam: Model of a Guerrilla Uprising." *Swiss Review of World Affairs*, March 1971, pp. 11-13.

Hinton, William. *Fanshen*. New York: Vintage Books, 1966.

"Intimidation of Witnesses to Police Atrocities." *EPW*, 10 September 1977, pp. 1601-3.

Jawaid, Sohail. *The Naxalite Movement in India*. New Delhi: Associated Publishing House, 1979.

"Killings in Guntur." *EPW*, 18 June 1977, pp. 971-973.

Mazumdar, Charu. "Srikakulam—Will it Be the Yenan of India?" *Liberation*, March 1969, pp. 66-69.

Meisner, Maurice. *Mao's China*. New York: The Free Press, 1977.

Mohanty, Manoranjan. *Revolutionary Violence: A Study of the Maoist Movement in India*. New Delhi: Sterling Publishers, 1977.

Nagi Reddy, T. "Genesis of Violence in Srikakulam: A Viewpoint." *How*, August 1978, pp. 5-11.

Naidu, N.Y. "Tribal Revolt in Parvatipuram Agency (Srikakulam)." *EPW*, 25 November 1972, pp. 2337-44.

Nair, V.M. "Extent of Naxalite Revolt in Andhra Pradesh." *The Statesman*, 10 December 1969.

——————. "Girijan Revolt: Marxists Organise Armed Action by Andhra Tribes." *The Statesman*, 12 April 1968.

——————. "Time Yet to Wean Girijans From the Naxalites." *The Statesman*, 11 December 1969.

"Ominous Silence on Killings." *EPW*, 11 June 1977, pp. 943-44.

"One Year of Revolutionary Struggle in Srikakulam." *Liberation*, December 1969, pp. 83-86.

Organization for the Protection of Democratic Rights, Andhra Pradesh, Fact Finding Committee, *Srikakulam Movement: A Report to the Nation*. Hyderabad: O.P.D.R., April 1978.

Prasada Rao, A.G. and Gopala Rao, N. *Tribal Development in Andhra Pradesh—With Special Emphasis on Girijan Development Agency, Srikakulam*. Occasional Paper No. 3, Andhra University, Waltair: Agro-Economic Research Centre, n.d.

Raghavaiah, V. *Tribal Revolts*. Nellore, Andhra Pradesh: Rashtra Adimajati Sevak Sangh, 1971.

Raghava Rao, Koka. *The Law Relating to Scheduled Areas in Andhra Pradesh*. Hyderabad: Andhra Pradesh Law Publisher, 1972.

Rai, Hardiwar and Prasad, K.M. "Naxalism: A Challenge to the Proposition of Peaceful Transition to Socialism." *Indian Journal of Political Science*, October-December 1972, pp. 455-80.

Rajeswara Rao, C. "Police Terror: Main Obstacle Towards Return to Normalcy in Affected Areas." *New Age*, 29 March 1970, p. 4.

———————. "Stop This Massacre of Naxalites." *New Age*, 24 August 1969, p. 3.

Ram, Mohan ("MR"). "Annihilating a Tactic." *EPW*, 3 November 1973, p. 1954.

———————. "The Communist Movement in Andhra Pradesh." *Radical Politics in South Asia*. Ed. Paul R. Brass and Marcus F. Franda. Cambridge, Mass.: MIT Press, 1973.

———————. "The Communist Movement in India." *Imperialism and Revolution in South Asia*. Ed. Kathleen Gough and Hari P. Sharma. New York: Monthly Review Press, 1973.

———————. "Five Years After Naxalbari." *EPW*, August 1972, pp. 1471-76.

———————. *Maoism in India*. Delhi: Vikas Publications, 1971.

———————. "Where is the Political Approach?" *EPW*, May 21, 1977, pp. 829-30.

Ramamurty, M.V. "Extremism in Andhra Pradesh." *Radical Humanist*, July 1970, pp. 12-16.

Rangaswami, Amrita. "And Then There Were None: A Report from Srikakulam." *EPW*, 17 November 1973, pp. 2041-42.

———————. "Making a Village: An Andhra Experiment." *EPW*, 7 September 1974, pp. 1524-27.

Roy, Asish Kumar. *The Spring Thunder and After: A Study of the Maoist and Ultra-Leftist Movements in India, 1962-1975*. Calcutta: Minerva Associates, 1975.

Sanyal, Kanu, et al. "Open Letter to Party Comrades." *Mainstream*, 21 October 1972, rpt in Manoranjan Mohanty, *Revolutionary Violence: A Study of the Maoist Movement in India*. New Delhi: Sterling Publishers, 1977, pp. 239-43.

Selden, Mark. *The Yenan Way in Revolutionary China*. Cambridge, Mass.: Harvard University Press, 1971.

Schram, Stuart R., ed. *The Political Thought of Mao Tse-tung*. New York: Praeger, 1971.

Sinha, Shanta. "Andhra Maoist Movement." *State Government and Politics in Andhra Pradesh*. Ed. G. Ram Reddy and B.A.V. Sharma. New Delhi: Sterling Publishers, 1979.

"Spring Thunder Breaks Over India." *People's Daily*, 5 July 1967, rpt in Manoranjan Mohanty, *Revolutionary Violence: A Study of the Maoist Movement in India*. New Delhi: Sterling Publishers, 1977.

Subba Rao, C. "Naxalite Threat in Andhra: Government's Indifference to Girijan Woes." *The Times of India*, 19 July 1972.

———————. "Revolt in Srikakulam." *The Times of India Magazine*, 4 January 1970.

————————. "Revolt in Srikakulam." *The Times of India Magazine*, 11 January 1970.

————————. "Srikakulam: The Bullet Beats the Bow." *The Times Weekly*, 21 March 1971.

Tarkunde, V.M. et al. *First Interim Report of Civil Rights Committee on Alleged Naxalite Encounters and Related Evidence*. Hyderabad: cyclotyled, 16 May 1977.

B. *Government Documents*

1. Government of Andhra Pradesh

*Andhra Pradesh District Gazetteers: Srikakulam*. Hyderabad, 1979.

Andhra Pradesh Legislative Assembly. *Report of the Committee of the House to Enquire into Matters Relating to Deficits and Misappropriations Etc. in Girijan Cooperative Corporation*. Hyderabad, 1976.

Andhra Pradesh Legislature (Assembly Secretariat), Committee on Welfare of Scheduled Tribes 1976-1977 (Fifth Legislative Assembly). *First Report on Educational Facilities, Representation in Services, Medical Facilities and Other Socioeconomic Schemes Implemented for the Welfare of Scheduled Tribes*. Hyderabad, 28 June 1977.

Information and Public Relations Department, The Director. *Tribals Join the Mainstream*. Hyderabad, September 1979.

————————. *Land Reforms in Andhra Pradesh*. Hyderabad, September 1979.

Integrated Tribal Development Agency, Srikakulam. *Medium Term Tribal Sub-Plan, 1978-83, Srikakulam District*. Hyderabad.

*Judgement, Parvathipuram Conspiracy Case*, 30 August 1976.

*Judgement, T. Nagi Reddy Conspiracy Case*. In the Court of the Additional Chief Judge-cum-Additional Sessions Judge (Temporary) City Civil Court, Hyderabad. Sri K. Venkata Ramana, Additional Sessions Judge. Sessions Case No. 106 of 1970 and Sessions Case No. 6 of 1971. 10 April 1972.

Rao, P. Kamala Manohar (Director of Tribal Welfare). *Assessment of the Tribal Development Blocks in Andhra Pradesh*. Hyderabad, 1968.

Revenue Department. *Report of the Committee on the Girijan Cooperative Corporation*. 1971.

Social Welfare Department. *Annual Plan for 1978-79 (Special Assistance Programmes)*. Hyderabad.

————————. *Draft Annual Plan 1980-81: Tribal Sub-Plan*. Hyderabad, November 1979.

————————. *Medium Term Tribal Sub-Plan: Annual Plan for 1979-80*. Hyderabad, April 1979.

————————. *Medium Term Tribal Sub-Plan 1978-83 (revised)*. Hyderabad, June 1979.

*Special Programme for the Development of Scheduled Areas and Scheduled Tribes of Andhra Pradesh in Fourth Five Year Plan*. Hyderabad, 1970.

Statement Filed by the Inspector General of Police on Behalf of the Police Department of Andhra Pradesh, 1977. (submitted to the Bhargava Commission).
Tribal Welfare Department. *Pilot Project for Tribal Development, Srikakulam District: Action Plan.* Hyderabad, 1971.
_____, Tribal Cultural Research and Training Institute [TCRTI]. *Indebtedness Among Scheduled Tribes of Andhra Pradesh.* Hyderabad, n.d.
Tribal Welfare Department, TCRTI. *Impact of Supplementary Feeding on the Tribals of Srikakulam District.* Hyderabad, 1976.
_____, TCRTI. *Statistical Compendium on Agricultural Sector of Sub-Plan Area in Andhra Pradesh.* Hyderabad, October 1978.
_____, TCRTI. *Study of Ashram Schools in Tribal Areas of Andhra Pradesh.* Hyderabad, 1971.
_____, TCRTI. *Survey of Tribal Development Block: Bhadragiri, Srikakulam District.* Hyderabad, 1969.

2. Government of India

Ministry of Home Affairs, Research and Policy Division. *The Causes and Nature of Current Agrarian Tensions.* August 1969.
Report of the Commissioner for Scheduled Castes and Scheduled Tribes, 1975-76 and 1976-77 (Twenty-fourth Report). Delhi, 29 December 1977.

C. *Unpublished Works: Typescripts and Ph.D. Dissertations*

Chandramowli, V., Managing Director Girijan Cooperative Corporation. "A Conspectus of the Corporation for the Girijans." 1970.
_____. "Highlights of the Girijan Problem (Srikakulam Since '64)." Inaugural Address at the Cooperation and Applied Economic Association, Andhra University, Waltair, 16 September 1971.
Kannabiran, K.G. "Who is Responsible for Explosive Situation in Srikakulam Area?" 1976.
"Naxalite Activities and the Police." Written for the Law and Order Seminar of the 19th Senior Officers Course, National Police Academy, October 1969-March 1970.
Sinha, Shanta. "Maoists in Andhra Pradesh." Dissertation, Jawaharlal Nehru University, New Delhi, 1976.

D. *Interviews*

Anonymous. Former Sub-divisional Magistrate, Srikakulam. Hyderabad, 26 March 1980.
V. Chandramowli. I.A.S.; Sub-Collector, Srikakulam, 1964-66; Managing Director of Girijan Cooperative Corporation, 1969-1972. Hyderabad, 2 April 1980 and 3 April 1980.
Lakshminarayana. Former Special Deputy Collector for Tribal Welfare, Srikakulam, 1968-69. Hyderabad, 29 March 1980 and 31 March 1980.
K.G. Kannabiran. Advocate; represented T. Nagi Reddy on appeal. Hyderabad, 25 March 1980.

## III. The Maharashtra Movements: Shramik Sanghatana and *Bhoomi Sena*

### A. *Books and Articles*

"Agricultural Workers in Action: The Story of the Shramik Sanghathan." *How*, June 1978, pp. 24-31.

"The Bhil Movement in Dhulia." *EPW*, February 1972, pp. 205, 207.

Brahme, Sulabha. "Drought in Maharashtra." *Social Scientist*, July 1973, pp. 47-54.

_____. "Economic Conditions of Agricultural Labour: A Study in Shahada Taluka of Dhulia District." *ICSSR Research Abstracts Quarterly*, January-June 1976, pp. 1-14.

Dalwai, Husain. "Bonded Labour Continues." *EPW*, 28 May 1977, pp. 868-69.

Dandekar, V.M. and Khudanpur, G.J. *Workings of Bombay Tenancy Act, 1948: Report of Investigation*. Pune: Gokhale Institute of Politics and Economics, 1957.

_____, and Rath, Nilakantha. "Poverty in India I: Dimensions and Trends." *EPW*, 2 January 1971, pp. 25-48.

De, Nitish R. "India's Agrarian Situation: Some Aspects of Changing the Context." *Agrarian Relations in India*. Ed. Arvind H. Das and V. Nilakant. New Delhi: Manohar, 1979.

Deshmukh, Sudam. "Employment Guarantee Scheme: Introduction and Review." *How*, October 1979, pp. 19-21.

de Silva, G.V.S., Mehta, N., Rahman, A., Wignaraja, P. "Bhoomi Sena: From the Village to the Global Order." *National Labour Institute Bulletin*, January-February 1979, pp. 14-22.

Frankel, Francine. *India's Green Revolution*. Princeton: Princeton University Press, 1971.

Gough, Kathleen. "Indian Peasant Uprisings." *EPW*, August 1974, pp. 1391-1412.

Gram Swarajya Samithi. *Shahada Chalwal*. Bombay: Gram Swarajya Samithi (Shahada) Publication, 1974.

Kanhare, Vijay. "A Meeting at Night." *How*, December 1979, pp. 24-28.

Kaufman, Michael T. "Social Activism Sprouts as India's Politics Decay." *The New York Times*, 15 June 1982, p. A2.

Kulkarni, S.D. "Adivasi Sub-Plan: A Mid-Term Appraisal." *EPW*, 15 January 1977, pp. 43-45.

_____. "Alienation of Adivasis' Lands: Government Not Serious." *EPW*, 31 August 1974, pp. 1469-1471.

_____. "Class and Caste in a Tribal Movement." *EPW*, February 1969, pp. 465-468.

_____. "Encroachments on Forest Lands: The Experience of Maharashtra." *EPW*, 10 November 1979.

_____. "Land Problems of the Adivasis." *New Quest*, July-August, 1978, pp. 286-90.

_____. "Letter to Editor: Organizing Tribals in Thane." *EPW*, 1 November 1980, p. 1873.

_____. "Over a Century of Tyranny." *EPW*, 9 March 1974, pp. 389-92.

_____. "Problems of Tribal Development in Maharashtra." *EPW*, 20 September 1980, pp. 1598-1600.

Kulkarni, Vijay Kumar. "Shramik Sangathana, Dhulia, Maharashtra: A Preliminary Report." *National Labour Institute Bulletin*, November 1975, pp. 13-16.

Limaye, Balmohan. "Adivasis in Maharashtra and their Movements." *Magoya*, May 1974, pp. 25-33. Translated from the Marathi in the BUILD Documentation Centre, Bombay. [Bombay Urban Industrial League for Development].

"The Long Haul." *EPW*, 20 April 1974, p. 615.

Mies, Maria. "The Shahada Movement: A Peasant Movement in Maharashtra (India): Its Development and Perspectives." *Journal of Peasant Studies*, July 1976, pp. 472-82.

"Offensive Against Poor Resumed." *EPW*, 18 March 1978, p. 516.

"Organizing the Adivasis." *EPW*, February 1974, pp. 173-76.

Parulekar, Godavari. *Adivasis Revolt*. Calcutta: National Book Agency Private, Ltd., 1975.

Parulekar, S.V. "The Liberation Movement Among Varlis." *Peasant Struggles in India*. Ed. A.R. Desai. Bombay: Oxford University Press, 1979. Reprinted from Parulekar, S.V. *Revolt of the Varlis*. Bombay: People's Publishing House, 1947.

_____. "The Struggle of 1946." *Peasant Struggles in India*. Ed. A.R. Desai. Bombay: Oxford University Press, 1979. Reprinted from Parulekar, S.V. *Revolt of the Varlis*. Bombay: People's Publishing House, 1947.

Patil, Sharad. "Famine Conditions in Maharashtra: A Survey of Sakri Taluka." *EPW*, 28 July 1973, pp. 1316-17.

_____. "Forest Development or Adivasi Oppression in Maharashtra?" *Social Scientist*, October 1974, pp. 51-56.

_____. "Government's War on Adivasis." *EPW*, 26 October 1974, pp. 1808-10.

_____. "On a Survey of Famine Conditions in Sakri Taluka of Maharashtra." *Social Scientist*, August 1973, pp. 69-73.

PB. "Organizing the Landless." *EPW*, 10 March 1973, pp. 501-4.

Rege, Mangesh. "Shahada: January 30 to May 1." *Magova*, June 1972. Translated from the Marathi in BUILD Documentation Centre, Bombay.

Reynolds, Norman and Sundar, Pushpa. "Maharashtra's Employment Guarantee Scheme: A Programme to Emulate?" *EPW*, 16 July 1977, pp. 1149-58.

"Rise to Support Our Friends in Shahada." *Magova*, October-November 1973. Translated from the Marathi in BUILD Documentation Centre, Bombay.

Sethi, Harsh. "Rural Development: Alternative Strategies." *Agrarian Relations in India*. Ed. Arvind N. Das and V. Nilakant. New Delhi: Manohar, 1979.

Srinivasan, Kannan. "Organising Tribals in Thane." *EPW*, 4 October 1980, pp. 1647-49.

Vohra, Gautam S.G. "Land Reforms a Failure in Maharashtra." *The Times of India*, 18 May 1976.

──────────. "Return of Land to Adivasis: Slow Pace of Progress." *The Times of India*, 18 May 1976.

"Where Bandhs Lead Further." *EPW*, 2 June 1973, pp. 970-71.

B. *Government Documents*

1. *Government of Bombay*

Symington, D. *Report on the Aboriginal and Hill Tribes*. Bombay, 1939.

2. *Government of Maharashtra*

Agriculture and Co-operation Department. *Report of the Committee on Relief from Rural and Urban Indebtedness*. V.S. Page, Chairman. Bombay, 22 October 1975.

Commissioner of Labour and Director of Employments. *Notifications Fixing/Revising Minimum Rates of Wages Under Minimum Wages Act, 1948 for Various Scheduled Employments in Maharashtra State 1976*. Bombay, 1976.

Department of Social Welare, Cultural Affairs, Sports and Tourism. *Draft Annual Tribal Sub-Plan (1980-1981)*. Bombay.

──────────. *Draft Sixth Five-Year Tribal Sub-Plan, 1978-83*. Bombay.

Directorate-General of Information and Public Relations. *Decade of Progress: Land Reforms*. Bombay, January 1976.

The Maharashtra State Co-operative Tribal Development Corporation, Ltd. *Annual Report for the Year 1978-79*. Pune.

*Maharashtra State Gazetteers: Dhulia District*. Bombay, 1974.

Page Committee. *Report of the Committee on Problems of Illicit Money-Lending and Bonded Labour*. V.S. Page, Chairman. Bombay, October 1977.

Planning Department. *Employment Guarantee Scheme in Maharashtra*. Bombay, n.d.

*Report of the Committee Appointed by the Government of Maharashtra for Evaluation of Land Reforms*. Bombay 1974.

*Report of the Study Committee on Employment Conditions of Agricultural Labour in Maharashtra State (with Reference to Minimum Wages).* V.S. Page, Chairman. Bombay, July 1973.

Sirsalkar, P.R., Tribal Research and Training Institute. *Land Alienation and Restoration of Land to Scheduled Tribes People in Maharashtra.* Full report is found in the Tribal Research and Training Institute, Pune. Summarized in *Tribal Research Bulletin,* September 1979, pp. 3-11.

Tribal Research and Training Institute. "Statistics on Scheduled Tribes." *Tribal Research Bulletin,* March 1979.

3. Government of India

Ministry of Home Affairs, Research and Policy Division. *The Causes and Nature of Current Agrarian Tensions.* August 1969.

National Archives of India. Home-Political File No. 18/1-18/12, 1946. Provincial Fortnightly Reports.

Planning Commission. *Draft Five Year Plan, 1978-1983.* New Delhi, 1978.

*Report of the Commissioner for Scheduled Castes and Scheduled Tribes, 1975-76 and 1976-77 (Twenty-fourth Report).* Delhi, 29 December 1977.

C. *Unpublished Typescripts*

Bhaduri, Amit; de Silva, G.V.S.; Mehta, Niranjan; Rehman, Anisur; and Wignaraja, Ponna. "The Emergence of People's Power in Palghar and Some Reflections Growing Out of It." August 1977. In files of BUILD Documentation Centre, Bombay.

Brahme, Sulabha and Upadhyaya, Ashok. *Study of Economic Conditions of Agricultural Labour in Dhulia District, Maharashtra.* Poona: Shankar Brahme Samajvidnyana Granthalaya, Poona, 1975.

Datar, Chhaya. "The Relationship Between the Women's Liberation Movement and the Class Movement in Shahada—A Case Study." 1975. In files of BUILD Documentation Centre, Bombay.

de Silva, G.V.S.; Mehta, Niranjan; Rahman, Anisur; Wignaraja, Ponna. *Bhoomi Sena: A Struggle for People's Power.* Bombay: National Intitute of Bank Management, August 1978. Prepublication draft.

Joint Action Committee. "Forests We Will Not Destroy. Our Lands We Will Not Quit: An Open Call/Challenge." Pamphlet, 14 August 1979. In files of BUILD Documentation Centre.

―――――――――. "Regarding Regularisation of Encroachments on Government Waste/Gairan/Forest Land in Maharashtra in reference to Government Resolution (GR) of 27th December 1978 and amendments to the GR announced in the assembly on the 13th July 1979." Press note, 18 July 1979. In files of BUILD Documentation Centre, Bombay.

Shramik Sanghatana (?). Untitled pamphlet regarding private army being raised by landlords of Dhule. 1974. In files of BUILD Documentation Centre, Bombay.

D. *Interviews*

See Appendix A for interviewees who requested anonymity.

Sudheer Bedekar. Former editor of *Magova*, a journal that had close ties to Shramik Sanghatana. Pune, 31 January 1980.

Sulabha Brahme. Gokhale Institute of Politics and Government. Author of several articles on agricultural labor in Dhule. Pune, 30 January 1980.

Chhaya Datar. Writer and Shramik Sanghatana supporter. Bombay, 29 January 1980.

Mrinal Gore. MLA representing northern Bombay, 1972-77, Socialist Party; imprisoned, 1975-77; MP, 1977-79, Janata Party. Bombay, 15 February 1980.

Vijay Kanhare. A founder of Shramik Sanghatana. Bombay, 5 February 1980.

S.D. Kulkarni. Director, Centre for Tribal Conscientization, and author of numerous articles on adivasis in Maharashtra. Pune, 13 February 1980.

Niranjan Mehta. National Institute of Bank Management. Co-author of several articles and a monograph on Bhoomi Sena. Bombay, 8 February 1980.

Godavari Parulekar. President of the Maharashtra Kisan Sabha; Member of Central Committee of CPI(M); leader of 1940s Communist movement in Thane. Bombay, 23 February 1980 and 26 February 1980.

Harsh Sethi. Indian Council for Social Science Research. New Delhi, 4 October 1979.

Navinit Shah. MLA representing Palghar, 1957-62, 1967-72. Formerly member Praja Socialist Party. In 1980, President of Palghar Janata Party. Bombay, 18 February 1980.

Vahru Sonawani. A Shramik Sanghatana activist. Bombay, 29 January 1980.

IV. Newspapers

*The Bombay Chronicle*
*The Deccan Chronicle*
*Economic and Political Weekly*, Bombay
*The Free Press Journal*, Bombay
*The Hindu*, Madras
*The Hindustan Times*, Delhi
*Liberation*, official publication of CPI(M-L), Calcutta
*The National Herald*, Lucknow and Delhi
*New Age*, journal of CPI

*The New York Times*
*The Patriot*
*People's Democracy*, official publication of CPI(M), Calcutta
*The Statesman*, Calcutta
*The Times of India*, Delhi and Bombay